Literacy Acquisitio
Social Context

THE DEVELOPING BODY AND MIND

Series Editor:
Professor George Butterworth, *Department of Psychology, University of Sussex*

Designed for a broad readership in the English-speaking world, this major series represents the best of contemporary research and theory in the cognitive, social, abnormal and biological areas of development.

Literacy Acquisition and Social Context

Edited by

Egbert M.H. Assink

Department of Psychology, Utrecht University, The Netherlands

HARVESTER WHEATSHEAF

New York   London   Toronto   Sydney   Tokyo   Singapore

First published 1994 by
Harvester Wheatsheaf
Campus 400, Maylands Avenue
Hemel Hempstead
Hertfordshire, HP2 7EZ
A division of
Simon and Schuster International Group

Typeset in 10/12pt Ehrhardt
by Photoprint, Torquay, Devon

Printed and bound in Great Britain by
TJ Press (Padstow) Ltd

British Library Cataloguing in Publication Data

A catalogue record for this book is available from the British Library

ISBN 0–7450–1354–6

1 2 3 4 5   98 97 96 95 94

Contents

Contributors

Cor Aarnoutse PhD, University of Nijmegen, Department of Education, Erasmusplein 1, Nijmegen, The Netherlands

Egbert M.H. Assink PhD, Utrecht University, Department of Psychology, Heidelberglaan 1, 3584 CS Utrecht, The Netherlands

Virginia Wise Berninger PhD, University of Washington, College of Education, Miller DQ-12, Seattle, WA 98195, USA

Wim H.J. Van Bon PhD, University of Nijmegen, Department of Special Education, PO Box 9103, 6500 HD Nijmegen, The Netherlands

Judith A. Bowey PhD, University of Queensland, Department of Psychology, Brisbane, Qld 4072, Australia

Adriana Bus PhD, Leiden University, Centre for Child and Family Studies, PO Box 9555, Leiden 2300 RB, The Netherlands

Anne E. Cunningham PhD, University of Washington, College of Education, Miller DQ-12, Seattle, WA 98195, USA

Usha Goswami PhD, University of Cambridge, Department of Experimental Psychology, Downing St, Cambridge CB2 3EB, United Kingdom

Giel Gresnigt PhD, Utrecht University, Department of Experimental Psychology, Heidelberglaan 1, 3584 CS Utrecht, The Netherlands

Göran Kattenberg PhD, Utrecht University, Department of Experimental Psychology, Heidelberglaan 1, 3584 CS Utrecht, The Netherlands

Jan J.F. ter Laak PhD, Utrecht University, Department of Developmental Psychology, Heidelberglaan 1, 3584 CS Utrecht, The Netherlands

Keith E. Stanovich PhD, Ontario Institute for Studies in Education, 252 Bloor St W., Toronto On M5S 1V6, Canada

Richard F. West PhD, James Madison University, Department of Psychology, Harrisonburg, VA 22807, USA

Introduction

Egbert M.H. Assink
Department of Psychology, Utrecht University

This volume presents an overview of current ideas on key issues in literacy acquisition, from early childhood to adolescence. These ideas have been developed in the social and behavioural sciences, in particular in the areas of experimental, developmental and educational psychology. The role of social context in the various stages of learning to read and write is the leading theme throughout the book. The contributions, all written by specialists in their field, present the reader with a broad sketch of reading acquisition, in particular with regard to the existing diversity in methods and approach of researchers.

The contributors present work conducted in research programmes currently in progress in the paradigm of mainstream cognitive psychology, as well as work of investigators working in the Vygotskian (socio-historic) research perspective. In the concluding chapter, Jan ter Laak, a specialist in the theoretical foundations of developmental psychology at Utrecht University, discusses the similarities and differences of the papers presented in this volume.

Over the past decade there has been growing interest in the work of L.S. Vygotsky, the early twentieth-century Russian psychologist. Several factors seem to have contributed to this. First is the fact that Vygotsky's ideas seem directly relevant to current issues in education and other applied fields (Moll, 1990). Another important factor is that Western scholars, especially in the United States, have been searching for new theoretical frameworks, and Vygotsky's ideas seem to address many of their issues of interest. Perhaps the main reason for Vygotsky's appeal in the West, however, is his analysis of the social origin of mental processes (Wertsch and Tulviste, 1992).

This view of the social origin of cognitive tools particularly holds for literacy acquisition. For this reason a number of the chapters that follow deal with the social aspects of becoming literate. Learning to become literate is a complex, socially rooted activity, which must be studied from a diversity of viewpoints in order to get a sufficiently complete view. This understanding was the basis for inviting the authors to contribute to the present volume, and this introduction summarizes the contributions presented here.

In Chapter 2, 'The role of social context in emergent literacy', Adriana Bus, of the Department of Educational Studies at the University of Leiden, discusses the fascinating period of early reading, the stage in which the child has not yet mastered the skill. As a consequence the child is wholly dependent on his or her social environment, in particular on parents or teachers. Early experience of (or exposure to) book reading takes place in the pre-school period. In this chapter recent research on emergent literacy is discussed. It focuses on adult–child interactions aimed at introducing the child to the world of books and texts. Special attention is devoted to the effect of story-book reading by parents and other educators on subsequently developing literacy skills in children.

One of the central and powerful ideas in Vygotsky's (1978) theory is that the adult acts as if the child is participating in a well-ordered social system, in which the adult gradually shifts more and more responsibility to the child as she or he develops. Bus elaborates this idea, taking literacy as her focus. The developmental studies presented suggest that in story-book reading mothers or other significant persons create a '*zone of proximal development*' for the child: activities children are not yet able to do by themselves are done with the assistance of others. It is shown that adults are highly sensitive to children's developmental abilities. Parents do not bring up information that is used unchanged by the child, but stimulate interactions on those things that children are not yet able to do themselves. The development of higher psychological processes, which enable the child to become a skilled, mature reader, is the result of the internalization of interpersonal exchanges to processes at the intrapersonal level. As will be argued in Chapter 10, this transformation is continuous in nature and never fully completed. Another major conclusion presented in Chapter 2 is that while book reading is an incentive to the learning process, this is not its main motive. The studies presented support the idea that reading only occurs when parents and children enjoy sharing a book; this underscores the importance of emotional factors in literacy acquisition.

Chapter 3 gives an account of the developmental changes in the use of oral and written language codes. In this contribution, entitled 'Codes, connections, context, and constructive processes: integrating the Vygotskian and Lurian perspectives', Virginia Berninger, of the College of Education, University of Washington, develops her thesis about what happens immediately after the stage of early reading. The child enters the period of formal schooling, and grasps the essentials of the written code. An intriguing question is how the interrelationships between oral and visible language codes develop as a function of cognitive growth. The importance of phonological skills in reading acquisition has been well established. Recent evidence shows, however, that it is not only phonological skills, but also orthographic skills that are important in learning to read. There has been a great deal of debate about what the basic perceptual unit or code is in word recognition. It has been shown that beginning readers initially learn to associate printed and spoken language at the unit of *words*. There is now evidence to suggest that we need to consider the role of at least two additional orthographic codes – the single *letter* and the *letter cluster* – in beginning reading. The purpose of this chapter is to elucidate how phonological and orthographic language codes interact in developing literacy acquisition.

Berninger discusses the Vygotskian perspective on the social foundations of cognitive development and the Lurian perspective on the individual working brain system. These perspectives are applied to understanding literacy acquisition. Her aim is to show that the social contextual perspective and the neuropsychological perspective are neither mutually exclusive nor incompatible, although the latter belief is widespread. The final goal is to build models of literacy acquisition that incorporate biological constraints in the individual learner as well as educational constraints in the social and cultural context.

In Chapter 4, 'Onsets and rimes as functional units in reading', Usha Goswami of the Psychology Department at the University of Cambridge, raises an interesting question in discussing developmental aspects of reading: Which unit or units are used in printed word identification? Recent research has shown that in word identification, not only letters and words may be used, but also letter clusters at the subword level. Studies conducted by Rebecca Treiman (Treiman, 1989, 1992) and her associates (Treiman and Chafetz, 1987; Treiman and Zukowski, 1989; Treiman *et al.*, 1990) have shown that onsets and rimes are important as units in word identification. Linguists view the syllable as having an ordered and hierarchical internal structure, being composed of an onset and a rime unit. The onset unit consists of the (optional) consonant group at the beginning of a syllable (e.g. /b/ in *book*, or /sk/ in *sky*); the rime unit consists of the vowel and the (optional) following consonant group (e.g. /uk/ in *book* and /aI/ in *sky*). Although initially introduced as linguistic concepts, there is now a growing body of evidence for a functional role of syllable onset and rimes as units in processing words.

Goswami argues that in the final stage of learning to read children become able to take advantage of orthographic units larger than single sound–letter associations. This involves the use of spelling sequences within words that are smaller than the whole word, but larger than the individual letters, such as '-at' in 'cat', or the 'tion' in 'station'. In this final stage of learning to read, children start to exploit larger orthographic units in words that have consistent pronunciations. The use of such orthographic strategies is thought to be fairly sophisticated and emerges relatively late in reading development. Goswami ends with a discussion of the implications of her findings for educational practice. Her conclusion is that instructional programmes should focus on training children to use orthographic analogies. Learning to read should be concentrated on analyzing written words in functional subunits.

Chapter 5, 'Literacy environment and the development of children's cognitive skills', by Anne Cunningham of the University of Washington, Keith Stanovich of the Ontario Institute for Studies in Education and Richard West of the James Madison University, highlights the effects of experience with printed materials. In the reading literature of the past few decades considerable attention has been paid to the role of phonological processes in reading acquisition (Brady and Shankweiler, 1991). An impressive amount of research has demonstrated critical linkages between the development of phonological abilities and the acquisition of word recognition skills (Rack *et al.*, 1992). Nevertheless, despite the importance of phonological processing in explaining differences in word identification skill, it is possible that additional factors may contribute to our understanding of the differences of interest. Recently, research has centred on orthographic processing abilities as a potential second source of variance in word recognition ability (Stanovich and West, 1989; Stanovich and Cunningham, 1993).

Individual differences in experience with printed materials originate not only from reading sessions in school, but also from the amount of the child's out-of-school reading. The authors argue that the effect of print exposure is not confined to decoding and word identification; it also accelerates the development of vocabulary knowledge and reading comprehension. Two investigations examining the complementary effects of print exposure on cognitive development are reported. The first deals with the relation between the first year of literacy environment and the development of children's orthographic and phonological skills. In the second study the authors followed a group of first-year school children and, ten years later, assessed their level of reading volume as well as their verbal intelligence, reading comprehension and general knowledge. In this longitudinal investigation, the widening achievement disparities and the relative contribution of print exposure in explaining these differences are highlighted.

Chapter 6, 'Basic mechanisms in learning to read', was compiled by Egbert Assink, in cooperation with Göran Kattenberg, both at the Psychology Department of Utrecht University. As there is already a vast amount of research literature dealing with the period of beginning reading, we have chosen to discuss the period following initial reading, rather than add another text to this well-documented topic. This period is completed when the child has learned the elementary sound–spelling correspondences and has progressed from decoding words on an individual letter basis to fluent reading by automatic word recognition. This goal is normally accomplished by the age of about 8 or 9 years.

After the stage of initial reading, the child enters the period of fluent reading. However, this does not mean that the child's reading skills are fully developed. For although a large proportion of words are readily recognized on the basis of their constituent letter patterns, the reading process is not yet fully automatized. The chapter discusses the developmental changes in accelerating word recognition, a topic discussed in relation to the issue of reading disability. Normal and poor readers are compared for their capacity to exploit fully the use of orthographic and phonological codes at the subword level. The training of word identification skills is also discussed. Attention is paid to the problem of achieving transfer in reading instruction. When the child identifies a string of letters as a word, he or she performs an amazingly complex skill. Word identification is concerned not only with discriminating single letters, but also involves extracting information beneath and beyond the single letter level (cf. Chapters 3, 4 and 5 in this volume).

In this chapter various levels of mechanisms involved in learning to read are investigated. First, we discuss the mechanisms working at the *letter feature level*, followed by a discussion of processes affecting the *individual letter level*. Subsequently, the *letter cluster level*, the intermediate stage between the single letter and the *whole word level*, is considered. We then present research focusing on identification mechanisms working at the *sentence context level*. The chapter concludes with a general discussion evaluating the results presented here. Performance profiles of poor readers and younger normal readers, selected for equal performance on standard reading tests, are compared. This type of experimental set-up, usually referred to as reading level design comparisons, allows us to make optimally interpretable comparisons between normal and poor readers (Goswami and Bryant, 1989). The differences established in our experiments are interpreted in terms of the model for the development of sightword reading, proposed by Ehri (1992).

Two central issues dominate the literature on reading disability. The first is concerned with the *role of orthographic and phonological information in reading*. The question under discussion is: Does reading disability originate primarily from a phonological deficit, or is it the result of an orthographic processing deficit? Is poor reading primarily a 'hardware' problem caused by dysfunctioning brain systems, or is it a failure in the acquisition of a culturally mediated cognitive skill, normally developing as a result of prolonged reading experience, or is it, perhaps, a combination of both accounts of poor reading?

The second issue is concerned with the question of whether poor readers show *qualitative differences in reading strategy*. An alternative to the phonological deficit hypothesis is the developmental lag or delay hypothesis (Treiman and Hirsh-Pasek, 1985). According to the phonological deficit hypothesis poor readers face a specific problem. The delay hypothesis denies this specificity aspect by claiming that poor readers do exactly what normally developing readers do in learning to read, only they do so more slowly. The data presented in this chapter have been collected to address these two issues.

In Chapter 7, 'Grammatical awareness and learning to read: a critique', Judith Bowey, of the Psychology Department at the University of Queensland, discusses the role of grammatical awareness in learning to read. There is an impressive body of research evidence dealing with the contributions of phonemic and word awareness in the acquisition of reading proficiency. In comparison, studies on the relationship between syntactic awareness and developing reading skill are relatively scarce. Most reading studies have focused on the development of phonemic and word awareness, and their relationship to reading proficiency.

Comparatively little research has dealt with children's awareness of grammatical well-formedness. It is not difficult to appreciate the theoretical significance of this issue. Bowey discusses the development of metalinguistic skill, as reflected in children's ability to identify and correct grammatically illegitimate sentences, and its relationship with both the use of linguistic structure in aural sentence memory and reading achievement.

Bowey begins with a critical examination of the tasks most frequently used to assess grammatical awareness, pointing to the difficulties involved in obtaining relatively pure estimates of this ability in beginning readers and the widespread contamination of grammatical awareness measures by semantic and other cognitive processes. Then comes a review of the literature examining the association between grammatical awareness and reading. It is argued that, although the available evidence supports the hypothesis that grammatical awareness contributes directly to reading disability, most studies permit alternate interpretations. Bowey claims that it has not yet been clearly demonstrated that poor readers show any deficit in grammatical awareness independent of more general delays in language development or other skills, and she critically examines the potential contribution of grammatical awareness to reading comprehension and word recognition processes, offering alternative interpretations of existing studies as well as suggestions for further work.

In Chapter 8, 'Remediation of reading problems: effects of training at word and subword levels', Wim van Bon, of the Department of Special Education at the University of Nijmegen, demonstrates that studies on remediation of reading problems can be classified according to various criteria, such as the type of training instruction used, the reading level under investigation, the seriousness of the reading problem and the type of reading problem involved. Van Bon adopts the approach of ordering the studies according to the linguistic processing level the remedial training is intended to influence and the linguistic performance levels that were studied in evaluating the effects of the treatment.

The review of experimental studies focused on the remediation of reading problems is restricted to studies at the word and subword levels. This constraint is justified by the availability of persuasive evidence for the role of context-free word decoding skill in basic reading problems (Stanovich, 1986; Siegel and Faux, 1989). The author discusses in turn studies with poor readers tackling decoding units of increasing size: grapheme–phoneme correspondences, sub-syllabic units consisting of more than one grapheme–phoneme, syllables and morphemes, and finally whole words. The chapter begins with a preliminary discussion of studies aimed at improving the basic phonological skills of phonemic segmentation and speech–sound discrimination.

The 'bottom-up' approach adopted here for discussing the effect of remedial programmes tackling decoding skills at specified linguistic processing levels closely parallels the approach followed in Chapter 7. This enables the reader to compare and assess the results and conclusions reported. In the discussion of Chapter 8 the author notes that, although the evidence is not yet conclusive, the effect of training at the syllabic and sub-syllabic levels looks promising and merits further exploration. Closely connected with this, two intriguing points should be studied further: the effect of training duration and the (long-term) duration of the induced training effects.

In Chapter 9, 'Learning higher-order reading skills: the cognitive perspective', Cor Aarnoutse, of the Department of Education at the University of Nijmegen, considers recent theoretical views on reading comprehension. His focus is on current theories and models developed in the framework of cognitive psychology. Schema theories are discussed as one of the important trends in information processing theories, since they most adequately describe the processing of information and the acquisition of knowledge from texts. Having evaluated the theories, Aarnoutse presents the results of his own work on teaching reading comprehension. In this approach a model of study-oriented reading, derived from the strategic discourse processing model of Kintsch and Van Dijk (1978), is central. Results of a large-scale training study in field settings are also reported.

The author concludes that future studies in teaching reading comprehension should be aimed at addressing at least three main issues: first, the long-term effects of the strategies taught in the experimental instruction conditions; second, the assessment of transfer effects of the reading comprehension strategies used in the experimental classes; and third, the design of new instructional programmes fostering the student's capabilities to integrate the various strategies used in the experimental course.

In Chapter 10, 'Learning higher-order reading skills: the Vygotskian perspective', Giel Gresnigt, of the Psychology Department at Utrecht University, discusses reading comprehension from a Vygotskian perspective; that is, primarily as a socially oriented activity. Analyzing complex text structures is considered as a basically social process in which the reader is a partner communicating with the originator of the text. The Vygotskian view that meaning is not accessed exclusively on the basis of linguistic information processing is elaborated. Understanding texts necessarily rests on a creative intellectual activity, which transcends linguistic processing. This activity is directed towards solving communication problems.

If social communication and thinking play an essential role in learning to read, this has important consequences for education. Teaching reading comprehension should contain models concerning the writer's intentions, including the function of the text given the social context and roles of writer and reader. Furthermore, basic thinking abilities, such as comparison, causality, analysis, etc., should be systematically taught. The consequences of this approach for designing instruction are described and contrasted with mainstream approaches. Results of empirical training studies using materials inspired by these ideas are reported.

In Chapter 11, 'Literacy acquisition and social context: approaches, emphases and questions', Jan ter Laak, of the Department of Psychology at Utrecht University, analyzes the theoretical perspectives presented in this volume. These are seen to be partly conflicting and partly complementary. It will be shown that learning to read and write is a very complex process, but one that is one of the fundamental conditions for becoming a member of late twentieth-century human society. However, this process cannot be described fully from the perspective of one discipline alone, and Ter Laak reviews the variety of orientations on the study of literacy acquisition presented in this book.

References

Brady, S.A. and Shankweiler, D.P. (1991), *Phonological Processes in Literacy. A tribute to Isabelle Y. Liberman.* Hillsdale, NJ: Lawrence Erlbaum.

Ehri, L.C. (1992), 'Reconceptualizing the development of sight word reading and its relationship to recoding'. In P.B. Gough, L.C. Ehri and R. Treiman (eds.) *Reading Acquisition.* Hillsdale, NJ: Lawrence Erlbaum, pp. 107–43.

Goswami, U. and Bryant, P. (1989), 'The interpretation of studies using the reading level design', *Journal of Reading Behavior, 21,* 413–24.

Kintsch, W. and van Dijk, T.A. (1978) 'Toward a model of text comprehension and production', *Psychological Review, 85,* 363–94.

Moll, L.C. (1990), *Vygotsky and Education: Instructional implications and applications of sociohistorical society.* Cambridge: Cambridge University Press.

Rack, J.P., Snowling, M.J., and Olson, R.K. (1992), 'The nonword reading deficit in developmental dyslexia: a review', *Reading Research Quarterly, 27,* 28–53.

Siegel, L.S. and Faux, D. (1989), 'Acquisition of certain grapheme–phoneme correspondences in normally achieving and disabled readers', *Reading and Writing, 1,* 37–78.

Stanovich, K.E. (1986), 'Matthew effects in reading: some consequences of individual differences in the acquisition of literacy', Reading Research Quarterly, *21,* 360–406.

Stanovich, K.E. and Cunningham, A.E. (1993), 'Studying the consequences of literacy within a literate society: the cognitive correlates of print exposure,' *Memory & Cognition, 20,* 51–68.

Stanovich, K.E. and West, R.F. (1989), 'Exposure to print and orthographic processing,' *Reading Research Quarterly, 24,* 402–33.

Treiman, R. (1989), 'The internal structure of the syllable.' In G.N. Carlson and M.K. Tanenhaus (eds.) *Linguistic Structure in Language Processing,* Dordrecht: Kluwer Academic Publishers, pp. 27–52.

Treiman, R. (1992), 'The role of intrasyllabic units in learning to read and spell'. In P.B. Gough, L.C. Ehri and R. Treiman (eds.) *Reading Acquisition,* Hillsdale, NJ: Lawrence Erlbaum, pp. 65–106.

Treiman, R. and Chafetz, J. (1987) 'Are there onset and rime-like units in written words?' In M. Coltheart (ed.) *Attention and Performance XII.* London: Lawrence Erlbaum, pp. 281–98.

Treiman, R., Goswami, U. and Bruck, M. (1990), 'Not all nonwords are alike: implications for reading development and theory', *Memory and Cognition, 18,* 559–67.

Treiman, R. and Hirsh-Pasek, K. (1985), 'Are there qualitative differences in reading behavior between dyslexics and normal readers?' *Memory & Cognition, 13,* 357–64.

Treiman, R. and Zukowski, A. (1989), 'Units in reading and spelling', *Journal of Memory and Language, 27,* 466–77.

Vygotsky, L.S. (1978). *Mind in Society. The development of higher psychological processes,* ed. M. Cole, V. John-Steiner, S. Scribner and E. Souberman, Cambridge, MA: Harvard University Press.

Wertsch, J.V. and Tulviste, P. (1992), 'L.S. Vygotsky and contemporary developmental psychology', *Developmental Psychology, 28,* 548–57.

2

The role of social context in emergent literacy

Adriana G. Bus
Centre for Child and Family Studies, Leiden University

Introduction

The beginning of learning to read does not coincide with reading instruction in the first year of formal schooling. In highly literate societies, children have already acquired knowledge on several components of reading and writing when they start school (e.g. Bus, 1986, 1991). In addition to acquiring letter knowledge, letter printing, writing and formal conventions of literacy, young children internalize the linguistic procedures which are characteristic of the written language register (Sulzby, in press a). Children familiarize themselves with the story script (Sulzby, in press b), they develop ways of thinking that enable them to transcend the immediate context (Pellegrini and Galda, 1991) and they become aware of a particular style of language employed in written stories (Pappas and Brown, 1987; Purcell-Gates, 1988; Pappas and Pettegrew, 1991).

Children have many incentives in their environment to explore written language: labels on drinks, sweets, shops and T-shirts, but also texts such as books, advertisements and journals (Teale, 1986; Sulzby and Teale, 1991). However, I assume that the presence of environmental print and the wide availability of printed material in a literate society is no guarantee that children will necessarily become readers (see also Sulzby and Edwards, in press). More important than the availability of printed material seems to be that children are involved in activity settings with ample scope to support emergent literacy, such as

The research reported in this chapter was partly supported by a PIONEER grant (PGS 59–256) from the Netherlands Organization of Scientific Research (NWO) to Marinus H. van IJzendoorn.

Address correspondence to Adriana G. Bus, Leiden University, PO Box 9555, NL–2300 RB Leiden, The Netherlands.

story-book reading and dinner table conversation (see also Lancy, in press). We claim that, in such situations, linguistic procedures characteristic of written language are internalized by children. In order to explain how children acquire knowledge about written language we did several studies with mothers and children reading interactively. We hypothesize that parents gradually 'scaffold' the child's language from dialogic exchanges into that of the story-book. This scaffolding involves the adult controlling those elements of the task that are initially beyond the child's individual capability, thus permitting the child to concentrate upon and complete only those elements that are within his or her range of competence (Sulzby and Teale, 1991). Assuming a key role of parental scaffolding in becoming literate, it seems plausible that children need to trust their parents in order to explore unfamiliar aspects of their environment, such as story-books, with confidence. From this perspective it is to be expected that there is a social explanation for the differences in children's interest and involvement in book reading, and therefore also in emergent literacy skills. In line with this argument, it is to be expected that negative responses to books are a consequence of a problematic parent–child relationship.

This chapter examines the parental role in the emergence of literacy. It focuses on the parental role as a function of children's growing competence. The discussion includes a description of the developmental character of interactive reading; it also focuses on the parental role in evoking children's interest. Do parents read to young children because of children's spontaneous interest? Or does sharing books prompt young children's interest in reading? I shall first argue that mothers reading simple books differ greatly in focus of attention for different age levels. In addition, I shall analyze the affective dimension of story-book reading. I shall discuss results that suggest a relationship between attachment security and the quality of story-book reading. In the next section I shall describe the strategies that parents follow successively when reading a text with all the characteristics of written language. I shall analyze the kinds of help given in consecutive stages of interactive reading, and the changes that occur as children gain in experience. I shall argue that the main incentive for book reading is not the child's reading interest, but the fact that parents are able to create an intimate situation in which parent and child share a book. In conclusion, I shall discuss some consequences of our findings for intergenerational literacy programmes.

The role of social support and mediating parental behaviour while reading simple books

The story-book reading paradigm adopts the *scaffolding* analogy to characterize the way in which literate adults enable a child to participate in book reading and thereby learn from it (Bruner, 1975). Those things children are not yet able to do themselves are done with the assistance of the mother. I believe that reading a book can better be described as a process in which mothers interpret events in dialogue with their child. Instead of a scaffolding analogy, which implies that the child uses parental information unchanged, mothers elicit comments from the child about the pictures or the text, and then respond to the child's comments (see also Elbers, 1991).

Mothers seem to adapt the topics of discussion to the child's level of understanding. In the process of reading the same book again and again, the character of the interactions between adult and child changes. Snow (1983) describes reading sessions with *Richard Scarry's Storybook Dictionary* over a period of approximately 11 months. She reports a transition from discussions concentrating on visible objects and events in the early and middle phases of the study, to a much greater focus on cause–effect relations at the end. From Sulzby and Teale's (1987) descriptions of Hannah and her mother in the course of reading *A Golden Story Book of Counting*, it appears that labelling and counting are emphasized at the beginning, whereas later the mother gets Hannah to discuss certain characteristics of the objects (e.g. colour, sounds they make), to examine synonyms for the words, and to link certain items in the text to her own experience and to family members. We examined whether the level of demands also changes when the book is new to the mother and child. This may offer evidence that reading functions are acquired independently of their application to a particular text.

Results of a cross-sectional study with 1½-, 3½- and 5½-year-olds

In a cross-sectional study on 1½-, 3½- and 5½-year-olds (Bus and Van IJzendoorn, 1988a) we studied interaction processes around two different booklets which were unknown to the mother–child dyads. The first was an expository book with letters of the alphabet and corresponding illustrations (A is an apple, B is a bear, etc.). The second book was a simple narrative about a mother dog looking everywhere in the house for her puppy, Spot. By looking behind flap-overs the children can decide for themselves whether Spot is under the table, in the drawer or somewhere else. Unlike the first book, this second book included a narrative, albeit at a very simple level. The text on every page ('Is Spot in the closet?') adds hardly anything to what can be deduced from the pictures and, as the book moves to the end, to what the child already knows about the story plot. We expected that, as children grow older and more competent, the focus of their attention would shift from simple to complex aspects of the book's content.

We did indeed find differences in the focus of attention. Younger and inexperienced children focus on the book's content while older and more competent children focus on the formal characteristics of the book.

The following illustration refers to the reading of the alphabet book and is characteristic of the younger and less experienced children:

(Child) [at the page with the picture of an eskimo and the letter *e*] 'Now read this.'
(Mother) 'This is a . . . What is it?' (C) 'I don't know.' (M) [surprised] 'Well?' (C)

[guessing] 'A farmer.' (M) 'Yes, something like that.' (C) 'What is it?' (M) 'An eskimo. That is someone from a country far away where it is cold, always cold, always snow, always ice. There they always wear thick clothes and there the eskimos live. An eskimo always wears thick clothes, gloves, big shoes, and a cap and a muffler.' (C) [turns page] . . .

Older children rarely discuss these aspects with their mothers, probably because they can easily interpret the pictures without any help. Attention shifts from the content to the form of written language, as is illustrated by the next example. This illustration also comes from reading the alphabet book:

(M) [page with *i* and a picture of an icecream] 'Ah, you like that.' (C) 'Icecream.' (M) 'Which letter is this?' [points to *i*]. (C) 'a.' (M) 'An acecream?' (C) [with much emphasis] 'An icecream.' (M) 'Which letter is this?' (C) 'a.' (M) 'a?' (C) 'Yes.' (M) 'An acecream?' (C) 'An icecream.' (M) 'A what?' (C) 'An icecream.' (M) 'Which letter is this?' (C) 'a.' (M) 'An acecream.' (C) [laughs]. (M) 'Did you eat an acecream yesterday? This is the letter . . .' (C) 'a.' (M) 'This is the letter i, from icecream.'

The shift in the focus of attention indicates that children learn how to extend the functional potential of story-books. By reading books a child's competence to understand books increases. However, we have to add that such a shift in attention also depends on the booklet. Differences in the focus of attention were less pronounced in reading Spot, a narrative. Here the main focus was on the story, for both the younger and the older and more competent 5½-year-olds. However, there was a difference in the number of explanations accompanying reading the story of Spot. With the older and more competent children, mothers were less likely to explain aspects of the book in addition to the reading. They seemed to consider the book content as self-evident. We subsequently recognized that a very simple plot with little text meant this study did not reveal much about the parental role in familiarizing children with characteristic patterns of written language. Reviewing the story-book reading literature we get the impression that most studies focus on expository texts with thematically related or unrelated pictures, particularly for the very young (e.g. Snow, 1983; Sulzby and Teale, 1987; Pellegrini *et al.*, 1990). In order to understand how book reading contributes to the process of understanding written language, we focused, in a follow-up study, on a story with all the characteristics of written language (Bus and Van IJzendoorn, 1993).

Problematic interactions and mother–child security

In line with the theory that the parental role is critical to the learning processes that occur as a result of book reading, it is plausible that negative responses to books are a consequence of a problematic parent–child relationship. In fact, I assume that children's interest in books is not the primary motive for interactive reading. The participants seem to be especially motivated to read by the pleasure of sharing a book. On several occasions I observed a 2-year-old willing to share his favourite toys with another child but not book reading with his mother. To test this assumption the cross-sectional study focused on the relation between attachment security on the one hand, and the quality of story-book reading on the other. The attachment relationship between children and parents (or other caregivers) is defined as a relatively enduring, affective relationship between a child and one or more adults with whom he or she regularly interacts.

From the secure basis of an attachment relationship children derive a feeling of trust in their social environment, especially in their parents, as well as in their own ability to influence this environment (Bretherton, 1985). From studies of learning processes, it appears that anxiously attached children are less enthusiastic and curious in difficult task settings, are less cooperative and obedient to adults, and that their parents are less effective teachers (e.g. Matas *et al.*, 1978; Bates, 1985). Though a relationship between quality and frequency of reading on the one hand, and the quality of the parent–child relationship on the other, seems plausible, there have been very few studies testing this hypothesis and showing a relationship between the affective dimension of the parent–child relationship and becoming literate. We therefore explored the assumption that attachment security is related to the quality of story-book reading. One consequence of an insecure parent–child relationship may be that parents are less able to stimulate interest and to deal with the child's signals of anxiety or curiosity. Insecure parents may also be less sensitive to the child's level of understanding.

In the cross-sectional study we described qualitative differences in book reading sessions in a group of middle-class mothers, and related the behaviour during the book reading sessions to the children's behaviour during a reunion session after a separation. To determine security of attachment, the 1½-year-olds were observed in the Strange Situation procedure. The 3½-year-olds and the 5½-year-olds were separated from their mothers for about 1 hour, during which they completed some tests. Security was scored on a scale during the first minute of reunion. We observed whether and how often the child smiled at the mother, showed toys, accepted initiatives for interaction, looked at the mother, evaluated what had happened in the meantime and offered to play together. From this cross-sectional study it appeared that the sessions were more problematic as children were less securely attached to their parents. These children showed more distracted behaviour and had to be disciplined more often by their mother. It appeared that the insecure children were less interested in reading the books, and that the mothers had more problems in focusing the children's attention on the books.

We also explored the hypothesis that insecure parents are less able to support children during the reading session, by studying the differences in the contents of the exchanges between parent and child. As the parent–child relationship was less secure mothers were more inclined to focus on the story than on the formal characteristics of written language, that is, to reading instruction and proto-reading. We interpreted this as indicating that mothers of secure children have higher expectations of their securely attached children, when it comes to reading. Yet we cannot exclude the possibility that the mothers of insecure children correctly focused on a 'lower' level, since their children were less advanced in reading comprehension as a consequence of less frequent book reading. Insecure pairs may be less inclined to read because the reading sessions are not as pleasant and rewarding as they are in the group of secure pairs. We explored this assumption in a follow-up study.

The interactive nature of reading narrative texts to 3-year-olds

The text used in this study has pictures, but the illustrations are mainly extensions of the text or linguistic message. The characteristic structure of the story-book itself, however, plays a major role in providing the clues to access meanings in that text. The text has all the characteristics of written language, i.e. it is continuous prose and has a disembodied quality to it. Unlike oral communication, where the situational context can also be used to interpret what is said, written communication focuses on the actual text as the carrier of meaning. To realize coherent text, written language includes forms that differ in varying degrees from the everyday language used in face-to-face situations (Bus and Sulzby, 1993; Feitelson *et al.*, 1993). Spoken Hebrew, for example, has undergone a very rapid process of modernization and has dropped conjugations of nouns, as well as many other usages that go back to ancient times, whereas these are largely retained in written texts, including in children's books (Feitelson *et al.*, 1991). Although the oral/written gap is less marked in English and Dutch than in Hebrew, these languages contain many differences as well (Sulzby, in press b).

The emergence of literacy implies that the linguistic procedures which are characteristic of the written language register are internalized by children. We expect children to develop ways of thinking that enable them to transcend the immediate context (Pellegrini and Galda, 1991), to become familiarized with the story script (Sulzby, in press b) and to learn language that is worded like written language (Pappas and Brown, 1987; Pappas and Pettegrew, 1991).

Sulzby (in press a) proposed and tested a developmental scheme of independent reading of narratives, i.e. younger and less experienced children recited books with a wording appropriate for oral situations; older and more experienced children used language that was expressed increasingly like written language and the book itself, and their intonation sounded like reading even before they began to pay attention to the text as the source of reading. Finally, children began to try reading from the printed text and to become conventional readers. Her scheme has eleven subcategories organized under five major categories:

1. Attending to pictures but not forming stories.
2. Attending to pictures and forming oral stories.
3. Attending to pictures, reading and storytelling speech mixed.
4. Attending to pictures and forming written-like stories.
5. Attending to print.

It seems reasonable to suppose that adults support the developmental scheme proposed by Sulzby and that there is, parallel to the developmental scheme of independent reading, a stage-like developmental sequence in the nature of interactive book reading. Thus, in the follow-up study we examined how the parental role changes as children become more experienced and knowledgeable. In this study three groups participated: 3-year-olds from a low socio-economic status (SES) with infrequent reading experience (at most once or twice a week); 3-year-olds from a low SES with frequent reading experience (at least once a day); and 3-year-olds from a high SES with frequent reading experience (at least once a day). The mothers read an illustrated story-book in a session at our laboratory.

Developmental nature of book reading

Most mothers followed a similar routine: after reading a page, or less, the text was extensively discussed, with the discussion mostly initiated by the mothers. Reading a text word by word is usually assumed not to be sufficient to make a book understandable for a young child, even if the book is very simple. The mothers seemed to assume that the pictures and text are not self-evident and that the child needs help to make inferences. I expect that mothers with a low level of literacy have difficulty in initiating such dialogues (e.g. Edwards, 1989, in press). Recently, we have made video tapes of a near-illiterate mother reading the same narrative to her 3-year-old son on several different occasions, which support this assumption. The sessions suggest that adults with a low level of literacy may consider reading to be verbalizing, and do not diagnose other obstacles to reading comprehension. The observations were made to test a procedure which is to be used in a study on the effect of repeated reading. We were unprepared for the fact that this mother had a low level of literacy when we asked her to read a complex illustrated story-book to her 3-year-old son. What struck us most forcibly was that she made no attempt to adapt the situation to her own level or to her son's comprehension. She took our request 'to read the book to her child' literally, and went right through the book, not reading fluently and with a poor intonation, and without paying any attention to her son or checking his level of comprehension. Only at the very end did she point once to two characters, saying: 'See, there are Bram and Karel.' During consecutive sessions following the same procedure she made even fewer attempts to adapt to her son's comprehension level, even though now she was familiar with the book, and the experimenter had explained to her that there was no need to read it word for word. It was quite clear that she did not appreciate that reading is not the same thing as pronouncing words from a book. She had no strategy to make the complex story-book comprehensible. During both sessions the child sat beside his mother paying hardly any attention to the book. His eyes focused on other objects in the room, and on no occasion did he respond, verbally or non-verbally, to the events which could be seen in the illustrations or were read by his mother.

Comparing the children who were read to daily and the children who were read to once or twice a week, we found significant differences in the quality of reading. The typical pattern of reading episodes with older and/or more competent children differed greatly from that with younger and/or less competent children. First, the comparison of frequently and infrequently reading mother–child pairs revealed significant contrasts in the number of explanations, suggesting that the digressive tactics are more characteristic of interaction with very young and/or inexperienced children (see also DeLoache and DeMendoza, 1987). As the children grow older and more experienced, there is much less elaboration of and communication on the pictures and/or text. Heath (1984) also reports that when children reach the age of about 3, her sample of middle-class and lower-income, white parents began to discourage the highly interactive dialogue readings which had been typical when their children were younger.

Second, the comparison revealed qualitative differences in the level of explanations. To test this assumption we focused on parts of the story which require inferences in order to understand the plot. For example, the story starts with Doedel, a mouse, looking everywhere for his 'special gloves'. In the text, no explanation is given of why he needs gloves to pick strawberries. The reader has to use schemes of strawberries (hairy) and mice (little feet) to understand that the hairs may hurt a little mouse. The book has a lot of decontextualization, i.e. saying everything in the text, but like many other children's books, it also has sections in which the text is contextualized by means of illustrations. Because the story is being told from the mouse's point of view the reader is required to link the text to the illustrations in some places. For example, the reader has to deduce from a picture that the 'big strawberry' mentioned in the text is in fact a dog's nose. In the next passage, it is not explained what happens to the mouse when he tries to pick this 'strawberry'. The explanation of Doedel's experience ('Suddenly the strawberry begins to shake violently') has to be deduced from the illustration of the dog shaking its head and the little mouse hanging on to its nose. Passages such as this usually prompt the mother to help with additional scaffolding. Most children, for example, take the text literally and look for the big strawberry. Most mothers made this point explicit, highlighting that the mouse *thinks* that there is a huge strawberry, but that the strawberry is really a dog's nose. Comparing frequently and infrequently reading dyads it appeared that inferences were more often explained in the latter group. There seems to be a decrease in the number of explicitly stated inferences as children become more experienced and more competent. However, the frequently reading dyads from a high SES made more inferences than both low SES groups and, in particular, more than the frequently reading dyads from a low SES. To explain this finding, we assumed that mothers from a high SES are more inclined to explain complex inferences even when children are quite experienced in reading complex story-books (see also Dickinson *et al.*, 1992).

Thirdly, we found no differences in textual changes as a function of past experience in being read to. We did find attempts to simplify the text by omitting or substituting words (Bus *et al.*, 1993). Grammatical changes, on the contrary, hardly ever occurred. But the number and kind of changes were similar for both groups. One explanation may be that the book contained many difficult words even for frequently read-to children.

On the basis of Sulzby's scheme of independent reading and the results reported here, we propose a scheme of four types of reading sessions:

1. Commenting on the pictures.
2. Extended discussions, primarily about the pictures.
3. Some discussion, primarily about the story plot.
4. Reading the text alone.

The following descriptions exemplify this variety of reading styles (Bus and De Groot, 1993). Because of the restricted age range and differences in reading experience, not all types were available to the same degree in the present data base.

Type 1

Only one mother ignored the text and made attempts to tell (parts of) the story, paraphrasing the text and commenting on the pictures. The story plot was ignored for the most part and mother and child mainly discussed the contents of the illustrations. This mother told us subsequently that she considered the book to be too difficult for her child and that she preferred simple stories like the Spot series with little text and a story told by the pictures. We suspected that in several cases this way of reading the book would be more productive than reading the text word for word. However, this style of story-book reading occurred quite rarely in the sample.

The mother of Lisanne, age 36 months, tells the story on the basis of the pictures. She starts to name objects and characters in the pictures and comments on the apparent behaviour or events. This mother never holds a monologue but continuously tries to elicit a response from her child. When the mother notices that her daughter does not understand, she does not make any further attempt to explain the story plot but confines the discussion to the details in the pictures. After reading the book once, the mother starts again, but this time in an even less story-oriented manner. All kinds of details (shelves, snail houses, little paws, nails, etc.) are discussed. The mother often relates the pictures to real-life experiences: 'Grandma also has strawberries.'

Type 2

Most mothers in this group read the text (more or less) literally but after a short piece of text the events on the page were discussed extensively. These mothers mostly discussed the details of the pictures.

Joyce, age 38 months, shows little interest to begin with, but after a while she participates actively in the reading session. Sometimes she initiates discussions on the text. Mother reads the text almost verbatim but with minor changes here and there. For example, instead of 'till the strawberry had disappeared', she reads 'till nothing of the strawberry was left.' After reading each piece of text there is a discussion, mostly initiated by the mother. Most discussions relate to details of the pictures: butterfly, mosquito, snail, glove, shelves, etc. The mother also tries to focus the child's attention on the story plot with the help of questions. However, when she notices that her daughter does not understand, she stops and confines herself to the details of the illustrations. The child is actively involved till the end.

Type 3

The third and fourth level were quite rare in this group of 3-year-olds. Mothers at the third level discussed only those events that were hard to infer from pictures and/or text.

Guido, 46 months old, responds to the story and not to the pictures during the whole session. If Guido does not understand the story line he asks for an explanation. Guido's responses indicate that he is able to understand the story and to anticipate the events that are going to happen. When the dog is visible in a picture and the text indicates that Doedel thinks that his nose is a strawberry, Guido calls out spontaneously: 'Oh, what will happen now?' At the same time he nestles close to his mother in a state of tension. The mother discusses only those events which are crucial to comprehend the story plot. She discusses the illustrations in so far as they are needed for story comprehension. For example, she points to the board 'Beware of the dog' before the dog is introduced in the text and later, when the dog is visible in a picture, she refers to the board again. If the mother feels that the story is not logical, she explains why. When she does not under-stand why Doedel needs gloves to pick strawberries, she comments: 'I don't understand this. Did you wear gloves when you went to pick strawberries?' When the child asks a question which cannot be answered with the available information ('Is he a nice dog?') she refers to the following text: 'We may read about that on the next page.' At the end of the book she speculates about what may happen in the future, together with Guido.

Type 4

At the fourth level children sat and listened like an audience. Few interruptions were made, either by adult or child, during the reading of the text. After the text had been read, however, mothers often asked questions about the book or engaged the child in extensive discussions.

Tom, 40 months old, concentrates during the book reading session but does not often respond verbally to the book. Mother reads the text more or less verbatim, only breaking off now and then with comments. During the whole session she quickly continues reading without making concerted attempts to elicit comments from the child. Only a few times does a somewhat longer discussion occur. In almost all cases these discussions focus on the story plot. When the whole book has been read, mother initiates a longer discussion recalling the main events of the story.

Mother–child security and the frequency of reading

Assuming that insecurely attached children have negative expectations of parental assistance during reading, in the light of their past experience, it is plausible to hypothesize that insecure children will show less interest in books because understanding depends strongly on parental help. Bus and Van IJzendoorn (1993) tested this assumption that attachment security is related to the frequency of book reading at the age of 3 years when most children – at least in the Netherlands – are read to by their mothers. We followed a procedure similar to that in the preceding study. After a separation mother and child were reunited and played together. We scored the child's behaviour during the first 5 minutes of the reunion. Most children experienced this separation as mildly stressful. The separation was discontinued if a child was very confused by the situation and refused to cooperate with the experimenter during the mother's absence. The results show that the frequency of story-book reading strongly depends on the security of the parent–child relationship. In a group of infrequent readers from a low SES, insecure children are strongly overrepresented (73 per cent) compared to the group of frequent readers from a low SES (33 per cent) or frequent readers from a high SES (13 per cent). This result is in line with previous research showing that insecure children are less inclined to share a book with their mother. We also explored qualitative differences in the reading process and the relationship between these results and the child's security. Surprisingly, the security of the attachment relationship between mother and child was not related to thematically irrelevant discussions, a finding that seems to contradict results of the cross-sectional study (Bus and Van IJzendoorn, 1988b). In the present study, however, we considered all discussions that were not related to the text as thematically irrelevant. In former studies we focused only on disciplining interactions. In addition, we did not find any relation between attachment security and instruction strategies. Differences in reading strategy appeared to be more strongly related to reading experience and competence than to the quality of the mother–child relationship.

Our results clearly support a relation between mother–child security and book reading; however, we have to consider alternative interpretations, such as an effect of the reading session on the child's behaviour during the separation–reunion session (Bus, 1993). We were also able to support our assumption that the child's behaviour during the reunion is an indicator of a fundamental characteristic of the parent–child relationship. In the study comparing frequently and infrequently reading dyads, we also measured the mother's mental representation of her own attachment experiences (Bus and Van IJzendoorn, 1992). We used the 'Adult Attachment Interview', developed by Main and her colleagues (1985). The 'Adult Attachment Interview' is a semi-structured interview in which questions about general characteristics of the subjects' relationship with their own parents are supplemented with questions about specific childhood events and about the current relationship with their parents. The coding system leads to a classification of the interview in terms of security of attachment. We found a strong relationship between the reunion score and an independent measure – the 'Adult Attachment Interview' – which has proved to be a strong predictor of the attachment relationship between parents and their own children. As a consequence of this finding, we can conclude that it is implausible that the children's behaviour during the reunion session shows situation-specific behaviour that is strongly influenced by events in the laboratory session.

Conclusions

We use the story-book reading paradigm to understand how children become literate in the pre-school period. The results may contribute to improving the teaching of children from disadvantaged homes. Sulzby (in press a; see also Feitelson and Bus, 1993) suggests that whereas many middle-class children are eventually successful even with educational programmes that are not developmentally appropriate, many less advantaged children do not progress as effortlessly. These children may require programmes that are more closely designed, like the kind of instruction and discovery that middle-class children receive via their informal instruction at home.

In the present chapter I have discussed some studies we have done on the parental role while reading story-books. Our descriptions of the developmental nature of interactive reading of new books supports the role of mediating parental behaviour. Parents discuss the parts of the book that children cannot comprehend by themselves. The results of both clearly suggest that adults show a high degree of sensitivity to their child's developing abilities. When reading alphabet books or very simple story-books attention shifts from a focus on the content of the pictures to the formal characteristics of the books, such as letters and words. The results of the study focused on the reading of a narrative suggest a developmental quality of interactive reading with attention shifting from explanations surrounding the reading of the text to simply reading the text, and from discussions about details of the pictures to discussions mainly focused on the story plot. The studies do not support the theory that parents instruct, in the sense that they supply information, which the child uses unchanged. However, parents do initiate interactions on those things that children are not yet able to do themselves.

The results of the current studies strongly support the idea that children's interest in reading is more dependent on the parent–child relationship than on the child's own characteristics. If the parent–child relationship is insecure, the sessions are often problematic and pairs are less inclined to engage in book reading. An explanation for these findings may be that insecure children lack trust in their parents and that insecure parents do not know how to excite their child's interest nor how to deal with the child's signals of anxiety or curiosity. In contrast to earlier studies (Matas *et al.*, 1978; Bates *et al.*, 1985), our studies did not reveal strong support for the assumption that mothers of insecure children are doing less well as teachers and that they have problems in adapting to different levels of emergent reading and in bridging the gap between the child's level of understanding and conventional reading. Experience with interactive book reading seems sufficient to affect the mother's attention-focusing behaviour and the level of the child's participation (see also Heath, 1984). Whatever the explanation for the relation between attachment security and frequency and quality of reading may be, our results strongly suggest that for children the main motive for reading story-books is the intimacy it affords with their parent during the reading session. Interest in story-books seems to be a result of sharing the book rather than a motive to read the book. We feel that we are on the right track in understanding the developing nature of interactive sessions and how learning processes are stimulated in consecutive stages. While studying the repeated reading of a story-book and the relationship between independent and interactive reading we will explore the emerging picture further (Bus *et al.*, in prep.).

The results of our studies support the assumption that parental help is a factor in children's literacy development. Intervention programmes aimed at stimulating story-book reading in the family should take into account the fact that the pleasure of sharing a book is the main incentive for book reading. In addition to evocative techniques to mediate between the child and the book content (e.g. Whitehurst *et al.*, 1988) parents may need examples that illustrate how to deal with their child's emotional responses and how to share the pleasure of reading a book. The developmental and emotional part of story-book reading may even argue against a prescriptive approach to describing and teaching book-sharing techniques. Our findings underline that intergenerational literacy programmes should focus on the pleasure of reading and on integrating reading into everyday routines, separately or in addition to didactic approaches (e.g. Eldridge-Hunter, 1992). However, our results also indicate that we have to be careful with interventions aimed at stimulating book reading in young children. We have to consider the possible disadvantages of insistence on engaging parents and children in an interactive situation, which they dislike. Continuation of book reading might even serve to solidify the child's negative attitude.

References

Bates, J.E., Maslin, C.A. and Frankel, K.A. (1985), 'Attachment security, mother–child interaction, and temperament as predictors of behavior-problem ratings at age three years'. In I. Bretherton and E. Waters (eds.) *Growing Points of Attachment Theory and Research. Monographs of the Society for Research in Child Development, 50* (1–2, Serial No. 209), 167–94.

Bretherton, I. (1985), 'Attachment theory: retrospect and prospect.' In I. Bretherton and E. Waters (eds.) *Growing Points of Attachment Theory and Research. Monographs of the Society for Research in Child Development, 50*, (1–2, Serial No. 209), 3–37.

Bruner, J.S. (1975), 'Language as an instrument of thought'. In A. Davies (ed.) *Problems of Language and Learning*, London: Heinemann.

Bus, A.G. (1986), 'Een onderzoek naar voorbereidend leesonderwijs: Een ontwikkelings-perspectief' [A study into pre-reading instruction: a developmental perspective]. In P. Reitsma, A.G. Bus and W. van Bon (eds.) *Leren lezen en spellen*, Lisse: Swets & Zeitlinger, pp. 33–8.

Bus, A.G. (1991), 'Kleuters op weg naar begrijpend lezen' [Kindergarten children on their way to reading comprehension]. In P. Reitsma and M. Walraven (eds.) *Instructie in begrijpend lezen*, Delft: Eburon, pp. 77–92.

Bus, A.G. (1993), 'Attachment and emergent literacy', *International Journal of Educational Research, 19*, 573–81.

Bus, A.G. and De Groot, I.M. (1993), *Voorlezen aan 3-jarigen. Vier leesniveaus en de wijze waarop moeders daarop inspelen.* [Reading to Three-year-olds. Four reading levels and the way mothers 'tune in' at the child's level of understanding], manual and video tape, Leiden: SARDES/Leiden University.

Bus, A.G., De Groot, I. and Van Dijk, I. (1993), *Vereenvoudiging van tekst als hulpmiddel bij voorlezen* [Simplifying Text as an Aid to Make Text Comprehensible], Leiden: Centre for Child and Family Studies, Leiden University.

Bus, A.G., and Sulzby, E. (1993), *The Role of Parent-Child Interactions in LSES Children's Refusals to Read Emergently*, unpublished manuscript, Leiden University/University of Michigan.

Bus, A.G., Sulzby, E. and Van IJzendoorn, M.H. (in prep.), *Children's Internalizations from Repeated Storybook Readings: A study of emergent literacy and attachments.*

Bus, A.G. and Van IJzendoorn, M.H. (1988a), 'Mother–child interactions, attachment, and emergent literacy: a cross-sectional study', *Child Development, 59*, 1262–73.

Bus, A.G. and Van IJzendoorn, M.H. (1988b), 'Attachment and early reading: a longitudinal study', *Journal of Genetic Psychology, 149*, 199–210.

Bus, A.G. and Van IJzendoorn, M.H. (1992), 'Patterns of attachment in frequently and infrequently reading dyads', *Journal of Genetic Psychology, 153*, 395–403.

Bus, A.G. and Van IJzendoorn, M.H. (1993), *The Reading of a New Story to Three-year-olds by their Mother: Validity of a social construction orientation*, Leiden: Centre for child and family studies, Leiden University.

Bus, A.G., Van IJzendoorn, M.H. and Pellegrini, A.D. (1993). *Joint Book Reading Makes for Success in Learning to Read: A meta-analysis of intergenerational transmission of literacy.* Unpublished manuscript, Leiden University, Leiden.

Bus, A.G., Van IJzendoorn, M.H. and Koole, P. (in prep.), *Stranger Anxiety and Children's Willingness to Pretend Reading*, unpublished paper, Centre for Child and Family Studies, Leiden University.

DeLoache, J.S. and DeMendoza, O.A.P. (1987), 'Joint picture book interactions of mothers and 1-year-old children', *British Journal of Developmental Psychology, 5*, 11–123.

Dickinson, D.K., De Temple, J.M., Hirschler, J.A. and Smith, M.W. (1992), 'Book reading with preschoolers: construction of text at home and at school', *Early Childhood Research Quarterly, 7*, 323–46.

Edwards, P.A. (1989), 'Supporting lower SES mothers' attempts to provide scaffolding for bookreading.' In J. Allen and J. Mason (eds.) *Risk Makers, Risk Takers, Risk Breakers: Reducing the Risks for Young Literacy Learners*, Portsmouth, NH: Heinemann, pp. 222–50.

Edwards, P.A. (in press), 'Responses of teachers and African-American mothers to a book reading intervention program'. In D. Dickinson (ed.), *Bridges to Literacy*, New York: Basil Blackwell.

Elbers, E. (1991), 'The development of competence and its social context', *Educational Psychology Review, 3*, 73–94.

Eldridge-Hunter, D. (1992), 'Intergenerational literacy: impact on the development of the storybook reading behaviors of hispanic mothers', *Yearbook of the National Reading Conference, 42*, 101–10.

Feitelson, D. and Bus, A.G. (1993), 'Introduction to a special issue on beginning reading instruction', *International Journal of Educational Research, 19*, 3–6.

Feitelson, D., Goldstein, Z., Eshel, M., Flasher, A., Levin, M. and Sharon, S. (1991), *Effects of Exposure to Literary Language on Kindergartners' Listening Comprehension and Use of Language*, unpublished manuscript, University of Haifa.

Feitelson, D., Goldstein, Z., Iraqi, J. and Share, D.L. (1993), 'Effects of listening to story reading on aspects of literacy acquisition in a diglossic situation', *Reading Research Quarterly, 28*, 70–9.

Heath, S.B. (1984), 'The achievement of preschool literacy for mother and child.' In H. Goelberg, A. Oberg and F. Smith (eds.) *Awaking to Literacy*, Portsmouth, NH: Heinemann, pp. 51–72.

Lancy, D.F. (in press), 'The conditions that support emergent literacy.' In D.F. Lancy (ed.) *Children's Emergent Literacy from Research to Practice*, Westport, CT: Praeger.

Main, M., Kaplan, N. and Cassidy, J. (1985), 'Security in infancy, childhood, and adulthood: a move to the level of representation.' In I. Bretherton and E. Waters (eds.) *Growing Points of Attachment Theory and Research. Monographs of the Society for Research in Child Development, 50*, 1–1 (Serial No. 209) 66–106.

Matas, L., Arend, R.A. and Sroufe, L.A. (1978), 'Continuity of adaptation in the second year: the relationship between quality of attachment and later competence', *Child Development, 49*, 547–56.

Pappas, C.C. and Brown, E. (1987), 'Learning to read by reading: learning how to extend the functional potential of language', *Research in the Teaching of English, 21*, 160–84.

Pappas, C.C. and Pettegrew, B.S. (1991), 'Learning to tell: aspects of developmental communicative competence in young children's story retellings', *Curriculum Inquiry, 21*, 419–34.

Pellegrini, A.D. and Galda, L. (1991), 'Longitudinal relations among preschoolers' symbolic play, metalinguistic verbs, and emergent literacy'. In J. Christie (ed.) *Play and Early Literacy Development*, Albany, NY: SUNY Press, pp. 47–68.

Pellegrini, A.D., Perlmutter, J.C., Galda, L. and Brody, G.H. (1990), 'Joint book reading between black Head Start children and their mothers', *Child Development, 61*, 443–53.

Purcell-Gates, V. (1988), 'Lexical and syntactic knowledge of written narrative held by well-read-to kindergartners and second graders', *Research in the Teaching of English, 22*, 128–60.

Snow, C.E. (1983), 'Literacy and language: relationships during the preschool years', *Harvard Educational Review, 53*, 165–89.

Sulzby, E. (in press a). 'Children's emergent reading of favorite storybooks: a developmental study'. In R. Ruddell and M. R. Ruddell (eds.) *Theoretical Model and Processes of Reading*, 4th edn, Newark, DE: International Reading Association. (Reprinted from *Reading Research Quarterly, 20*, 458–81.)

Sulzby, E. (in press b), 'Roles of oral and written language as children approach conventional literacy.' In C. Pontecorvo and M. Orsolini (eds.) *Early Text Construction in Children*, Hillsdale, NJ: Lawrence Erlbaum.

Sulzby, E. and Edwards, P. (in press), 'The role of parents in supporting literacy development of young children'. In B. Spodek and O.N. Saracho (eds.) *Yearbook in Early Childhood Education.* Vol. 4: *Early Childhood Language and Literacy.* New York: Teachers College Press.

Sulzby, E. and Teale, W.H. (1987), *Young Children's Storybook Reading: Longitudinal study of parent–child interaction and children's independent functioning*, Final report to the Spencer Foundation, Ann Arbor, MI: The University of Michigan.

Sulzby, E. and Teale, W.H. (1991), 'Emergent literacy'. In R. Barr, M.L. Kamil, P. Mosenthal and P.D. Pearson (eds.) *Handbook of Reading Research*, Vol. II New York: Longman, pp. 727–57.

Teale, W.H. (1986), 'Home background and young children's literacy development.' In W.H. Teale and E. Sulzby (eds.) *Emergent Literacy. Writing and Reading*, Norwood, NJ: Ablex, pp. 173–206.

Whitehurst, G.J., Falco, F.L., Lonigan, C.J., Fischel, J.E., DeBaryshe, B.D., Valdez-Menchaca, M.C. and Caulfield, M. (1988), 'Accelerating language development through picture book reading', *Developmental Psychology, 24*, 552–9.

3

Codes, connections, context and constructive processes: integrating the Vygotskian and Lurian perspectives[1,2]

Virginia Wise Berninger
College of Education, University of Washington

In this chapter I shall discuss the Vygotskian perspective on the social foundations of cognitive development and the Lurian perspective on the individual working brain system. Then, I shall apply both perspectives to understanding literacy acquisition. My aim is to show that the social contextual perspective and the neuropsychological perspective can be integrated into theoretical models of reading and writing acquisition and in educational practice. These perspectives are neither mutually exclusive nor incompatible, although the belief that they are is widespread. This misconception permeates not only the educational and cognitive fields, but also artificial intelligence, which is divided as to whether intelligence should be modelled in terms of the individual thinking machine (e.g. Minsky, 1986) or in terms of the social network (e.g. Roschelle and Clancey, 1992) with which that individual machine interfaces.

The Vygotskian perspective

Vygotsky believed that the scientific psychology of his time needed to go beyond the behaviourists' reductionism to the cultural context in which the mind develops. To make the transition he proposed the ontogenetic method, which has two major tenets. The first is that human behaviour should be studied as a process by tracing developmental change over time. The second is that changes

1. Direct correspondence to 322J Miller DQ-12, University of Washington, Seattle, WA 98195, USA.
2. Research reported in this chapter was supported by Grant No. 25858–02 from the National Institute of Child Health and Human Development.

in culture lead to changes in human nature (Olswang *et al.*, 1992). He applied this method to show how social interaction between dyads or within small groups leads to higher mental functioning in the individual (Wertsch, 1985).

Vygotsky's claim that the mechanism of individual change is rooted in culture (Cole and Scribner, 1978) and social interactions (Vygotsky, 1960) has often been pitted against Piaget's claim that the origin of intelligence is in the interactions between the nervous system and the sensorimotor activities of the infant (Piaget, 1970). These views are not necessarily contradictory. Social interactions may facilitate verbal intelligence and declarative knowledge, whereas sensorimotor interactions with the physical environment may facilitate nonverbal intelligence and procedural knowledge (Berninger, 1988a; Berninger *et al.*, 1988; Berninger and Hart, 1992).

Vygotsky identified two key phenomena in cultural development: internalization and the zone of proximal development. He believed that higher mental functions were rooted in the transition from inter-individual activity to intra-individual activity (Vygotsky, 1981a). However, the internal representation within the individual is not a simple copy of the social processes leading to it, but rather it is a transformation of those processes (Vygotsky, 1981b). The zone of proximal development is the distance between the child's independent problem-solving ability and the child's ability to solve problems under guidance from adults or more able peers (Vygotsky, 1986). Instruction tailored to this zone moves mental development forward. The notion of a zone of proximal development has influenced research and practice in psychology and education for more than thirty years (Olswang *et al.*, 1992).

Although Vygotsky's emphasis on the influence of social interaction on cognitive development is well known, it is less well known that Vygotsky believed that 'the biological significance of mind is a necessary condition of scientific psychology' (1982, p. 76). As Wertsch (1985) pointed out, Vygotsky, who was familiar with a broad range of disciplines, rejected single-factor explanations of development. Influenced by the study of physiology, Vygotsky viewed higher mental processes as functional systems. He thought that scientific child psychology should be based on a solid biological foundation despite the fact that biological forces could not be viewed as the sole force of change. According to Vygotsky, social factors operate within a biological framework, but development cannot be reduced to biological factors – both biological and social factors are needed to explain mental development. Vygotsky and Luria (1930) proposed that behaviour should be studied within the context of *evolutionary, historical* (cultural) and *ontogenic* (individual) development, each of which has its own unique set of explanatory principles. Although Vygotsky envisaged a natural or biological line of development as well as a social line of development, he focused almost exclusively on social or cultural development in his own research. It was his pupil, Luria, who was explicit about the biological line of development and added to our knowledge of it.

The Lurian perspective

Using the clinical method with patients with neurological disorders, Luria focused on individual development independent of its cultural context. Luria (1973) identified three functional units of the individual working brain and five stages of their development: (1) the *arousal unit* regulates arousal and responsiveness to the environment; (2) the *information processing unit* obtains, stores and processes incoming information; and (3) the *programming/regulating unit* makes and carries out plans of action directed to the future, and performs executive functions for self-regulation. Hooper and Boyd (1986) charted the neuro-developmental stages in which these functional units develop. These stages overlap to some degree, but differ as to which functional units or neural substrates of functional units mature when. For example, the first and second stages (see below) develop concurrently, but differ as to which unit is developing (arousal or information processing) and as to when full maturity is reached (1 year or 2 years).

The arousal unit is working during the *first stage* (birth to 1 year) when infants learn to regulate their sleep–awake cycle. The primary zones (which mediate sensory and motor functions) of the information processing unit mature and begin to work during the *second stage* (birth to 2 years) when infants and toddlers are developing their perceptual and motor skills. The secondary zones (which integrate sensory and motor functions) of the information processing unit become functional during the *third stage* (2 to 5 years) when pre-schoolers develop their perceptual-motor skills. The tertiary zones (which integrate input from the secondary zones and are abstract and not modality-specific) of the information processing unit develop during the *fourth stage* (5 to 12 years) when children acquire the abstract reasoning skills necessary for learning academic subjects. The programming/regulating unit develops during the *fifth stage* (6 to adult years) when ability to plan and regulate behaviour increases.

Of these stages, the fourth and fifth are the most important for literacy acquisition. Shurtleff *et al.* (1993) used structural equation modelling to test Hooper and Boyd's (1986) hypothesis that the fourth stage is a prerequisite for learning academic subjects. In the first grade (6 to 7 years of age) the model treating Stages 3 and 4 as a single factor in predicting the reading/spelling factor provided the best fit, suggesting that most children had achieved Stage 4 neuro-development. There is a good biological reason why children begin formal schooling and literacy instruction about the same time in all cultures (around 5 or 6 years) – that is, when the tertiary zones of the information processing unit become functional (Hooper and Boyd, 1986). The fifth stage contributes to literacy learning by allowing the child to monitor and regulate behaviour during reading and writing activities.

Although Luria added to our understanding of the biological framework in which literacy learning occurs, he did not explicitly investigate the process of learning to read and write. Over the past ten years my colleagues and I have investigated reading and writing acquisition from the developmental neuropsychological perspective, which postulates both biological constraints and educational constraints on the literacy acquisition process (Berninger, 1994). Below I provide an overview of those findings of that research programme that are relevant to the theme of this chapter – the importance of considering both the individual learner and the social context in which learning occurs.

Representations and operations

The brain can be analyzed at many levels, including its microstructure (e.g. single neurons and their connections) and macrostructure (e.g. collections of neurons in larger systems such as the lobes of cerebral cortex) and its microfunctions (activity of individual neurons) and macrofunctions (activity of collections of neurons). Within the macrofunctions, a distinction is made between representations – data structures – and operations that act upon those data structures (Berninger, 1994, Table 1.1). This distinction is relevant to the theme of this chapter because social interaction may exert a greater influence on the content of the stimulus representations than on the lower-level microfunctions of the brain, which are biologically constrained.

Much research in experimental psychology manipulates stimulus variables, which are indices of representation, while keeping tasks, an index of operations, constant. In contrast, Berninger (1988b) systematically varied tasks while keeping stimuli constant. Of interest was whether significant interactions occurred between the linguistic tasks (lexical decision, naming and written reproduction) and the stimuli, showing that procedures for operating upon stimulus words exist independently of stimulus representations. Significant task–stimulus interactions occurred for pseudowords[1] at the beginning, middle and end of the first year of schooling but did not occur for phonically regular real words or for phonically irregular real words after the beginning of the first year. These results suggest that stimulus representations and processing operations are independent of one another for novel words that must be decoded, but that stimulus representations and processing operations may be integrated for real words in the sight vocabulary that are recognized automatically.

More recently, a similar analysis was conducted as part of a large-scale psychometric study of reading and writing acquisition (Berninger *et al.*, 1994). A set of eighteen pseudowords of varying difficulty was selected from the 'Word Attack' subtest of the Woodcock Reading Mastery Test – Revised (Woodcock, 1987). Ninety-two fourth-graders were asked to perform four different tasks with the same set of words. Order of the target tasks was kept constant across children: spelling, phonological, orthographic and reading. Several other tasks with different stimuli were interspersed between each of these target tasks using the constant set of stimulus words. For the spelling task, children wrote the pseudowords from dictation. For the phonological task, children were asked to repeat the pseudoword and then to say it again deleting a designated phoneme or rime unit (the part of the syllable remaining when the onset phoneme is deleted).

Table 3.1 Percentage correct on each task for the same stimulus word

	Phonological (%)	Orthographic (%)	Reading (%)	Spelling (%)
raff	79	89	98	64
bim	99	93	99	78
pog	99	99	97	57
plip	76	88	86	58
dud's	93	97	86	76
vunhip	60	47	78	24
bufty	74	83	86	65
than't	74	96	71	51
tadding	23	89	91	18
twem	66	89	76	53
adjex	73	78	80	38
zirdn't	43	64	79	51
knoink	57	61	49	29
cigbet	87	48	38	57
bafmotbem	25	39	47	10
translibsodge	32	91	50	4
monglustamer	5	62	37	21
pnomocher	60	7	9	52
M	62.5%	73.3%	69.8%	44.8%
SD	27.3	25.2	25.5	22.2

For the orthographic task, the target pseudoword was displayed briefly then removed, and the children were asked to reproduce the entire pseudoword or a designated letter or a designated letter cluster in the pseudoword. For the reading task, children were asked to pronounce the pseudoword aloud.

Results in Tables 3.1–3.6 are reported by stimulus words, which are organized according to difficulty level on the *Woodcock Reading Mastery Test – Revised*. Clearly, on all tasks some words were more difficult than others.

Overall, the orthographic task was the easiest and the spelling task was the most difficult (see means and standard deviations, Table 3.1). On the average, children tended to be successful across all four tasks for a given stimulus word only about 25 per cent of the time (see Table 3.2). About 40 per cent of the time they were successful on only two tasks or only one task for a given stimulus word (see Table 3.2). These results suggest that children may be successful in applying some but not all operations to the same stimulus word.

To show that success was not just a function of task difficulty, conditional probabilities were computed for every possible combination of tasks taken two at a time, summed over subjects for a particular stimulus item. If a child was successful on the phonological task, the probability was about 0.75 that the child would also be successful on the orthographic or reading task, but only about 0.50 that the child would also be successful on the spelling task (see Table 3.3). If a child was successful on the orthographic task, the probability was again 0.75, or close to that value, that the child would be successful on the phonological or

Table 3.2 Percentage of successes across different tasks for the same stimulus word

	Number of tasks correct				
	4(%)	3(%)	2(%)	1(%)	0(%)
raff	49	37	11	2	1
bim	74	21	4	1	0
pog	52	47	1	0	0
plip	39	37	17	5	1
dud's	62	26	10	2	0
vunhip	11	31	22	26	10
bufty	43	30	17	4	4
than't	31	38	22	8	1
tadding	7	26	53	11	3
twem	24	45	16	13	2
adjex	24	40	20	13	3
zirdn't	16	34	25	20	5
knoink	7	28	28	28	9
cigbet	16	27	33	18	5
bafmotbem	0	6	33	36	25
translibsodge	2	16	42	35	4
monglustamer	0	9	31	36	24
pnomocher	0	11	28	38	23
M	25.4%	28.3%	22.9%	16.4%	6.7%
SD	23.1	12.0	12.9	13.6	8.5

Table 3.3 Conditional probability of success on orthographic, reading, and spelling tasks if phonological task is successful

	Orthographic	Reading	Spelling
raff	0.92	0.99	0.64
bim	0.92	0.97	0.79
pog	0.99	0.97	0.56
plip	0.90	0.87	0.66
dud's	0.97	0.90	0.73
vunhip	0.60	0.87	0.27
bufty	0.90	0.91	0.69
than't	0.97	0.76	0.59
tadding	1.00	0.95	0.33
twem	0.85	0.85	0.46
adjex	0.82	0.73	0.45
zirdn't	0.75	0.88	0.80
knoink	0.60	0.60	0.27
cigbet	0.50	0.63	0.78
bafmotbem	0.35	0.57	0.04
translibsodge	0.93	0.66	0.07
monglustamer	0.80	0.40	0.80
pnomocher	0.09	0.13	0.56
M	0.77	0.76	0.53
SD	0.25	0.23	0.24

Table 3.4 Conditional probability of success on phonological, reading, and spelling tasks if orthographic task is successful

	Phonological	Reading	Spelling
raff	0.82	0.99	0.61
bim	0.98	0.99	0.80
pog	0.99	0.97	0.58
plip	0.78	0.89	0.60
dud's	0.93	0.89	0.72
vunhip	0.74	0.91	0.33
bufty	0.80	0.92	0.68
than't	0.75	0.72	0.50
tadding	0.26	0.94	0.20
twem	0.89	0.80	0.46
adjex	0.79	0.89	0.44
zirdn't	0.51	0.85	0.58
knoink	0.54	0.55	0.34
cigbet	0.89	0.52	0.61
bafmotbem	0.22	0.53	0.11
translibsodge	0.32	0.51	0.06
monglustamer	0.05	0.46	0.21
pnomocher	0.83	0.17	0.67
M	0.67	0.75	0.47
SD	0.29	0.23	0.22

reading task, but again only about 0.50 that the child would also be successful on the spelling task (see Table 3.4). If the child was successful on the reading task, the probability was again close to 0.75 that the child would also be successful on the phonological or orthographic tasks, but again only about 0.50 that the child would also be successful on the spelling task (see Table 3.5). If the child was successful on the spelling task, the probability was in the range 0.7–0.8 that the child would also be successful on the phonological, orthographic or reading tasks (see Table 3.6).

Taken together, these results, like those of Berninger (1988b), provide evidence that representation of stimulus words and operations for acting upon those representations may be separable processes for novel words. Much of our research over the past decade has focused on yet another level of representation – the low-level procedures for representing words in memory; that is, the codes involved in representation.

Codes

Definitional issues

Johnson (1978) reviewed the concept of codes in the cognitive psychology literature. Codes are procedures for transforming incoming stimulus information

         Virginia Wise Berninger

Table 3.5 Conditional probability of success on phonological, orthographic and spelling tasks if reading task is successful

	Phonological	Orthographic	Spelling
raff	0.80	0.90	0.82
bim	0.97	0.93	0.79
pog	0.99	0.99	0.55
plip	0.77	0.89	0.59
dud's	0.96	0.96	0.77
vunhip	0.67	0.56	0.77
bufty	0.80	0.89	0.66
than't	0.80	0.97	0.57
tadding	0.25	0.92	0.20
twem	0.74	0.93	0.50
adjex	0.81	0.86	0.41
zirdn't	0.48	0.68	0.55
knoink	0.71	0.71	0.31
cigbet	0.91	0.66	0.71
bafmotbem	0.33	0.44	0.09
translibsodge	0.39	0.91	0.09
monglustamer	0.06	0.74	0.26
pnomocher	0.88	0.13	0.88
M	0.68	0.78	0.50
SC	0.27	0.22	0.25

Table 3.6 Conditional probability of success on phonological, orthographic and reading tasks if spelling task is successful

	Phonological	Orthographic	Reading
raff	0.76	0.95	1.00
bim	1.00	0.94	1.00
pog	0.98	1.00	0.94
plip	0.89	0.91	0.89
dud's	0.96	0.97	0.93
vunhip	0.73	0.68	0.95
bufty	0.80	0.87	0.87
than't	0.81	0.96	0.74
tadding	0.41	0.94	0.94
twem	0.69	0.88	0.88
adjex	0.80	0.77	0.86
zirdn't	0.51	0.72	0.85
knoink	0.70	0.74	0.56
cigbet	0.90	0.58	0.52
bafmotbem	0.67	0.67	0.44
translibsodge	0.50	1.00	1.00
monglustamer	0.11	0.63	0.42
pnomocher	0.67	0.10	0.15
M	0.72	0.80	0.77
SD	0.22	0.22	0.25

into unitary mental representations. Codes are not the same as the information they represent – the content of a code becomes available only after the coding process is complete. Two kinds of code have been identified: integrative codes for rule-governed processes, and representative codes for processes governed by examples or specific cases rather than rules. For example, phonics relies on rule-governed codes, whereas sight word recognition relies on word-specific representative codes.

Biological basis

Both rule-governed codes, as measured by pseudoword reading, and representative codes, as measured by the homophone/pseudohomophone choice task, are heritable or genetically constrained to some degree (Olson, in press). Positron emission tomography (PET) studies show that different codes are activated in specific brain regions. For example, Posner *et al.* (1988) showed that visual coding for written words occurred in five areas of the occipital lobe. Semantic coding for spoken words occurred in the anterior left frontal lobe. Phonological coding for spoken words occurred in the primary auditory cortex and an area of the left temporoparietal cortex. Thus, coding procedures are lower-level micro-functions of the individual's brain that have a biological basis.

Multiple orthographic codes

Visual codes specific to written words are orthographic codes and cannot be equated with visual perception or visual memory, which is usually measured with non-orthographic stimuli such as geometric figures, line drawings or non-alphabetic symbols. Different brain processes are associated with orthographic skills and visual skills not involving orthographic stimuli (Berninger, 1990, 1991, 1994). Multiple orthographic codes – for whole printed words, for a component letter in a word and for letter clusters in a word – are involved in literacy acquisition (Berninger, 1990; see also Assink and Kattenberg, Chapter 6 this volume). Both accuracy and reaction-time data supported a developmental pattern in kindergarten (age 5) children and first-year school children (age 6) in which whole-word coding emerges first, followed by letter coding, then by letter-cluster coding (Berninger, 1987). Accuracy data replicated this developmental pattern in first-, second- and third-graders (Berninger *et al.*, 1991). However, individual differences have been observed in this developmental pattern. For example, 6 per cent of the first-year sample met absolute criteria for disability in whole-word coding, but were not disabled in letter or letter-cluster coding. Four per cent of the first-year sample were disabled in letter coding but not in letter-cluster coding or whole-word coding (Berninger and Hart, 1992).

Berninger *et al.* (1991) examined the relationship between each of the multiple orthographic codes and reading and writing acquisition in the primary grades. To reduce Type 1 errors the alpha level was set at $p < 0.001$. In the first grade each of the orthographic codes was correlated with each of the component reading skills (reading real words, reading pseudowords and reading comprehension) and each of the component writing skills (handwriting, spelling and compositional fluency). In the second grade each of the orthographic codes was correlated with each component reading skill; for the component writing skills, whole-word coding was correlated with spelling, letter coding was correlated with handwriting and spelling, and letter-cluster coding was correlated with handwriting, spelling and compositional fluency. In the third grade, letter coding and letter-cluster coding were correlated with each component reading skill; for the component writing skills, letter coding was correlated with spelling and letter-cluster coding was correlated with handwriting and spelling. Thus, all orthographic codes, including whole-word coding, are important early in reading and writing acquisition, but letter and letter-cluster coding are most important later in reading and writing acquisition.

Using multiple regression, Berninger and Abbott (1992b) found that for *reading real words*, whole-word coding contributed unique variance beyond that contributed by zero-order correlations in the first grade; whole-word and letter coding contributed unique variance in the second grade; and letter-cluster coding contributed unique variance in the third grade. For *reading pseudowords*, letter-cluster coding contributed unique variance in the first grade, whole-word and letter coding contributed unique variance in the second grade, and letter-cluster coding contributed unique variance in the third grade. Using multiple regression, Berninger *et al.* (1992) found that whole-word coding and letter-cluster coding contributed unique variance to handwriting, and letter-cluster coding contributed unique variance to compositional fluency in the primary grades. Taken together, these results show that multiple orthographic codes contribute to literacy acquisition.

Multiple phonological codes

Phonological coding is not the same as auditory processing (Studdert-Kennedy, 1974). Auditory processing is the preliminary, non-linguistic analysis of the frequency and intensity of the incoming acoustic signal. Phonological coding is linguistic processing of aural/oral words.

The field of reading has tended to use phonological coding to refer nonspecifically to any kind of sound coding (La Berge and Samuels, 1974) or to refer to decoding as in reading pseudowords (e.g. Olson, in press). In our research we refer to reading pseudowords as *phonological recoding or decoding* (see Perfetti and Hogaboam, 1975; Ehri, 1992) and use the term *phonological coding* to refer only to coding of spoken language. The reason is that both orthographic coding and phonological coding contribute unique variance to reading pseudowords (Berninger and Abbott, 1992b, 1994). Furthermore, spoken language can be phonologically coded at different unit sizes: name or phonetic codes at the whole-word level; and syllables, phonemes or rimes (part of syllable remaining when onset is deleted) at the subword level (Berninger, 1994). The name code is sometimes referred to as the phonetic/semantic code because the phonetic code for real words activates the semantic code.

Like orthographic codes, phonological codes exhibit a normal developmental pattern of acquisition. Pre-schoolers can produce and understand whole words (phonetic codes). Kindergarten children can rhyme (Vellutino and Scanlon, 1987), which requires segmenting monosyllabic words into onsets and rimes and matching rimes across words, and can segment polysyllabic words by syllable (Liberman *et al.*, 1974). First-year school children can segment words into constituent phonemes (Liberman *et al.*, 1974). Intermediate grade children (grades 4 to 6) can segment polysyllabic words into rime units within constituent syllables (Berninger *et al.*, 1994). However, as in the case of orthographic coding, individual differences have been observed in this developmental pattern. For example, 2 per cent of the first-year children were disabled in syllable segmentation but not phonemic segmentation (Berninger and Hart, 1992).

Berninger and Abbott (1992b) used multiple regression to examine the relationship between each of three phonological codes – phonetic/semantic (word defining), syllabic and phonemic – and two component reading skills – reading real words and reading pseudowords in isolation – in a primary grade sample. In the first, second and third grades, each phonological code contributed significant variance to each of the reading skills. For *reading real words* in the second and third grades the phonemic code contributed unique variance beyond that in the zero-order correlations. For *reading pseudowords* in the first, second and third grades the phonemic code contributed unique variance, and in the second grade the syllabic code also contributed unique variance.

Berninger *et al.* (1992) used regression to examine the relationship between each of three phonological codes – phonetic/semantic (word finding), syllabic and phonemic – and three component writing skills – handwriting, spelling and compositional fluency – in a primary grade sample. Each phonological code contributed variance to each writing skill, with the exception of the phonetic/semantic code and spelling. However, in the intermediate grades phonological coding contributed unique variance only to spelling and not to handwriting or compositional fluency (Berninger *et al.*, 1994).

Taken together the Berninger and Abbott (1992b, 1994) and Berninger, Yates *et al.* (1992) studies show that multiple phonological codes contribute to reading and writing acquisition. Phonological coding is not a unitary process. Reading researchers should avoid referring to phonological coding nonspecifically as any kind of sound coding and specify the unit of sound coding involved.

Independent contribution of orthographic and phonological coding

Normal reading depends on orthographic and phonological processing (see Assink and Kattenberg, Chapter 6, Experiment 5, this volume). In normal reading, orthographic and phonological codes function together rather than independently (see Multiple orthographic–phonological code connections, pp. 37–9 below). However, in disabled reading a deficit in either an orthographic or phonological code can interfere with connections forming between these codes (Berninger and Hart, 1992; Berninger, 1994). Both direct brain measures and statistical techniques can be used to tease apart the independent contribution of procedures that are normally functionally interrelated.

Two kinds of direct brain measures are relevant in this regard. *PET studies* (e.g. Posner *et al.*, 1988; Petersen *et al.*, 1989) have shown that different brain regions are activated by phonological coding tasks for auditory words than by orthographic coding tasks for written words. *Electrophysiological studies* show that the brain responds differently to orthographic tasks than it does to phonological tasks. Sanquist *et al.* (1980) asked subjects to match words on the basis of phonological, semantic or orthographic information. A component centred around 500 ms discriminated match from no-match conditions, whereas a peak in the region of 300 ms discriminated the orthographic from the phonemic and semantic comparisons. Kramer and Donchin (1987) noted the greatest increase in the N200 event-related component (ERP)[2] when tokens were presented in which both the orthography and phonology did not match, a smaller increase when there was a mismatch in only one of these dimensions, and the smallest increase when tokens matched on both dimensions.

Structural equation modelling, which combines the advantages of factor analysis and multiple regression (Biddle and Marlin, 1987), is also relevant in this regard. Unlike multiple regression, but like factor analysis, this technique can model latent factors based on the covariance of the measured variables; unlike factor analysis, but like multiple regression, this technique can describe the degree of relationship among predictor latent factors and criterion latent factors (Lunneborg and Abbott, 1983). Structural equation modelling can be used to test competing models to determine which provides the best fit for the data. For example, in one model the covariance between predictor factors may be freely estimated with no constraints on the data, whereas in another model the covariance may be constrained by arbitrarily setting it to zero thereby creating orthogonal (independent) factors. Structural equation modelling can also be used to test the statistical significance of a path from a predictor factor to a criterion factor.

Berninger, Abbott and Shurtleff (1990) found that the best fitting model at the beginning of the first grade did not treat visible language coding (orthographic coding) and oral language coding (phonological and semantic) as orthogonal factors in predicting reading and spelling. However, the best fitting models at the end of the first grade did treat orthographic coding and oral language coding as orthogonal factors in predicting reading and spelling. They concluded that visible language coding and oral language coding systems differentiate and make independent contributions to reading and spelling as children's literacy skill increases. They also evaluated the statistical significance of the paths from the visible language coding factor and from the oral language factor at the end of the first grade (when they were independent) to reading and spelling single words. The path from the oral language coding factor was significant for both reading tasks (lexical decision and naming) and the spelling task (reproducing briefly presented words, pseudowords or letter-strings from memory). However, the path from the visible language coding factor was significant only for one reading task (naming). The investigators concluded that the orthographic coding factor contributed directly only to pre-lexical processes, whereas the oral language coding factor contributed to both pre-lexical (tapped by the naming task) and post-lexical processes (tapped by the lexical decision and written reproduction tasks).

In subsequent studies Berninger and Abbott (1992b) and Abbott and Berninger (1993) used *multiple group structural equation modelling*, which tests whether the fit of a model is significantly different at different age levels. In these studies, like the study by Berninger *et al.* (1990), visible language coding was based on orthographic coding, but, unlike the study by Berninger *et al.* (1990), oral language coding was based only on phonological coding and not semantic coding. In the first, second and third grades both the orthographic coding factor and the phonological coding factor contributed to the fit of the model for predicting reading (Berninger and Abbott, 1992b, 1994) and spelling (Abbott and Berninger, 1993). However, the statistical significance and relative contribution of the path between a predictor factor and a criterion factor depended on the criterion task and level of skill acquisition. For reading, the path from the orthographic coding was more sizeable than the path from phonological coding only in the first grade; in the second and third grades, the path from the phonological coding factor was more sizeable than the path from the orthographic coding factor (Berninger and Abbott, 1992b). For spelling, on the other hand, consistently in the first, second and third grades, only the path from the orthographic coding factor was statistically significant. Unlike the Berninger *et al.* (1990) study, this spelling task required spelling words from long-term memory in dictated lists or compositions.

Taken together, the structural equation modelling studies show that ortho- graphic coding and phonological coding make independent contributions to reading and spelling over and beyond their covariance. This finding, based on individual differences in the level to which orthographic and phonological coding skills are developed, does not imply that orthographic coding and phonological coding function independently. In normal reading and spelling, orthographic and phonological coding are functionally interrelated. I now turn to how this functional interrelationship is achieved.

Multiple orthographic-phonological code connections

According to the 'Multiple Connections Model' (Berninger *et al.*, 1988; Berninger and Abbott, 1992b; Berninger, 1994, Table 4.1), learning to read and spell involves forging multiple orthographic–phonological code connections of corresponding size: whole written word–phonetic/name codes; letter–phoneme codes; letter-cluster–syllable codes; letter-cluster–rime codes; and letter-cluster–phoneme(s) codes. Berninger *et al.* (1988) compared first-year school children with large discrepancies (1 standard deviation or greater between corresponding orthographic and phonological codes), which could interfere with formation of orthographic–phonological code connections at three unit sizes (whole written word–whole spoken word, letter-cluster–aural syllable, letter–phoneme). Large discrepancies between letter-cluster coding and syllable coding occurred in 40 per cent of the sample; large discrepancies between whole-word and phonetic/ semantic coding occurred in 26 per cent of the sample; and large discrepancies between letter and phoneme coding occurred in 24 per cent of the sample. Children with large discrepancies between whole-word orthographic and whole-word phonological coding and between letter-cluster coding and aural syllable coding read significantly worse than children with small discrepancies (1/3 standard deviation or less) between these same orthographic and phonological codes.

The number of large discrepancies, which reflects the number of dysfunctional orthographic–phonological code connections, affected level of reading achievement. Children with no large discrepancies or only 1 read above the mean (range + 0.5 to + 0.2 standard deviation units) compared to children with 2 or 3 large discrepancies who read substantially below the mean (range −0.7 to −1.2 standard deviation units).

Berninger and Abbott (1992b, 1994) further tested the Multiple Connections Model by (1) testing the significance of main effects and interaction terms in multiple regressions in which three orthographic codes – whole-word, letter, letter-cluster – and three phonological codes – phonetic/semantic, phoneme, syllable – were entered to predict reading or spelling achievement; and (2) evaluating whether the level of reading and spelling achievement decreases as the number of functional orthographic–phonological code connections decreases. For *reading real words* all the orthographic and phonological codes contributed unique variance. For *reading pseudowords* all the orthographic codes, except letter coding, and all the phonological codes contributed unique variance. This finding substantiates our claim that pseudoword reading is not a purely phonological task in that two orthographic coding skills contributed independent variance over and beyond that contributed by three phonological coding skills. Of the interaction terms, only the letter-cluster–syllable interaction explained a significant increment of unique variance – in pseudoword reading and spelling real words. Thus, letter-cluster coding and syllable coding may need to be developed to comparable levels more so than the other corresponding orthographic and phonological codes.

Berninger and Abbott (1992b, 1994) used a different, and more stringent, approach to defining dysfunctional code connections than Berninger *et al.* (1988). Level of development of one code had to be significantly different from level of development of the corresponding code based on the Mahalanobis Statistic (Stevens, 1986); and one or both codes had to fall in the bottom 5 per cent of the normal distribution. Nevertheless, they reached the same conclusion that reading achievement is related to the number of functional orthographic–phonological code connections. On the average, the group with all code connections functional read real words and pseudowords about 0.9 standard deviations better and spelled about 0.7 standard deviations better than the group with only 2 code connections functional. On the average, the group with 2 code connections functional read only slightly better but spelled about 0.5 standard deviations better than the group with only 1 code connection functional. On the average, the group with 1 code connection functional read real words over 1 standard deviation better, read pseudowords about 0.8 standard deviations better, and spelled about 0.5 standard deviations better than the one child with zero functional code connections, who could hardly read or spell. The major difference in findings across studies was that use of less stringent criteria for dysfunctional code connections suggested that one dysfunctional code connection did not impair reading, whereas use of more stringent criteria suggested that just one dysfunctional code connection could substantially impair reading. In both studies the most dramatic differences in achievement were between children with all code connections functional and those with only one or zero functional code connections; their achievement tended to differ by more than one standard deviation.

Berninger (1989) administered an experiment with on-line processing tasks which showed multiple code connections are involved in reading single words. In both Study 1 (end of first grade) and Study 2 (mid-second and mid-fourth grades) speed of naming phonically irregular words, in which every letter cannot be translated into a phonemic code but the whole word can be translated into a phonetic or name code, and speed of naming phonically regular words, in which every letter can be translated into a phonemic code, were not significantly different. In both studies, naming phonically regular real words was faster than naming phonically regular pseudowords, thus showing that naming is facilitated when two connections – whole word–phonetic code and whole word–semantic code – are activated. These and other results suggested that reading involves active orchestration of multiple codes and their connections rather than passive access to a static lexicon.

Social context of literacy acquisition

Just because there is a biological basis for coding procedures in the individual working brain, it does not follow that instruction does not influence their development or that the social context in which literacy is acquired does not affect their development. Our intervention and field studies to date show that instruction can remediate orthographic or phonological coding deficits and facilitate development of code connections. However, the nature of the instructional programme – that is, the cultural context in which literacy is acquired – may influence which code connections are forged. At the same time, literacy learning also appears to depend on the constructive processes of learners, who use instructional cues in varying ways, and not only on their coding procedures or their instructional programme. An overview of these studies is provided in the next section.

Development of codes and code connections during literacy instruction

Berninger and Traweek (1991) investigated the effect of a two-phase, theory-based intervention on the reading achievement of twenty second-graders at risk for word recognition problems (on average about 1 standard deviation below the mean and no more than 1 functional orthographic–phonological code connection). In Phase I (18 sessions) orthographic and phonological coding skills were trained, but no explicit reading instruction was provided. In Phase II (17 sessions) explicit reading instruction was provided which emphasized three of the orthographic–phonological code connections: whole-word–phonetic/semantic, letter–phoneme and letter-cluster–syllable/sub-syllable. Each child served as his or her own control. Changes in relative standing among grade-equivalent peers on standard scores on a standardized test (Woodcock Reading Mastery Test – Revised, WRMT–R, Woodcock, 1987) were evaluated at pre-test, mid-test (end of Phase I) and post-test (end of Phase II). Effects due to maturation over the course of the year-long study were controlled in that changes are expected in absolute scores on these tests, but not in relative standing among grade peers on standard scores.

From pre-test to post-test children improved on the average about 1 standard deviation in reading real words and 1 standard deviation in reading pseudowords. The relative amount of improvement was greater for Phase I than for Phase II treatment, suggesting that pre-treatment in orthographic/phonological coding may result in greater gains than explicit reading instruction for 'at risk' beginning readers. Regression to the mean did not account for the results. To analyze results for individuals, the standard error of measurement of the WRMT–R was used to set confidence intervals at the 0.95 probability level. From pre-test to post-test 70 per cent of the sample showed significant gains in reading real words and 90 per cent showed significant gains in reading pseudowords. Although only 20 per cent had one functional orthographic–phonological connection prior to treatment, by the end of treatment, 45 per cent had developed all three, 25 per cent had developed two, 20 per cent had developed one, and 10 per cent still had zero connections, showing that they were treatment non-responders. The letter–phoneme code connection was relatively more resistant to treatment because of persisting phonemic coding problems than the whole-word–phonetic/semantic code connection or letter-cluster–syllable code connection.

For over a century the question of how best to teach beginning reading has been debated emotionally (Aaron and Joshi, 1992). Currently, researchers are advocating a code approach (e.g. Adams, 1990), but practitioners are increasingly adopting a 'whole language' meaning emphasis approach (e.g. Blachowicz and Lee, 1991; Vogt, 1991). We advocate a balanced approach (Wise, 1991), which teaches to all levels of language, including explicit code instruction and meaning-oriented instruction and experience in reading excellent children's literature (Berninger, 1994).

Traweek *et al.* (1992) tested the hypothesis that individual differences in orthographic coding and in phonological coding were a better predictor of reading achievement than was the instructional method (code-oriented or meaning-oriented). The rationale was that in a code-emphasis programme children may lack the orthographic or phonological coding skills needed to make sense of the explicit instruction in phonics rules. For example, a child may learn by rote association in a code-oriented instructional programme that the letter *c* says /k/, the letter *a* says /a/, and the letter *t* says /t/; but, if that child cannot selectively attend to and code each letter embedded in the whole word pattern (letter coding), and cannot segment the spoken word *cat* into its component phonemes, then the child will not be able to synthesize the sequential letter–phoneme code connections to apply the phonics rules productively. In a meaning-emphasis programme in which children must abstract the letter–sound correspondences from repeated exposure to the same words, the child may have the same deficits, inability to code letter and/or phonemic information in repeatedly encountered printed words. Consequently, the child does not abstract inductively the letter–sound correspondences.

Results confirmed the hypothesis. Individual differences in phonological coding and in orthographic coding predicted reading achievement at the end of the first grade, but the nature of the instructional programme – code-oriented DISTAR or meaning-oriented integrated reading writing – did not. However, the nature of the instructional programme did affect which orthographic–phonological code connections children tended to acquire. Children in the integrated reading-writing programme, who write stories using Sunshine Cards[3] to learn grapheme–phoneme associations, tended to acquire whole-word as well as subword (letter–phoneme and letter-cluster–syllable) connections. Children in DISTAR, who were given systematic phonics instruction, tended to acquire subword (letter–phoneme connections).

Constructive processes of the learner

Wittrock (1974) demonstrated that learning is a generative process. Generative processes are especially important in reading comprehension (Wittrock, 1990), but may also play a role in constructing orthographic–phonological code connections. Berninger and Abbott (1992a) compared instructional groups at the beginning, middle and end of the first grade on experimental measures which manipulated variables related to orthographic and phonological processing. Within an instructional group (high, middle, low), the instructional programme (materials, lessons, assignments) was as constant as an instructional intervention can be outside the research laboratory. The goal was to evaluate individual differences within the same group in response to the same instructional pro-gramme. First, variation among children in an instructional group was treated as systematic variance in an analysis of variance design. Data were aggregated over individual stimulus items rather than over individual subjects and individual response over stimulus trials was used to estimate error. Not only the main effect for individuals but also all the two-way and three-way interactions involving individuals were statistically significant. These results justified a re-analysis of the data for each individual.

Next, a separate analysis of variance was performed on the stimulus trials for each subject. Within a session and across the three sessions, children within the same instructional group did vary considerably as to which main effects or interactions were statistically significant and as to the pattern of the levels of a variable. Berninger and Abbott attributed this variation in response to the same instruction to the constructive processes of the learner. Children are not programmed externally as computers are, and may vary in how they use external instructional cues to construct procedures for representing and reproducing printed words.

Integrating the Vygotskian and Lurian perspectives

Understanding the reading acquisition process will, in keeping with the Vygotskian perspective, depend on social and cultural variables. Given current cultural practices, beginning readers first interact with print in a social context – initially on their parent's lap during shared reading of books and subsequently in a small or large group in the classroom during didactic instruction or skill practice. The progression is from social interaction to the individual reading independently for pleasure or for assigned activities. This progression fits with Vygotsky's emphasis on the transition from inter-individual activity to intra-individual activity of the learner. Culture exerts an influence on the intra-individual activity. When the culture favours meaning-oriented reading instruction, children learn to focus on meaning. When the culture favours code-oriented reading instruction, children learn to focus on spelling and sound patterns. The reading material determines what words, text structures and content become represented in memory.

At the same time, a complete understanding of the reading acquisition process will, in keeping with the Lurian perspective, depend on biological variables. Procedures for coding and representing stimulus words in memory have a biological basis in the individual learner. *Whereas the social variables affect what gets represented, the biological variables affect how the content is represented.* As Johnson (1978) noted, codes should not be confused with content. Individual differences in the coding procedures affect the mechanisms for representing words in memory – the code connections.

At present, research on the social and cultural variables in literacy acquisition and research on the biological variables in literacy acquisition proceed, for the most part, like parallel play with no interaction between the two traditions. Researchers in the two traditions attend different meetings and read and publish in different journals. If we are to further our understanding of reading acquisition, and writing acquisition too, we need to integrate these contrasting approaches. For example, we might apply microgenetic analysis to teachers' instructional language while interacting with children during reading lessons to show how it may or may not promote development of specific codes or their connections. We might then investigate the zone of proximal development for developing specific codes and their connections. We need to build theoretical models of literacy acquisition which incorporate both biological constraints in the individual learner and educational constraints in the social and cultural context (Berninger, 1994). To diagnose and remediate reading and writing disabilities we need to assess (1) specific coding abilities in individual learners, (2) components of the instructional programme and teacher practice in the classroom, and (3) the teacher–pupil interactions during reading/writing instruction. We also need to design intervention programmes that take into account both learner characteristics – the individual – and the ecology of the classroom – the social and cultural context in which learning occurs. Literacy acquisition research would benefit from a meeting of the minds from the Vygotskian tradition, with its focus on the social and cultural context of literacy learning, and the Lurian tradition, with its focus on the individual and the biology of the working brain.

Notes

1. Pseudowords refer to pronounceable letter-strings that do not have meaning. In other papers I have also referred to them as nonwords.
2. Negative amplitude 200 msec after stimulus onset.
3. Each alphabet letter is paired with a picture the first sound of which is associated with that letter.

References

Aaron, P.G. and Joshi, R.M. (1992), *Reading Problems, Consultation and Remediation*, New York: Guilford.

Abbott, R. and Berninger, V. (1993), 'Structural equation modeling of relationships among developmental skills and writing skills in primary and intermediate grade students', *Journal of Educational Psychology, 85 (3)*, 478–508.

Adams, M. (1990), *Beginning to Read: Thinking and learning about print,* Urbana, IL: Center for the Study of Reading, University of Illinois.

Berninger, V. (1987), 'Global, component, and serial processing of printed words in beginning reading', *Journal of Experimental Child Psychology, 43,* 387–418.

Berninger, V. (1988a), 'Development of operational thought without a normal sensorimotor stage', *Intelligence, 12,* 219–30.

Berninger, V. (1988b), 'Acquisition of linguistic procedures for printed words: neuro-psychological implications for learning'. *International Journal of Neuroscience, 42,* 267–81.

Berninger, V. (1989), 'Orchestration of multiple codes in developing readers: an alternative model of lexical access', *International Journal of Neuroscience, 48,* 85–104.

Berninger, V. (1990), 'Multiple orthographic codes: key to alternative instructional methodologies for developing orthographic–phonological connections underlying word identification', *School Psychology Review, 19,* 518–33.

Berninger, V. (1991), 'Overview of "bridging the gap between developmental, neuro-psychological, and cognitive approaches to reading" ', *Learning and Individual Differences, 3,* 163–80.

Berninger, V. (1994), *Reading and Writing Acquisition: A neurodevelopmental perspective,* DuBuque, IA: Brown and Benchmark.

Berninger, V. and Abbott, R. (1992a), 'The unit of analysis and the constructive processes of the learner: key concepts for educational neuropsychology', *Educational Psychologist, 27,* 223–42.

Berninger, V. and Abbott, R. (1992b), *Multiple Orthographic and Phonological Codes and Code Connections in Reading and Spelling Single Words,* American Educational Research Association, San Francisco.

Berninger, V. and Abbott, R. (1994), 'Multiple orthographic and phonological codes in literacy acquisition: an evolving research program'. In V. Berninger (ed.), *The Varieties of Orthographic Knowledge I: Theoretical and Development Issues,* Kluwer, The Netherlands, pp. 277–317.

Berninger, V., Abbott, R., and Shurtleff, H. (1990), 'Developmental changes in interrelationships of visible language codes, oral language codes, and reading or spelling', *Learning and Individual Differences, 2,* 45–67.

Berninger, V., Cartwright, A., Yates, C., Swanson, H. and Abbott, R. (1994), 'Developmental skills related to writing and reading in the intermediate grades: Shared and unique functional systems', *Reading and Writing: An Interdisciplinary Journal, 6,* 161–96.

Berninger, V., Chen, A. and Abbott, R. (1988), 'A test of the multiple connections model of reading acquisition', *International Journal of Neuroscience, 42,* 283–95.

Berninger, V., Gans, B., St James, P. and Connors, T. (1988), 'Modified WAIS-R for patients with speech and/or hand dysfunction', *Archives of Physical Medicine and Rehabilitation, 69,* 250–5.

Berninger, V. and Hart, T. (1992), 'A developmental neuropsychological perspective for reading and writing acquisition', *Educational Psychologist, 27,* 415–34.

Berninger, V. and Swanson, H.L. (in press), 'Modifying Hayes and Flower's model of skilled writing to explain beginning and developing writing'. In E. Butterfield (ed.) *Children's Writing: Toward a process theory of development of skilled writing.* JAI Press.

Berninger, V., Thalberg, S., DeBruyn, D. and Smith, R. (1987), 'Preventing reading disabilities by assessing and remediating phonemic skills', *School Psychology Review, 16,* 554–65.

Berninger, V. and Traweek, D. (1991), 'Effects of a two-phase reading intervention on three orthographic–phonological code connections', *Learning and Individual Differences*, *3*, 323–38.

Berninger, V., Yates, C., Cartwright, A., Rutberg, J., Remy, E. and Abbott, R. (1992), 'Lower-level developmental skills in beginning writing', *Reading and Writing: An Interdisciplinary Journal*, *4*, 257–80.

Berninger, V., Yates, C. and Lester, K. (1991), 'Multiple orthographic codes in reading and writing acquisition', *Reading and Writing: An Interdisciplinary Journal*, *3*, 115–49.

Biddle, B. and Marlin, M. (1987), 'Causality, confirmation, credulity, and structural equation modeling', *Child Development*, *58*, 4–17.

Blachowicz, C. and Lee, J. (1991), 'Vocabulary development in the whole literacy classroom', *The Reading Teacher*, *45*, 188–204.

Cole, M. and Scribner, S. (1978), 'Introduction'. In M. Cole, V. John-Steiner, S. Scribner and E. Souberman (eds.) *L.S. Vygotsky, Mind in Society*, Cambridge, MA: Harvard University Press, pp. 1–14.

Ehri, L. (1992), 'Reconceptualizing the development of sight word reading and its relationship to reading.' In P. Gough, L. Ehri and R. Treiman (eds.) *Reading Acquisition*, Hillsdale, NJ: Lawrence Erlbaum, pp. 107–43.

Hooper, S. and Boyd, T. (1986), 'Neurodevelopmental learning disorders'. In J.E. Obrzut and G.W. Hynd (eds.) *Child Neuropsychology*, Vol. 2, *Clinical Practice*, San Diego: Academic Press, pp. 15–58.

Johnson, N. (1978), 'Coding processes in memory.' In W.K. Estes (ed.) *Handbook of Learning and Cognitive Processes* Vol. 6, Hillsdale, NJ: Lawrence Erlbaum, pp. 87–129.

Kramer, A. and Donchin, E. (1987), 'Brain potentials as indices of orthographic and phonological interaction during word matching', *Journal of Experimental Psychology: Learning, memory, and cognition*, *13*, 76–86.

La Berge, D. and Samuels, S.J. (1974), 'Toward a theory of automatic information processing in reading', *Cognitive Psychology*, *6*, 293–323.

Liberman, I., Shankweiler, D., Fischer, F. and Carter, B. (1974), 'Explicit syllable and phoneme segmentation in the young child', *Journal of Experimental Child Psychology*, *18*, 201–12.

Lunneborg, C. and Abbott, R. (1983), *Elementary Multivariate Analysis for the Behavioral Sciences*, New York: North–Holland.

Luria, A.R. (1973), *The Working Brain*, New York: Basic Books.

Minsky, M. (1986), *Society of Mind*, New York: Simon & Schuster.

Olson, R. (in press), 'Language deficits in "specific" reading disability'. In M. Gernsbacher (ed.) *Handbook of Psycholinguistics*, New York: Academic Press.

Olswang, L., Bain, B. and Johnson, G. (1992). 'Using dynamic assessment with children with language disorders'. In S. Warren and J. Reichle (eds.), *Causes and Effects in Communication and Language Intervention*, Baltimore, MD: Paul H. Brookes Publishing Co., pp. 187–215.

Perfetti, C. and Hogaboam, T. (1975), 'The relationship between single word decoding and reading comprehension skill', *Journal of Educational Psychology*, *67*, 461–9.

Petersen, S., Fox, P., Posner, M., Mintun, M. and Raichle, M. (1989), 'Positron emission tomography studies of the processing of single words', *Journal of Cognitive Neuroscience*, *1*, 153–70.

Piaget, J. (1970), 'Piaget's theory'. In P.H. Mussen (ed.) *Carmichael's Manual of Child Psychology*, Vol. I, 3rd edition, New York: John Wiley, pp. 703–32.

Posner, M., Petersen, S., Fox, P. and Raichle, M. (1988), 'Localization of cognitive operations in the human brain', *Science*, *240*, 1627–31.

Roschelle, J. and Clancey, W. (1992), 'Learning as social and neural', *Educational Psychologist*, *27*, 435–53.

Sanquist, T., Rohrbaugh, J., Syndulko, K. and Lindsley, D. (1980), 'Electrocortical signs of levels of processing: perceptual analysis and recognition memory', *Psychophysiology*, *17*, 568–76.

Shurtleff, H., Abbott, R., Townes, B. and Berninger, V. (1993), 'Luria's neurodevelopmental stages in relation to intelligence and academic achievement in kindergarten and first grade', *Developmental Neuropsychology*, *9*, 55–75.

Stevens, J. (1986), *Applied Multivariate Statistics for the Sciences*, Hillsdale, NJ: Lawrence Erlbaum.

Studdert-Kennedy, M. (1974), 'The perception of speech'. In T. Sebeok (ed.) *Current Trends in Linguistics*, Vol. 12, The Hague: Mouton, pp. 2349–85.

Traweek, D., Cartwright, A. and Berninger, V. (1992), *Effects of Integrated Reading–Writing Instruction versus Direct Instruction in Phonics on Achievement Outcome and Orthographic–Phonological Processes*. American Educational Research Association, San Francisco.

Vellutino, F. and Scanlon, D. (1987), 'Phonological coding, phonological awareness, and reading ability: evidence from a longitudinal and experimental study', *Merrill-Palmer Quarterly*, *33*, 321–63.

Vogt, M. (1991), 'An observation guide for supervisors and administrators: moving toward integrated reading/language arts instruction', *The Reading Teacher*, *45*, 206–11.

Vygotsky, L.S. (1960), 'Razvitie vysshykh psikhicheskikh funktsii' [The development of higher-order mental functions], Moscow: Izdatel'stvo Akademii Pedagogiches-kikh Nauk.

Vygotsky, L.S. (1981a), 'The genesis of higher mental functions'. In J. Wertsch (ed.) *The Concept of Activity in Soviet Psychology*, Armonk, NY: M.E. Sharpe.

Vygotsky, L.S. (1981b), 'The instrumental method in psychology'. In J. Wertsch (ed.) *The Concept of Activity in Soviet Psychology*, Armonk, NY: M.E. Sharpe.

Vygotsky, L. (1982), *Collected Works*, Vols 1 and 2, Moscow: Izdatel'stvo Pedagogika.

Vygotsky, L. (1986), *Thought and Language*, ed and transl. A. Kozulin, Cambridge, MA: MIT Press. (First published in 1934.)

Vygotsky, L.S. and Luria, A.R. (1930), *Essays in the History of Behavior: Ape, primitive, child,*. Moscow and Leningrad: Gosudarstvennoe Izdatel'stvo.

Wertsch, J. (1985), *Vygotsky and the Social Formation of Mind*, Cambridge, MA: Harvard University Press.

Wise, B. (1991), 'What reading disabled children need: what is known and how to talk about it', *Learning and Individual Differences*, *3*, 307–21.

Wittrock, M. (1974), 'Learning as a generative process', *Educational Psychologist*, *11*, 87–95.

Wittrock, M. (1990), 'Generative processes in comprehension', *Educational Psychologist*, *24*, 345–76.

Woodcock, R. (1987), *Woodcock Reading Mastery Test – Revised*, Circle Pines, MN: American Guidance Service.

4

Onsets and rimes as functional units in reading

Usha Goswami
Department of Experimental Psychology, University of Cambridge

Children who are beginning to learn to read are faced with a daunting task: they have to work out the connection between sequences of letters – printed words – and the sounds of those words in their spoken language. Traditionally, psychologists have proposed two ways in which children may set about this task. The first is to begin to read by learning associations between entire letter-strings and spoken words ('look-and-say' reading strategies). This approach has been called the *logographic* route to reading. Children using a logographic strategy are thought to learn connections between relatively unanalyzed visual units and individual words in spoken language. For example, a child reading logographically may read a nonsense word like 'cime' as 'cats', guessing at the pronunciation of the word on the basis of its first letter (e.g. Marsh *et al.*, 1981).

The second way to try to relate printed letter-strings to the sounds of spoken words is to learn the associations between individual letters and their sounds, and then to blend these separate sounds into a word. This approach has been called the phonological or *alphabetic* route to reading (a 'phonics' strategy). A child reading alphabetically who knows the sounds associated with the letters 'c', 'a' and 't' should be able to derive the spoken word 'cat'. This child will read the nonsense word 'cime' as 'kime', using the phoneme usually associated with the letter 'c' to produce a hard 'k' sound at the beginning of the word (Marsh *et al.*, 1981).

According to traditional approaches, then, children either identify words as holistic units when they read, or they segment words into their constituent alphabetic letters. Two recent influential models of reading development have proposed that these different strategies emerge sequentially as young children learn to read (Marsh *et al.*, 1981; Frith, 1985). According to these models, young children begin learning to read by applying a logographic strategy. At the next stage of reading development, children progress to using an alphabetic strategy. Finally, children become able to use a third strategy as well to link spelling patterns with the sounds of spoken language. This third strategy is an 'orthographic' one. It involves the use of spelling sequences within words that are smaller than the whole word, but larger than the individual letters, such as the '-at' in 'cat', or the '-tion' in 'station'. At this final stage of learning to read, children become able to take advantage of larger orthographic units in words that have consistent pronunciations. The use of such orthographic strategies is thought to be fairly sophisticated, emerging relatively late in the development of reading.

This chapter is largely concerned with children's use of this third strategy for linking print to sound, a strategy that has also been called orthographic analogy (e.g. Glushko, 1979). The term analogy has been used because a child who reads new words by comparing their spelling patterns with those of known words and then using those shared spelling patterns as a basis for making a prediction about pronunciation is making an analogical comparison based on the *orthographic* similarity of the two words. For example, a child who knows how to pronounce the written word 'cat' should be able to use this knowledge as a basis for reading words that share letter clusters with 'cat', such as 'mat', 'hat', and 'fat'. A child who knows how to pronounce the written word 'light' should be able to make analogies to words like 'fight', 'night' and 'tight'. A child who can read the word 'beak' should be able to read analogous words like 'peak', 'weak' and 'speak', and possibly 'bean', 'bead' and 'beat' as well. This orthographic analogy strategy is very different from logographic reading. In order to work out the consistent connection with sound, the children must *analyze* the spelling patterns of the analogous words. In logographic reading, the spelling patterns of different words are learned as relatively unanalyzed units.

By studying the characteristics of the orthographic analogies that young children make, we can try to understand how the child approaches the task of linking spelling patterns to the sounds of spoken language. In fact, research on children's orthographic analogies suggests that the connections that they make between letter clusters reflect their *phonological* knowledge about spoken language, and are not based simply on the degree of orthographic similarity between words. In particular, it seems that their knowledge of the phonological units that linguists call *onsets* and *rimes* have an important role to play in analogizing. Take the example of the words with analogous spelling patterns to the word 'beak'. Both 'peak', 'weak' and 'speak', and 'bean', 'bead' and 'beat' share a letter cluster with 'beak', but the first set of words also rhymes with 'beak'. This factor turns out to be important. As we shall see, children are more likely to use shared spelling sequences in words as a basis for pronouncing new words when these spelling sequences correspond to distinctive phonological units such as rhyme. Research has shown that children's early orthographic analogies are intimately related to their phonological knowledge at the onset–rime level.

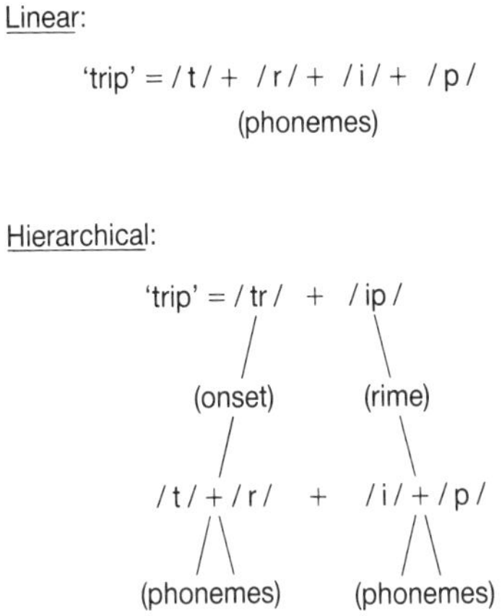

Linear:

'trip' = / t / +   / r / +   / i / +   / p /

(phonemes)

Hierarchical:

'trip' = / tr /   +   / ip /

(onset)   (rime)

/ t / + / r /   +   / i / + / p /

(phonemes)   (phonemes)

Figure 4.1 Linguistic structure of the syllable.

Onsets, rimes and orthographic analogies in reading

What are onsets and rimes?

Traditional linguistic analyses of the structure of spoken words have identified two distinct sub-lexical units: *syllables* and *phonemes* (e.g. Treiman, 1988). A word like 'wigwam' has two syllables, 'wig' and 'wam', whereas a word like 'butterfly' has three. Each syllable can be further subdivided into phonemes. A phoneme is the smallest unit of sound that changes the meaning of a word. For example, 'pig' and 'wig' differ by one phoneme, and each word is made up of three separate phonemes. This is the traditional *linear* view of syllabic structure.

More recently, however, it has been proposed that there is a level of analysis intermediate between the syllable and the phoneme. According to this *hierarchical* view of syllabic structure, there are distinct linguistic units which are larger than phonemes but smaller than syllables, namely onsets and rimes. Onsets correspond to any initial consonants in the syllable, whereas rimes correspond to the vowel and any following consonants. The onset of a word like 'wig' corresponds to the initial consonant 'w-', and the rime corresponds to the unit made up of the vowel and the final consonant, '-ig'. The onset of a word like 'trim' corresponds to the consonant blend 'tr-', and the rime to the vowel and final consonant, '-im'. Onsets and rimes can also correspond to single phonemes (e.g. 'do', 'tea'), and some words have no onsets (e.g. 'ear', 'ice'). However, rimes are obligatory in syllables, and it is more usual for rimes to correspond to groups of phonemes than to single phonemes (e.g. 'beak', 'dish', 'last'). Onsets may correspond to groups of phonemes, too (e.g. 'trim', 'clasp', 'spring', 'straight'). The linear and hierarchical views of syllabic structure are contrasted in Figure 4.1.

Children's knowledge about onsets and rimes

Research has shown that onsets and rimes are the phonological units that young children find it easy to recognize. In fact, according to some researchers, these units are more accessible to beginning readers than phonemes are. Such claims raise the intriguing possibility that onsets and rimes may provide the most natural way into reading for young children. If children are aware of onset and rime units before they begin learning to read, but become aware of phonemes largely as a consequence of reading, then the most useful way for a child to begin analyzing the connections between spelling patterns and sounds may be to think about the connections between onsets and rimes and sequences of letters in words. Orthographic analogies may provide an entry strategy to reading, rather than emerging only in the final stages of learning to read.

Evidence that young children are aware of onsets and rimes as distinct units of sound comes from at least two sources. One is research on children's awareness of rhyme and alliteration. Young children's pleasure in nursery rhymes and rhyming games at home, at school, and in the playground has been widely documented (e.g. Chukovsky, 1963; Opie and Opie, 1987). More recently, psychologists have studied young children's awareness of rhyme experimentally, and have also asked whether rhyme awareness is related to the progress that individual children make in learning to read. Lenel and Cantor (1981), for example, asked 4-, 5- and 6-year-old children to judge whether pairs of words such as 'bed' and 'sled' rhymed. They found that all the children they tested scored significantly above chance in this task. Bradley and Bryant (1983) asked children of a similar age to find the odd word out in sets of words that either rhymed ('pin', 'win', *'sit'*, 'fin') or had a different beginning sound ('rock', 'rot', 'rod', *'box'*). They also found above-chance performance in their task.

Furthermore, Bradley and Bryant's work established that there was a strong connection between rhyming skill and reading progress. Bradley and Bryant measured the reading skills of the children initially seen at 4 and 5 years of age when they were 8 and 9 years old, and found a strong predictive relationship between pre-reading rhyming and alliteration scores and later reading development. This relationship held even when individual differences in memory and IQ were controlled, and the relationship was specific to reading – a similar relationship between early rhyming and later academic progress was not found for mathematics. So children's rhyming ability is strongly related to the progress that they make in learning to read. More recently, Maclean *et al.* (1987) have found that nursery rhyme knowledge measured at 3 years of age is also significantly related to later reading progress.

How can we be sure that tests of rhyming and alliteration are measuring onset–rime skills? In the original rhyming oddity task designed by Bradley and Bryant (1983), the odd word out differed by only one phoneme from the other three words ('pin', 'win', *'sit'*, 'fin'). All four words shared part of the rime, as they all had a vowel sound in common. To check that children were making oddity judgements on the basis of onset–rime units rather than on the basis of phonemes, Kirtley *et al.* (1989) devised a more fine-grained version of the oddity task. This new task compared judgements based on a difference in a single phoneme with judgements based on onsets and rimes. Kirtley *et al.* expected phonemic judgements to be more difficult than onset-rime judgements.

Phonemic judgements coincide with onset–rime judgements when CVC (consonant/vowel/consonant) words share an opening sound, but not when they share a final sound. Accordingly, Kirtley *et al.* had two types of oddity task. In the *opening sound* judgement task, 5-year-old children were asked to find the odd word out in sets of CVC words like '*cap*', 'doll', 'dog' (same CV); or 'doll', 'deaf', '*can*' (same initial C), both of which can be solved on the basis of the onset. In the *end sound* judgement task, the children were asked to find the odd word out in sets of words like 'top', '*rail*', 'hop' (same VC); or 'mop', '*lead*', 'whip' (same final C). Here only the 'VC pair' can be solved on the basis of the rime. The 'same C' pair share only a final phoneme, requiring segmentation of the rime, and so this judgement should be relatively difficult.

This was exactly what Kirtley *et al.* found. While there was no difference in the ease with which children made their judgements in the two opening sound tasks, there was a considerable difference between the two end sound tasks, the task requiring phonemic judgements being much more difficult. Kirtley *et al.* also argue that this study shows that the original oddity task based on rhyme and alliteration is an onset–rime task rather than a phonemic one. So the phonological knowledge that young children have prior to learning to read seems to be largely about onsets and rimes.

The second source of evidence for young children's awareness of onsets and rimes comes from experiments that specifically ask children to manipulate onset–rime units. The first experimenter to do this was Rebecca Treiman. In one early study (Treiman, 1985), she asked 8-year-old children to perform a difficult sound manipulation game in which they had to substitute either entire onsets and rimes in spoken words (e.g. 'fog–ful', 'fru–slu'), or had to make substitutions that required segmenting the onset or the rime (e.g. 'fru–fli', 'fog–lug'). She found that the children were much better at the game when the onset or the rime could be preserved. She also showed that younger children (4–6 year-olds) were better at recognizing the first sound in words when this corresponded to the entire onset. For example, the children were better at recognizing the sound /s/ in a word like 'san' than in a word like 'sna'. Treiman argued that their difficulty with words like 'sna' lay in segmenting the onset.

More recently, Treiman and Zukowski (1991) have provided more direct evidence that onset and rime judgements are easier than phonemic judgements for young children. They designed a same–different task, in which the 'same' word pairs shared either one or the other phonological unit. For example, in their 'shared initial sound' task, a same onset pair might be 'plea' and 'plank', while a same phoneme pair might be 'plea' and 'pray'. In their 'shared final sound' task, a same rime pair might be 'spit' and 'wit', whereas a same phoneme pair might be 'rat' and 'wit'.

Using this task, Treiman and Zukowski showed that 5-, 6- and 7-year-old children all found the onset–rime judgements easier than the phoneme judgements. There was also a clear improvement in the children's ability to make the phoneme judgements with age. Only 25 per cent of the 5-year-olds and 39 per cent of the 6-year-olds could reach criterion on the phoneme task, compared to 100 per cent of the 7-year-olds. It seems plausible to propose that this remarkable increase in phonemic awareness by the age of 7 was related to being taught to read, although reading was not measured in this study. Other authors have found similar changes in phonemic awareness once reading is taught, supporting the idea that phonemic awareness may emerge partly as a consequence of learning to read (e.g. Liberman *et al.*, 1974; Morais *et al.*, 1979; Cossu *et al.*, 1987).

The use of onsets and rimes in reading

We have seen that there are good grounds for believing that onsets and rimes are phonological units that have psychological reality for young children; and that children's awareness of onsets and rimes is initially better than their awareness of phonemes. Although this view is not without its opponents (e.g. Morais *et al.*, 1987; Morais, 1991), it raises an interesting pedagogical question, namely, how might onset–rime knowledge be useful to a child who is learning to read? We have already seen that there is a strong connection between a child's rhyming ability and that child's reading progress (Bradley and Bryant, 1983; Maclean *et al.*, 1987), a relationship that has been found by other authors (e.g. Lundberg *et al.*, 1980). The question for those interested in the acquisition of literacy is *how* the two skills may be related, that is, how onset–rime knowledge might help a child to recognize printed words.

As mentioned earlier, research on children's use of orthographic analogies in reading has shown at least one way in which this relationship might work. To make an orthographic analogy in reading, a child must use a shared spelling sequence to make a prediction about a shared pronunciation. For example, a child who knows how to read a word such as 'beak' could use the spelling–sound relationship represented by this word as a basis for reading other words with spelling patterns analogous to 'beak', such as 'peak', 'weak' and 'speak', or 'bean', 'bead' and 'beat'. These connections between shared spelling sequences like '-eak' and 'bea-' and shared sounds would appear to be relatively simple for children to make. However, in the models of reading development discussed earlier, the use of analogy was seen to be a fairly sophisticated strategy in reading. It was thought to emerge late in development, after the child had passed through the logographic and the alphabetic stages of reading (Marsh *et al.*, 1981; Frith, 1985).

The belief that the use of analogy emerged late was based on data showing that

7- and 10-year-old readers make very little use of analogy when reading nonsense words. For example, Marsh and his co-workers had given children of varying ages nonsense words like 'puscle' and 'biety' to read, words that could either be read on the basis of grapheme–phoneme correspondences ('puskle', 'beety'), or by analogy to the real words 'muscle' and 'piety'. They found that most children used alphabetic strategies to read these words. For example, in one study only 14 per cent of the 7-year-olds and 34 per cent of the 10-year-olds read the nonsense words by using analogies (Marsh *et al.*, 1981). The problem with these studies, however, was that the younger children may not have had words like 'muscle' and 'piety' in their reading vocabularies. They may therefore have been failing to use orthographic analogies, not because they were cognitively incapable of doing so, but because they had no basis for making an analogy in the first place.

In order to discover how early in the reading process children can use analogies to read new words, it is thus necessary to ensure that they have a basis for analogy available. My early experiments attempted to do this by introducing the analogy task as a word game about working out words. In this game, children were taught to read 'clue' words such as 'beak' which could form the basis for analogies to new words like 'peak' and 'bean'. These clue words remained visible during the testing phase, to make sure that the children did not simply forget them. The children were also tested prior to learning the clue words, to make sure that they could not already read the analogous words that were the focus of interest. Performance with the clue words (analogy test) was then compared to this pre-test performance.

Three types of test word were presented in each experimental trial. Some of the test words did not share analogous spelling patterns with the clue words. These non-analogous words either shared grapheme–phoneme correspondences with the clue words (e.g. 'bank', 'bask'), or were analogous in spelling pattern to a clue word used in a different experimental trial (e.g. 'rain', 'tail' [clue = rail]). A minority of test words in each case were analogous to the taught clue word. If young children can use analogies in reading, then there should be a significant difference between the analogous and the non-analogous words at analogy test. However, if young children are unable to use analogies in reading, then no difference between reading the analogous and the non-analogous words would be predicted. The clue word task is depicted in Figure 4.2.

The results showed quite clearly that even young children in the earliest phases of learning to read could use analogies to decode new words (Goswami, 1986, 1988). Six- and 7-year-old readers used the clue word to help them to read analogous words like 'peak' and 'bean', but did not improve in reading non-analogous words like 'bank' and 'rain'. The use of analogy did not vary with reading level, but analogous words like 'peak' were read more frequently than analogous words like 'bean' by both age groups. This pattern of results also extended to reading nonsense words ('beak'–'neak', 'beak'–'beap'). Younger children who did not yet score on a standardized test of reading were able to

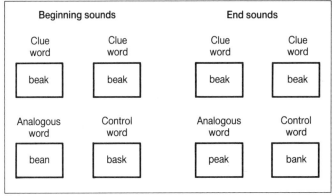

Note:
The first analogy experiment (Goswami, 1986): the children were given a clue word on each trial, which remained visible throughout the trial; they were then asked to read a succession of test words (analogous and control words).

Figure 4.2 The clue word task (*source*: Goswami and Bryant, 1990).

make a (very few) analogies, but they only made connections between spelling patterns at the ends of words ('beak'–'peak', 'beak'–'neak'). Finally, the older children also used orthographic analogies when the clue words were taught as part of the title of different stories, and the test words were embedded in the stories themselves. So the analogy effect was not restricted to single-word reading.

Two interesting findings thus emerged from the early clue word studies. The first was that children's ability to use analogies did not seem to vary with reading level. Even beginning readers could make analogies between spelling sequences to read new words. The second was that there was a qualitative difference between the analogies that the children made. Analogies between the spelling patterns at the ends of words, such as 'beak'–'peak', were not only easier for the children, they also emerged first developmentally. This suggested that the *phonological status* of the shared spelling sequence might affect the orthographic analogies that children notice.

Onset–rime analogies and phonological skills

If shared spelling sequences in words correspond to rimes, then children seem to make more analogies. This finding implies that there is a connection between orthographic analogies and onset–rime knowledge. In order to use a word like 'beak' as a basis for reading a new word like 'peak', the child must make a prediction about the pronunciation of the new word which is based on the spelling sequence that corresponds to the *rime* of the clue word. The shared spelling sequence ('-eak') thus corresponds to a 'natural' phonological unit. In order to use 'beak' as a basis for reading 'bean', however, the child must make a prediction about the pronunciation of a spelling unit that crosses the onset–rime boundary. The shared spelling sequence 'bea-' in 'beak' and 'bean' corresponds to the onset and part of the rime. So if a child's phonological knowledge partly determines how that child analyzes the spelling patterns of words during the early phases of learning to read, then rime analogies like 'beak'–'peak' should be easier than onset-and-part-of-the-rime analogies like 'beak'–'bean'.

This idea about the role of onsets and rimes in early analogies gives rise to a number of predictions. First, if the phonological knowledge that children bring with them to the reading task affects the way that they set about trying to link spelling to sound, then children with better onset–rime skills should make more analogies. Second, if it is onset–rime knowledge that particularly underlies this process of linking spelling and sound, then children should be more likely to make connections between spelling sequences that reflect onsets than between spelling sequences that reflect part of the rime, just as they are more likely to make connections between spelling sequences that reflect the rime than between spelling sequences that reflect the onset-and-part-of-the-rime. Finally, if the analogy process is truly orthographic, and is based on similarities in spelling rather than on rhyming sound, then children should not use analogies between words like 'head' and 'said'. Although these words share phonology (the rhyming sound), they differ in orthography (representing the rime with different spelling sequences), and so there is no basis for an orthographic analogy. Each of these predictions will be examined in turn.

The prediction that children with better onset–rime knowledge should make more analogies turns out to be correct. In my first study of this question (Goswami, 1990a), I gave children the clue word analogy task, and two different phonological tasks, the Bradley and Bryant oddity task (an onset–rime task) and a phoneme deletion task developed by Content *et al.* (1982), in which children are asked to delete either the first ('beak'–'eak') or the last ('beak'–'bea') phoneme in spoken words. I also gave the children a general test of verbal skills (the British Picture Vocabulary Scale, or BPVS) and the WISC digit span subtest.

Preliminary analyses showed that whereas memory scores were not significantly related to analogies, the phonological and the verbal scores were. I then examined whether these phonological relationships remained significant after controlling for verbal skills in a series of three-step multiple regression equations. Each equation controlled for verbal skills at step 1, and then either entered a deletion (phoneme) score or an oddity (onset–rime) score at steps 2 and 3. It turned out that the oddity task scores were still significantly related to rime analogies even after controlling for vocabulary skills and phoneme skills, whereas phoneme deletion did not retain a significant relationship with analogy after controlling for vocabulary skills and onset–rime (oddity) performance. So there seemed to be a specific relationship between onset–rime skills as measured by the oddity task and children's use of analogies between the spelling patterns corresponding to the rimes in words. The rhyme oddity task accounted for 20 per cent of the variance in rime analogies even after taking out the variance accounted for by verbal and phonemic skills.

The picture for onset-and-part-of-the-rime analogies ('beak'–'bean') was rather different. Here oddity task performance failed to retain a significant relationship with analogy performance after controlling for verbal and phonemic skills. This is not really surprising, of course, as these analogies do not utilize onsets and rimes. In order to use the spelling sequence shared between 'beak' and 'bean' as a basis for an analogy, children must segment the rime. However, it should be noted that the phoneme test used in this study was somewhat ambiguous, as initial phoneme deletion ('beak'–'eak') is also onset deletion. In a later study (Goswami and Mead, 1992), we decided to look at the pattern of relationships between phonological skills at different levels and beginning and end analogies in more detail.

In this second study, we included more phonological measures, such as syllable and phoneme segmentation as well as onset–rime segmentation, and we included a test of nonsense word reading ('vep', 'hig') as well. The nonsense word reading test was included to measure phonological recoding. Again, preliminary analyses showed that all our phonological measures were significantly related to analogizing, including nonsense word reading. In this study, we also found that reading age (Schonell score) was significantly related to analogizing, whereas verbal skills (BPVS) were not. Better readers made more analogies, although the end (rime) effect was maintained.

Two different sets of multiple regression equations were then used to analyze the results. The first set looked at the contribution made by the different phonological variables after controlling for reading age. The second set looked at the contribution made by the different phonological variables after controlling for both reading age and nonsense word reading. Each set of equations produced a consistent set of results. If reading age was controlled, then the onset–rime measures retained a significant relationship with rime analogies (the rhyme oddity task and onset deletion), but the phonemic measures did not (final consonant deletion and phoneme segmentation). In contrast, both the phonemic and the onset–rime measures retained significant relationships with beginning ('beak'–'bean') analogies. When reading age and nonsense word reading were controlled, then the only variables to retain a significant relationship with rime analogies were the oddity rhyme measures. The only variables to retain a significant relationship with beginning analogies were the consonant deletion measures. So knowledge about rhyme seems to have a strong and specific relationship with rime analogies, whereas analogies between spelling sequences corresponding to the onset-and-part-of-the-rime are related to more fine-grained phonological knowledge about phonemes.

The second prediction made by the phonological status hypothesis was that children should make more analogies between spelling sequences of equal length that reflect the onset than between spelling sequences that reflect part of the rime. We have already seen that analogies between clue words like 'beak' and test words like 'peak' (rime) are easier than analogies between clue words like 'beak' and test words like 'bean' (onset-and-part-of-the-rime), even though both share the same number of letters with the clue word. However, in order to check that this effect is due to phonological status and is not simply related to the position of the shared letter clusters, we need to reverse our prediction. The appropriate comparison is provided by consonant clusters. Shared consonant clusters at the beginnings of words correspond to the onset ('trim'-'trot'), whereas shared consonant clusters at the ends of words correspond to part of the rime ('desk'-'risk'). So analogies between words like 'trim' and 'trot' reflect a natural and early developing phonological unit, the onset, whereas analogies between words like 'desk' and 'risk' do not. Thus for consonant clusters, the onset–rime hypothesis would predict that children should make more analogies between shared spelling sequences at the beginnings of words than at the ends of words.

In a study examining the use of consonant cluster analogies by 6-year-old children (Goswami, 1991), I found exactly the effect predicted by the phonological status hypothesis. The children made a significant number of analogies between clue words like 'trim' and 'flan' and test words like 'trot' and 'flop'. They did not use analogies between clue words like 'desk' and 'loft' and test words like 'risk' and 'tuft', even though these words also shared consonant clusters with the clue words. So the phonological (onset–rime) status of the shared spelling sequence had a clear effect on the children's analogies. However, if the clue and the test words shared a vowel as well as a consonant cluster (e.g. 'trim'-'trip', 'loft'–'soft'), then both beginning and end analogies were found, replicating the effect found for clue and test words like 'beak' and 'bean'. Without a shared vowel, however, the children were only prepared to make connections between shared consonant clusters and sounds corresponding to onsets.

The third prediction made earlier was that the use of analogies in early reading should be truly orthographic in nature. That is, the analogies should reflect children's attempts to make connections between shared spelling patterns and shared sounds, and should not arise from some kind of phonological priming. For example, it could be argued that the extremely robust rime analogy effect found in the clue word studies is an artefact of the fact that the clue and the test words rhyme. It may have nothing to do with the fact that they also share a spelling sequence.

The simple form of this criticism cannot be right, as we have never observed children in the clue word studies simply guessing rhyming pronunciations for random test words. Such guessing does not even occur to test words that share phonemes with the clue words, such as 'bank'. However, the best way to test the phonological priming hypothesis directly is to measure children's use of analogy when the test words rhyme with the clue words, but have different spelling patterns. For example, if the clue word is 'head', then children should not use this word as a basis for analogies to words like 'said'. If the clue word is 'bone', children should not use this word as a basis for analogies to words like 'moan'. In another clue word study with 6-year-old readers, I compared analogies between clue and test words like 'head'–'bread'/'said', and 'bone'–'cone'/'moan' (Goswami, 1990b).

This 'phonological priming' study showed a clear and significant orthographic effect in rime analogies. The children made significantly more analogies when the clue and the test words shared a spelling sequence ('head'–'bread', 'bone'–'cone') than when they did not ('head'–'said', 'bone'–'moan'). In a second study using passages of prose, the only analogies that occurred were between words with shared spelling sequences. So in 'real reading' – that is, reading passages of connected prose – children restrict their use of analogies to words that have analogous spelling patterns. This prose study supports the claim that children spontaneously use orthographic strategies even in the earliest phases of learning to read.

The orthographic analogy work has thus established three important facts. The first is that children can make connections between spelling patterns in words from the beginning of learning to read. In fact, analogy seems to be a strategy that they *bring with them* to the reading task. The second is that the analogies that children make reflect their phonological knowledge. Children are more likely to make connections between spelling sequences that reflect the phonological units of the onset and the rime than to make connections between spelling sequences that cross the onset–rime boundary. The third is that children's phonological awareness of onsets and rimes affects the number of analogies that they make. Children with better onset–rime skills make more analogies. Onsets and rimes are thus important functional units in reading.

Theoretical implications

It is worth pointing out that the implications of this research extend beyond the importance of onsets and rimes as functional units in children's reading. The nature of the analogies that children make as they learn to read suggests that reading development is an inherently *interactive* process. Children bring phono-logical knowledge to the task of learning to read, and as they learn more about the orthography, the nature of their phonological knowledge changes (from onsets and rimes to phonemes). This interactive view stands in marked contrast to traditional models of learning to read, which (as discussed earlier) are stage models. In the two best-known stage models (Marsh *et al.*, 1981; Frith, 1985), children are thought to begin to read by using holistic strategies (the logographic stage), then to progress to using letter–sound correspondences (the alphabetic stage), and finally, to become able to use orthographic strategies. According to these models, the approach that children take to the task of learning to read is qualitatively different at successive stages of the process (although the earlier strategies do remain available).

An analogy model of learning to read is quite different (Goswami, 1993). Instead of conceptualizing learning to read as a sequential emergence of strategies, the analogy model proposes that children use the *same* strategy from the earliest phases: they try to work out the connection between orthography and phonology by comparing and contrasting spelling patterns and sounds. As we know from the research discussed in this chapter, children do not begin the task of learning to read as blank slates. Instead, they bring a lot of useful knowledge about the language with them, both in terms of its meaning and, more importantly, in terms of its sound. It is this *phonological* knowledge that will be especially important in learning to read. Orthographic knowledge may be *founded* in phonological skills, at least for phonologically able children (see also Stuart and Coltheart, 1988). Children thus begin learning to read by trying to work out the relationship between the sound categories that they already possess – the categories of syllables, onsets and rimes – and the orthography. Even the earliest recognition units that the child establishes may have phonological coding, and this coding will be at the onset–rime level.

However, this initial focus on onset–rime knowledge will not prevent children from learning something about phonemes too. Onsets in particular will often correspond to individual phonemes, and so will some rimes. So this basic interactive process will give children some insight into grapheme–phoneme relationships as well as knowledge about larger spelling sequences in words. While early orthographic recognition units may only have onset–rime coding, as reading develops the comparisons that children make between spelling patterns and sound will become increasingly fine-grained. Orthographic recognition units will eventually be coded in terms of all the constituent phonemes in the words, enabling the development of an increasingly well-specified orthographic lexicon.

This interactive analogy model does not include a logographic stage, in contrast to the interactive model of reading development proposed by Ehri (1992). It also begins with onset–rime units rather than with partial phonemic analyses, in contrast to other interactive models (Stuart and Coltheart, 1988; Ehri, 1992; Perfetti, 1992). The advantages of these changes are two-fold. First, the analogy model represents more closely our current knowledge of the process of phonological development, with onset–rime knowledge preceding phonemic development. Second, orthographic recognition units with onset-rime coding can act as a basis for analogies, whereas logographic recognition units, or units with partial phonemic specification, cannot. An initial focus on rime offers large potential gains in reading development. Stanback (1992) has analyzed a corpus of 17,602 words, and has found that 616 rime families account for almost all the 43,041 syllables in these words. So coding letter clusters in terms of rimes and then making analogies would enable the rapid growth of a child's reading vocabulary.

Onsets and rimes in the classroom

Learning words using onset–rime segmentation

The claim that onsets and rimes are important functional units in reading makes a clear prediction about teaching children to read new words. If children are shown how to segment words into onsets and rimes when they learn to read them rather than into other units such as phonemes, then their reading should benefit. A research programme based on a computerized system for teaching reading has shown that this is indeed the case (e.g. Wise *et al.*, 1990; Wise, 1992). Children who are taught to read words with the help of onset-rime segmentation seem to benefit more than children who are taught to read words via other segmented sub-syllabic units.

The computerized teaching system used by Wise and her colleagues is based on a system called DECtalk, which can pronounce either whole words or sub-units within those words in recognizable synthesized speech. The system presents children with individual words to read on the computer screen, and when the children activate a given word the computer pronounces different phonological segments of that word, highlighting the letters associated with each segment as it does so. For example, for a word like CLAP with onset–rime segmentation, the CL- will be highlighted and pronounced, followed by the -AP. This process enables the relationship between spelling patterns and sound to be neatly and concretely demonstrated to young children.

If onset–rime segmentation is more beneficial than other kinds of segmentation in helping children to learn new words, then children should learn to read words most easily when they are segmented at the onset–rime boundary. However, in order to test this prediction properly, it is necessary to equate the subword segments that are being compared for the amount of orthographic and phonological information that they contain. The rime usually contains more information than other subword segments of single-syllable words, as it often constitutes a larger unit within the word (e.g. '-eak' in 'beak', '-at' in 'cat').

To get round this problem, Wise *et al.* (1990) decided to compare single-syllable words that were either CVCC words or CCVC words. When CVCC words are segmented at the onset–rime boundary (e.g. D-ISH), then the rime has three letters and the onset one letter, but when CCVC words are segmented at the onset–rime boundary (e.g. CL-AP), then each unit has two letters. In the control condition, the same words were segmented after the vowel (CLA-P, DI-SH). For CVCC words, each unit again has two letters, so if the initial bigram is important in learning new words, then post-vowel segmentation of CVCC words should be equivalent to onset-rime segmentation of CCVC words. However, if it is the onset–rime division that is the important one, then onset–rime segmentation should prove most helpful for learning both kinds of words.

Wise *et al.* gave the children (6-year-olds) three trials on each word. The child's job in each trial was to blend the different sub-syllabic units (onset–rime or post-vowel) into a pronunciation. Learning was measured both immediately after receiving a block of eight segmented words, and in a delayed post-test in which all the words (32) learned during a particular half-hour session were presented to be read a second time. The results showed a clear effect of segmentation type on learning. Children who received onset–rime segmentation consistently learned to read more words than children who received post-vowel segmentation, and this enhanced learning was found at both the short-term and the long-term post-tests. However, the strength of the effect was reduced at the long-term post-test, being non-significant in some analyses. Wise *et al.* speculated that this was because learning to read 32 new words presented in isolation during a half-hour period is an unusual and difficult task for young children.

In a further set of studies using the computerized reading teacher, Wise (1992) compared the effects of phonemic segmentation and whole word pronunciation with onset–rime segmentation in word learning. This comparison is a particularly interesting one for teachers, as phonemic segmentation is analogous to a phonics method of teaching reading (letter-by-letter), whereas whole word pronunciation is analogous to a holistic method ('look-and-say'). However, the comparison has a serious drawback. Not only is it impossible to equate these different segmented units for the amount of orthographic and phonological information that they contain, the different units also carry different memory loads. The memory load imposed by having to remember and blend together the five phonemes in a single-syllable word like BLAST is greater than that imposed by having to remember and blend together the two units of the onset and the rime (BL-AST), and the memory load involved in simply remembering the correct pronunciation for the whole word (BLAST) is even lighter.

Wise (1992) did find differences between these three comparisons. Children who received onset–rime segmentation learned more words than children who received phoneme segmentation, and children who received whole word pronunciations learned more words than either of these two groups once the words were longer than one syllable. The problem with this result is that it can be explained on the basis of differences in memory load alone. It is not necessarily due to the difference between the phonological units of the onset and the rime versus phonemes and whole words. However, for single-syllable words, Wise found no learning differences between the whole word group and the onset–rime group, despite the greater memory load imposed by the latter manipulation. So learning was equivalent whether the children learned about onset–rime segments or whether they were simply given the pronunciation for the whole word. This is a heartening result. Not only is there no cost associated with learning onset–rime segments, there might actually be a distinct advantage. The advantage is that onset–rime segmentation might be a better way to encourage transfer.

Teaching children to use onset–rime analogies

The claim that onsets and rimes are important functional units in reading makes a clear prediction about training studies too. Training children to segment words into onset–rime units and showing them that words share a similar spelling pattern for the rime should help them to generalize pronunciations to other analogous words. Recently, a number of studies have attempted to test this prediction (White and Cunningham, 1990; Bruck and Treiman, 1992; Peterson and Haines, 1992), with rather mixed results. While some studies find a significant effect of training (e.g. Peterson and Haines, 1992), others do not (e.g. Bruck and Treiman, 1992). The reasons for this seem to depend on the length and the depth of the training that the children receive. The better the training, the stronger the effect on reading.

Let us begin with an example of a positive result. A training study carried out in Canada with 5- to 6-year-old children by Peterson and Haines (1992) found a clear effect of orthographic analogy training on reading. Training lasted for a period of one month, and was given to children individually. During training, the children were introduced to ten different rime units (for example, '-all' in 'ball', 'fall'; '-ump' in 'jump', 'bump'). In each case, a clue word (such as 'ball') would be placed on an easel, and the child would be told 'This word is "ball"'. The child was then shown that the three letters '-all' stayed together to make the sound 'all', and that adding the 'b' (onset) made the word say 'ball'. Letters and sounds within the rime were never presented as isolated units. An analogous word like 'fall' would then be placed below 'ball', and the children were told this new word. The experimenter pointed out the orthographic similarity between the two words, removing and replacing the onsets ('f' and 'b'). Four new analogous words were then added to the easel ('wall', 'mall', 'hall', 'gall'), using the same technique. Over the month of training, the children learned ten clue words and their associated test words.

Prior to receiving this training, the children had been tested on a different set of clue and test words, and these words were used as a post-test to assess the effects of analogy training. Peterson and Haines found a highly significant effect of their training programme on the children's performance in this post-test. The trained group showed a significant increase in the number of words that they could read compared to a control group who had received normal classroom teaching for the same period. Analogy training benefited other reading-related skills as well. The experimental group improved more than the control group on a test of sentence and word segmentation (TALS, Test of Awareness of Language Segments; Sawyer, 1987), and on a test of letter-sound knowledge. This finding implies that learning about onset–rime analogies also benefits other skills that are important for reading progress.

In fact, this relationship between analogy and segmentation may be a reciprocal one. Peterson and Haines also found that initial segmentation skills had an effect on the benefits derived from analogy training. Children who had entered the study with good segmentation skills as measured by the TALS benefited more from analogy training than those who did not. Similar results have been reported by Ehri and Robbins (1992), in a study using an artificial orthography. They found that children with better nonsense word reading skills (e.g. 'kin', 'fop') benefited more from analogy training than children who were poor at reading nonsense words. However, they concluded from this that children can only use analogies if they can already segment words *phonemically*, an assertion that can be questioned. The good readers in their study may have been reading the nonsense words by analogy rather than by grapheme–phoneme rules, as most of their nonsense words had many orthographic neighbours (e.g. 'kin' has 18, and 'fop' has 21; see Treiman *et al.*, 1990). So their results could also show that the children who were already better at making analogies benefited more from the analogy training.

Two researchers who are not convinced that analogy training is useful in helping young children's reading are Bruck and Treiman (1992). They taught 6-year-old children to read a list of ten clue words (such as 'pig'), and then trained one group (the rime group) to read ten analogous rime words ('big'), another group (the CV group) to read ten words sharing the same CV ('pin'), and a third group (the vowel group) to read ten words sharing the same vowel ('rib'). Training was provided in two to four 10–15-minute sessions given on consecutive days. During this training, the analogous portions of the clue and the test words were highlighted in coloured pen. The experimenter asked the child to decode the analogous segment in isolation first, and then to derive a pronunciation for the whole test word. If the child was unable to do either of these tasks, the experimenter told the child the answer, and training continued until the child pronounced the test word correctly on two consecutive trials. This procedure was then repeated without the colour prompt, after which retention of the test words was measured. Finally, the children were given ten analogous nonsense words ('nig', 'pim') to try to read as a measure of transfer.

Bruck and Treiman found that although the children in the rime group learned to read the test words significantly more quickly than the children in the other two groups, the advantage for rime training was not maintained at the retention test. Here the rime group's performance was poorer than the other two groups – they remembered significantly fewer test words and performed less well in the generalization test, generalizing to three nonsense words on average compared to six nonsense words for the vowel group. Because the vowel group fared better in this study, Bruck and Treiman's conclusion was that 'a whole-hearted embrace of rime-based analogies as a method of teaching children to read may be premature'.

It is too early to reach this conclusion, however, for two reasons. The principal problem with Bruck and Treiman's study is that the experimental groups did not receive equal amounts of training. Because the children in the rime group learned to read the transfer words faster than the children in the other two groups, they actually received significantly *less* training than the children in these comparison groups. So without equating the groups for the amount of time spent in teaching them the different decoding strategies, it cannot be concluded that the benefits of onset–rime analogy training were relatively limited. The rime group may simply have needed more practice. The second problem is that the amount of training given to the groups was actually rather small (40–60 minutes in total), and did not stress the connection between orthography and phonology. Although the analogous segments of the clue and the test words were highlighted in colour for part of the training, there was no focus on rhyme. Yet this connection between orthography and phonology is exactly what a rime-based training programme needs to emphasize. Peterson and Haines' study appears to have succeeded where Bruck and Treiman's study failed because the former used a fairly lengthy training period, and because Peterson and Haines also taught children about the connection between rhyme and the spelling patterns of rimes by using different 'word families'.

Peterson and Haines' study is not the only one to demonstrate a clear effect of analogy training on reading new words. A study carried out by White and Cunningham (1990) with a much larger group of children found similar results. White and Cunningham used a whole school district in Hawaii for their study, and their training programme lasted for an entire year. The analogy training was provided by the class teachers themselves, who had been trained to use an analogy-based reading programme by the experimenters. White and Cunningham were thus able to compare the reading progress of the children in these 'analogy' classrooms to the progress of children in control classrooms, who did not receive analogy-based teaching. The 290 children taking part in the study were from minority and low-SES groups, and were aged from 6 to 7 years (first and second grades).

The analogy training was based on 200 key words which were chosen to reflect major spelling patterns, thereby providing a basis for analogy to many other words (e.g. 'look' – 'book', 'took', 'cook' . . . ; 'nine' – 'mine', 'pine', 'fine' . . .). These key words were gradually taught to the children throughout the year, and were written up on a 'word wall' in the classroom as they were learned, colour-coded by vowel. The children also received instruction about analogy. The analogy instruction began with work on rhyming, and was followed up by systematic teaching about word 'families'. For example, the children might learn about the 'nine', 'mat' and 'job' families by being presented with a new word from one family, such as 'spine'. They would have to decide which family this new word belonged to, and how to pronounce it. Similar instruction was then given in spelling. So information about how to categorize words on the basis of their spelling patterns and about the way in which spelling categories were linked to sound categories formed the main analogy training.

When White and Cunningham compared the reading progress of the children in the 'analogy' classrooms to that of the children in the control classrooms, they found that the former were significantly ahead in measures of both decoding and comprehension. A replication study carried out the following year with a further 305 5- to 6-year-old children found similar results. So analogy training works well in the normal classroom setting. It is not limited to use with individual children who receive individualized training. Furthermore, the children in this study were from a disadvantaged group, a group that would generally be expected to make slow progress in learning to read. White and Cunningham's conclusion was that analogy training was an effective way of teaching disadvantaged children to learn to read.

Backward readers, onsets and rimes

White and Cunningham's work with disadvantaged children is particularly important for the question of whether onset–rime analogies can help children who have been diagnosed as dyslexic readers. Dyslexic children are known to have poor phonological skills (see Rack *et al.*, 1992, for a recent review). In particular, their rhyming skills are known to be significantly poorer than those of much younger children reading at equivalent levels (the stringent 'reading level match' experimental design; see Bryant and Goswami, 1986). For example, Bradley and Bryant (1978) showed that 10-year-old backward readers found the rhyme oddity task significantly more difficult than 7-year-old normal readers. These children were also significantly poorer at generating sets of words that rhymed with simple words provided by the experimenter, like 'dog' and 'dish'. Specific difficulties with rhyme for dyslexic readers have also been reported by other authors using reading level match studies (e.g. Olson *et al.*, 1985; Holligan and Johnston, 1988).

A child who has a problem in recognizing rhymes in spoken words is not in a good position to start making connections between shared spelling sequences in words and rhyming sounds. On the basis of the interactive model of reading development proposed earlier, therefore, dyslexic children might be expected to be rather poor at using analogies in reading. Research suggests that this is indeed the case. Lovett and her group have been investigating this question for some time, and they consistently find that dyslexic children do not use analogies spontaneously when they read new words. For example, dyslexic children who are taught to read words like 'beak' and 'part' do not read more words in a list of analogous words like 'peak' and 'cart' than control children who do not learn the first list (Lovett *et al.*, 1990). This lack of transfer is found even though the children can remember the spelling patterns of the words in the training list when shown them later. So the difficulty in using analogy does not seem to be based on an inability to remember spelling sequences. Instead, it seems to arise from poor phonological skills, which prevent the children from making the connection between shared spelling patterns and rhyming sounds.

One way to test the idea that poor rhyming skills are at the root of this failure to use analogies would be to give dyslexic children some training in rhyme, and then to see whether this training affects their use of analogy. Although such a study remains to be done, suggestive evidence comes from Bradley and Bryant (1983), who gave rhyme training to some children with phonological difficulties (these children, who were pre-readers, were not actually dyslexic). They found that rhyme training had large benefits on the children's later reading progress, especially when the training was given in conjunction with instruction about spelling categories using plastic letters. After two years of training, the experimental group were a staggering 23 months ahead of an unseen control group in spelling, and 12 months ahead of them in reading. Another group of children who received training in rhyme alone were also ahead of the control group, but their advantages were less marked.

The results of Bradley and Bryant's study are extremely interesting for our hypothesis about rhyme and analogy. The plastic letter and rhyme training group were effectively learning to use analogies. They spent the first year of training learning about phonological categories, and the second year making links between these rhyming categories and shared orthography. This implies that a *combination* of orthographic and phonological training has the greatest effect in improving reading in a group of children with poor phonological skills. In fact, an analogy-based training programme has been developed in Philadelphia specifically for use with dyslexic children (Gaskins *et al.*, 1986). So onsets and rimes may be functional units in the reading of dyslexic children, too.

Conclusion

The research reviewed here has established a number of important facts about children's use of onsets and rimes when they learn to read. First, experiments on phonological development have shown that knowledge about onsets and rimes appears to develop before children learn to read. Second, the clue word analogy experiments have shown that children's onset–rime knowledge feeds directly into their early reading, as they make connections between shared spelling patterns in words that reflect onset–rime units before they make connections between shared spelling patterns in words that cross the onset–rime boundary. Third, the level of a child's onset–rime skills is significantly related to that child's use of orthographic analogies, and this appears to be true of backward readers as well as of normal readers. Finally, training children to use onset–rime units when they read can benefit their reading progress, and learning new words with the help of onset–rime segmentation can facilitate the acquisition of new words.

These findings provide clear evidence that onsets and rimes are functional units in young children's reading. They can also be used to argue that it is time to think about the process of reading development in a different way. Rather than focusing on stage models of development, in which children progress through qualitatively different stages of reading, a more interactive model of development can be proposed (Goswami, 1993). According to this model, reading development is based on the interaction of phonological and orthographic knowledge from its earliest phases. Children are active learners, busy trying to make connections between phonology and the orthography from the very beginning of learning to read. After all, children do not come to the task of reading without any relevant knowledge at all. They actually have quite a lot of relevant knowledge, and this is *phonological* knowledge. In order to relate this phonological (onset–rime) knowledge to print, they must begin to analyze the correspondences between phonological categories like rhyme and spelling categories, and analogy provides them with a strategy for beginning such an analysis. The evidence suggests that the use of orthographic analogies is an important entry strategy to the process of learning to read, and that onsets and rimes are the important functional units in this process.

References

Bradley, L. and Bryant, P.E. (1978). 'Difficulties in auditory organisation as a possible cause of reading backwardness', *Nature, 271*, 746–7.

Bradley, L. and Bryant, P.E. (1983), 'Categorising sounds and learning to read: a causal connection', *Nature, 310*, 419–21.

Bruck, M. and Treiman, R. (1992), 'Learning to pronounce words: the limitations of analogies', *Reading Research Quarterly, 27* (4), 374–89.

Bryant, P.E. and Goswami, U. (1986), 'The strengths and weaknesses of the reading level design: comment on Backman, Mamen and Ferguson', *Psychological Bulletin, 100*, 101–3.

Chukovsky, K. (1963), *From Two to Five*, Berkeley: University of California Press.

Content, A., Morais, J., Alegria, J. and Bertelson, P. (1982), 'Accelerating the development of phonetic segmentation skills in kindergarteners', *Cahiers de Psychologie Cognitive, 2*, 259–69.

Cossu, G., Shankweiler, D., Liberman, I.Y., Tola, G. and Katz, L. (1987), *Awareness of Phonological Segments and Reading Ability in Italian Children*, Haskins Labs Status Report on Speech Research, No. SR–91.

Ehri, L.C. (1992), 'Reconceptualising sight word reading'. In P.B. Gough, L.C. Ehri and R. Treiman (eds.) *Reading Acquisition*, Hillsdale, NJ: Lawrence Erlbaum, pp. 107–43.

Ehri, L.C. and Robbins, C. (1992), 'Beginners need some decoding skill to read words by analogy', *Reading Research Quarterly, 27* (1), 12–28.

Frith, U. (1985), 'Beneath the surface of developmental dyslexia'. In K. Patterson, M. Coltheart and J. Marshall (eds.) *Surface Dyslexia*, Cambridge: Academic Press, pp. 301–30.

Gaskins, I.W., Downer, M.A. and Gaskins, R.W. (1986), *Introduction to the Benchmark School Word Identification/Vocabulary Development Program*, Media, PA: Benchmark Press.

Glushko, R.J. (1979), 'The organisation and activation of orthographic knowledge in reading aloud', *Journal of Experimental Psychology, Human Perception and Performance, 5*, 674–91.

Goswami, U. (1986), 'Children's use of analogy in learning to read: a developmental study', *Journal of Experimental Child Psychology, 42*, 73–83.

Goswami, U. (1988), 'Orthographic analogies and reading development', *Quarterly Journal of Experimental Psychology, 40A*, 239–68.

Goswami, U. (1990a), 'A special link between rhyming skills and the use of orthographic analogies by beginning readers', *Journal of Child Psychology and Psychiatry, 31*, 301–11.

Goswami, U. (1990b), 'Phonological priming and orthographic analogies in reading', *Journal of Experimental Child Psychology, 49*, 323–40.

Goswami, U. (1991), 'Learning about spelling sequences: the role of onsets and rimes in analogies in reading', *Child Development, 62*, 1110–23.

Goswami, U. (1993), 'Towards an Interactive Analogy Model of Reading Development:

68   *Usha Goswami*

decoding vowel graphemes in beginning reading', *Journal of Experimental Child Psychology*, *56*, 443–75.

Goswami, U. and Bryant, P.E. (1990), *Phonological Skills and Learning to Read*. Hillsdale, NJ: Lawrence Erlbaum.

Goswami, U. and Mead, F. (1992), 'Onset and rime awareness and analogies in reading', *Reading Research Quarterly*, *27* (2), 152–62.

Holligan, C. and Johnston, R.S. (1988), 'The use of phonological information by good and poor readers in memory and reading tasks', *Memory and Cognition*, *16*, 522–32.

Kirtley, C., Bryant, P., MacLean, M. and Bradley, L. (1989), 'Rhyme, rime and the onset of reading,' *Journal of Experimental Child Psychology*, *48*, 224–45.

Lenel, J.C. and Cantor, J.H. (1981), 'Rhyme recognition and phonemic perception in young children', *Journal of Psycholinguistic Research*, *10*, 57–68.

Liberman, I.Y., Shankweiler, D., Fischer, F.W. and Carter, B. (1974), 'Explicit syllable and phoneme segmentation in the young child', *Journal of Experimental Child Psychology*, *18*, 201–12.

Lovett, M.W., Warren-Chaplin, P.M., Ransby, M.J. and Borden, S.L. (1990), 'Training the word recognition skills of dyslexic children: treatment and transfer effects', *Journal of Educational Psychology*, *82*, 769–80.

Lundberg, I., Olofsson, A. and Wall, S. (1980), 'Reading and spelling skills in the first school years predicted from phonemic awareness skills in kindergarten', *Scandinavian Journal of Psychology*, *21*, 159–73.

MacLean, M., Bryant, P.E. and Bradley, L. (1987), 'Rhymes, nursery rhymes and reading in early childhood', *Merrill-Palmer Quarterly*, *33*, 255–82.

Marsh, G., Friedman, M.P., Welch, V. and Desberg, P. (1981), 'A cognitive–developmental approach to reading acquisition.' In G.E. MacKinnon and T.G. Waller (eds) *Reading Research: Advances in theory and practice*, Vol. 3, New York: Academic Press, pp. 199–221.

Morais, J. (1991) 'Constraints on the development of phonemic awareness'. In S.A. Brady and D.P. Shankweiler (eds.) *Phonological Processes in Literacy: A tribute to Isabelle Liberman*, Hillsdale, NJ: Lawrence Erlbaum, pp. 5–27.

Morais, J., Alegria, J. and Content, A. (1987), 'The relationships between segmental analysis and alphabetic literacy: an interactive view', *Cahiers de Psychologie Cognitive*, *7*, 415–38.

Morais, J., Cary, L., Alegria, J. and Bertelson, P. (1979), 'Does awareness of speech as a sequence of phonemes arise spontaneously?' *Cognition*, *7*, 323–31.

Olson, R.K., Davidson, B.J., Kliegl, R. and Foltz, G. (1985), 'Individual and developmental differences in reading disability'. In G.E. MacKinnon and T.G. Waller (eds.) *Reading Research: Advances in theory and practice*, Vol. IV, New York: Academic Press, pp. 1–64.

Opie, I. and Opie, P. (1987), *The Lore and Language of Schoolchildren*, Oxford: Oxford University Press.

Perfetti, C. (1992), 'The representation problem in reading acquisition'. In P.B. Gough, L.C. Ehri and R. Treiman (eds.) *Reading Acquisition*, Hillsdale, NJ: Lawrence Erlbaum, pp. 145–74.

Peterson, M.E. and Haines, L.P. (1992), 'Orthographic analogy training with kindergarten children: effects on analogy use, phonemic segmentation, and letter–sound knowledge', *Journal of Reading Behaviour*, *24*, 109–27.

Rack, J.P., Snowling, M.J. and Olson, R.K. (1992), 'The nonsense word reading deficit in developmental dyslexia: a review', *Reading Research Quarterly*, *27*, 28–53.

Sawyer, D.J. (1987), *Test of Awareness of Language Segments*, Rockville, MD: Aspen.

Stanback, M.L. (1992), 'Syllable and rime patterns for teaching reading: analysis of a frequency-based vocabulary of 17,602 words', *Annals of Dyslexia*, *42*, 196–221.

Stuart, M. and Coltheart, M. (1988), 'Does reading develop in a sequence of stages?' *Cognition*, *30*, 139–81.

Treiman, R. (1985) 'Phonemic awareness and spelling: children's judgements do not always agree with adults', *Journal of Experimental Child Psychology*, *39*, 182–201.

Treiman, R. (1988), 'The internal structure of the syllable'. In G. Carlson and M. Tanenhaus (eds.), *Linguistic Structure in Language Processing*, Dordrecht: Kluger, pp. 27–52.

Treiman, R., Goswami, U. and Bruck, M. (1990), 'Not all nonwords are alike: implications for reading development and theory', *Memory and Cognition*, *18*, 559–67.

Treiman, R. and Zukowski, A. (1991), 'Levels of phonological awareness'. In S. Brady and D. Shankweiler (eds.) *Phonological Processes in Literacy*, Hillsdale, NJ: Lawrence Erlbaum.

White, T.G. and Cunningham, P.M. (1990), *Teaching Disadvantaged Students to Decode by Analogy*, Paper presented at the annual meeting of the American Educational Research Association, Boston, MA, April.

Wise, B.W. (1992), 'Whole words and decoding for short-term learning: comparisons on a "Talking Computer" system', *Journal of Experimental Child Psychology*, *54*, 147–67.

Wise, B.W., Olson, D.K. and Treiman, R. (1990), 'Subsyllabic units as aids in beginning readers' word learning: onset–rime versus post-vowel segmentation', *Journal of Experimental Child Psychology*, *49*, 1–19.

5

Literacy environment and the development of children's cognitive skills

Anne E. Cunningham, College of Education, University of Washington;
Keith E. Stanovich, Ontario Institute for Studies in Education; and
Richard F. West, Department of Psychology, James Madison University

Early literacy development: Matthew effects

The role played by experiential factors in determining variation in children's cognitive growth has been at the heart of much theorizing in developmental psychology. Multiple factors have been cited as contributing to children's cognitive development. For example, individual differences in home and family environment are hypothesized to play a large role in children's cognitive growth (e.g. Hewison and Tizard, 1980; Alwin and Thornton, 1984; Hess et al., 1984; Iverson and Walberg, 1984).

When speculating about variables in people's ecologies, which could account for cognitive variability, in an attempt to supplement purely genetic accounts of mental ability (e.g. Ceci, 1990), we should focus on variables that have the requisite potency to perform their theoretical roles. A class of variable that might have such potency would be one that has long-term effects because of its repetitive and/or cumulative action. Schooling is obviously one such variable (Morrison, 1987; Cahan and Cohen, 1989; Ceci, 1990, 1991). In this chapter we shall argue that another experiential factor which, like schooling, has long-term cumulative effects is exposure to print.

Reading is a very special type of interface with the environment, providing the child with unique opportunities to acquire declarative knowledge. Furthermore, the processing mechanisms exercised during reading receive an unusual amount

This research was supported by a James S. McDonnell Foundation Fellowship to Anne E. Cunningham and by a grant from the Social Sciences and Humanities Research Council of Canada to Keith E. Stanovich. We thank Gary F. Carson for his assistance in data collection and coding. We are most appreciative to William Neff, Assistant Superintendent, for all his help in arranging the study and to the students at Clarkston Community Schools.

of practice. Certain microprocesses of reading which are linked to words or groups of words are repeatedly exercised. For example, from the time of at least the fifth grade, an avid reader is seeing literally millions of words a year (Anderson *et al.*, 1988). Thus, whatever cognitive processes are engaged over word or word-group units (phonological coding, semantic activation, parsing, induction of vocabulary items) are being exercised hundreds of times a day. It is surely to be expected that this amount of cognitive muscle-flexing will have some specific effects. Differential participation in such a process should result in large individual differences not only in reading ability but other cognitive skills as well.

Biemiller (1977–8) found large ability differences in exposure to print within the classroom as early as midway through the first year of school. Convergent results have been obtained by Allington (1984). In his sample of first-grade school children, the total number of words read during a week of school-reading group sessions ranged from a low of 16 for one of the children in the less skilled group to a high of 1,933 for one of the children in the skilled reading group. The average skilled reader read approximately three times as many words in the group reading sessions as the average less skilled reader. Nagy and Anderson have estimated that in the case of in-school reading

> the least motivated children in the middle grades might read 100,000 words a year while the average children at this level might read 1,000,000. The figure for the voracious middle grade reader might be 10,000,000 or even as high as 50,000,000. If these guesses are anywhere near the mark, there are staggering individual differences in the volume of language experience, and therefore, opportunity to learn new words. (Nagy and Anderson, 1984, p. 328)

There are, of course, also differences in the volume of reading outside the classroom which are linked to reading ability (Fielding *et al.*, 1986), and these probably become increasingly large as schooling progresses.

It is these individual differences in out-of-school reading volume and their resulting effects that we have attempted to model in our research programme. Although it has been shown that cognitive processes influence children's ability to read, very little attention has been focused on what might be considered a form of reciprocal causation – that is, on the possibility that differences in exposure to print affect the development of cognitive processes and acquisition of knowledge.

The effect of reading volume on cognitive processes and declarative knowledge bases, combined with the large skill differences in reading volume, could mean that a 'rich get richer' or cumulative advantage phenomenon is almost inextricably embedded within the developmental course of reading progress (see Stanovich, 1986). For example, we can see these 'the rich get richer' (and their converse 'the poor get poorer') effects in vocabulary development. The very children who are reading well and have good vocabularies will read more, learn more word meanings and hence read even better. Children with inadequate vocabularies – who read slowly and without enjoyment – read less, and as a result have slower development of vocabulary knowledge, which inhibits further growth in reading ability.

These educational sequences where early achievement in literacy spawns faster rates of subsequent achievement have been termed 'Matthew effects' by Stanovich (1986; see also Walberg and Tsai, 1983). The term 'Matthew effects' derives from the Gospel according to Matthew (XXV: 29): 'For unto every one that hath shall be given, and he shall have abundance: but from him that hath not shall be taken away even that which he hath' – and refers to the rich get richer and the poor get poorer effects embedded in the socio-developmental context of schooling. Reading comprehension provides an example of this effect – children who are already good comprehenders may tend to read more, thus spurring further increases in their reading comprehension abilities and increasing the achievement differences between them and their age cohorts who are not good comprehenders and not avid readers (Stanovich, 1986; Share and Silva, 1987; Juel, 1988; Share *et al.*, 1989; van den Bos, 1989; Chall *et al.*, 1990).

We shall attempt to examine these reciprocal effects in children's early reading development and evaluate their subsequent cognitive growth in the two studies reported in this chapter. Our first investigation delineates the relation between first-grade literacy environment and the development of children's orthographic and phonological skills. In our second study, we have followed a group of first-grade children and, ten years later, assessed their level of reading volume as well as their verbal intelligence, reading comprehension and general knowledge. In this longitudinal investigation, we have been able to observe the widening achievement disparities and the relative contribution of print exposure in explaining these differences.

An analytic logic for tracking the specific effects of print exposure

Over the past several years, our research group has attempted to develop and validate measures of individual differences in print exposure (e.g. Stanovich and West, 1989; Cunningham and Stanovich, 1990, 1991; West and Stanovich, 1991; Stanovich, 1992, 1993; Stanovich and Cunningham, 1992, 1993). We first examined the relation between print exposure and cognitive growth among adults (Stanovich and West, 1989) and later among children (e.g. Cunningham and Stanovich, 1990). In our methodology, we attempt to correlate differential engagement in reading with various cognitive outcomes that have been associated with the acquisition of literacy (Stanovich and West, 1989; Cunningham and Stanovich, 1990, 1991; West and Stanovich, 1991; Stanovich and Cunningham, 1992, 1993). However, such a logic, if not supplemented with additional methodological controls, is subject to the same problem that has plagued historical investigations of literacy's effects – the problem of spurious correlation. That is, degree of print exposure is correlated with various reading skills such as word decoding and with cognitive abilities generally. Simply and obviously, individuals with superior reading skills read more. This correlation is problematic because it raises the possibility that an association between amount of print exposure and any criterion ability, skill or knowledge base might arise not because of the unique effects of print exposure, but because of individual differences in general ability or in specific reading subskills such as decoding.

This point can be illustrated using vocabulary as an example. The counter-argument to the claim that print exposure is a major mechanism determining vocabulary growth (Nagy and Anderson, 1984; Stanovich, 1986; Hayes, 1988) is that superior decoding ability leads to more print exposure, and that decoding abilities are themselves related to vocabulary development because better decoding ensures an accurate verbal context for inducing the meanings of unknown words. Thus, according to this argument, vocabulary and print exposure are spuriously related via their connection with decoding ability: good decoders read a lot and have the best context available for inferring new words. Decoding ability could also in part reflect the efficiency of the phonological short-term memory which Gathercole and Baddeley (1989) have argued is critical to early oral vocabulary acquisition. Finally, vocabulary and print exposure could be spuriously linked through general cognitive abilities which are associated with both print exposure and the ability to induce meaning from context (Sternberg, 1985).

We have utilized a regression logic to deal with this problem. In the analyses to be discussed, we shall first control statistically for the effects of general ability before examining the relationship between print exposure and criterion variables. This procedure of reducing possible spurious relationships by first partialling out relevant subskills and abilities and then looking for residual effects of print exposure has been used in our earlier investigations. For example, in previous work we have demonstrated that independent of decoding ability, variation in print exposure among adults predicts spelling ability and orthographic knowledge (Stanovich and West, 1989). Similarly, in a previous study of children's performance (Cunningham and Stanovich, 1990) we found that after partialling IQ, memory ability and phonological processing abilities, print exposure accounted for additional variance in orthographic knowledge and word recognition. The logic of our analytic strategy is quite conservative because we partial out variance in abilities that are likely to be developed by print exposure itself (Stanovich, 1986, 1993). Yet even after print exposure is robbed of some of its rightful variance, it remains a unique predictor (Stanovich and West, 1989).

Assessing print exposure

There are numerous difficulties involved in assessing individual differences in exposure to print. Time diary methods, in which daily activity records are filled out by subjects (see Greaney, 1980; Greaney and Hegarty, 1987; Anderson *et al.*, 1988; Taylor *et al.*, 1990), result in estimates of the absolute amount of time spent on literacy activities. Other techniques are available if one wants only an index of relative differences in exposure to print. For example, a variety of questionnaire and interview techniques has been used to assess relative differences in print exposure (e.g. Estes, 1971; Sharon, 1973–4; Lewis and Teale, 1980; Guthrie, 1981; Guthrie and Greaney, 1991; Guthrie and Seifert, 1983), but many of these are encumbered with social desirability confounds: responses are distorted due to the tendency to report socially desirable behaviours (Paulhus, 1984; Furnham, 1986) – in this case, the tendency to report more reading than actually takes place (Ennis, 1965; Sharon, 1973–4). This problem is particularly acute within the context of the present study where primary and secondary school children are being asked questions about a socially valued activity such as reading.

In this chapter, we report further data on three recognition measures of print exposure – the Author Recognition Test, the Magazine Recognition Test and the Title Recognition Test – measures that have proved to be robust predictors in earlier studies (Stanovich and West, 1989; Cunningham and Stanovich, 1990, 1991; West and Stanovich, 1991; Allen *et al.*, 1992; Cipielewski and Stanovich, 1992; Stanovich and Cunningham, 1992, 1993; West *et al.*, 1993).

The first measures we developed were designed for use with adult subjects (Stanovich and West, 1989). The Author Recognition Test (ART) and the Magazine Recognition Test (MRT) both exploited a signal detection logic whereby actual target items (real authors and real magazines) were embedded among foils (names that were not authors or magazine titles, respectively). Subjects simply scan the list and check the names they know to be authors on the ART, and the titles they know to be magazines on the MRT. The measures thus have a signal detection logic. The number of correct items checked can be corrected for differential response biases which are revealed by the checking of foils. Although checklist procedures have been used before to assess print exposure (Chomsky, 1972), our procedure is unique in using foils to control for differential response criteria (see Stanovich and Cunningham, 1992, for examples of the stimuli).

In constructing the ART list, authors were selected who were most likely to be encountered outside the classroom, so that the ART would be a proxy measure of out-of-school print exposure rather than of curriculum exposure. Thus, an attempt was made to avoid authors who are regularly studied in the school curriculum. For example, none of the authors that we have employed appeared in Ravitch and Finn's (1987) survey of secondary school curriculum literature. In short, the ART was intentionally biased towards out-of-school reading, because it was intended as an indirect measure of amount of free reading. The ART is dominated by 'popular' authors. That is, it is not composed of 'highbrow' writers who would be known by only the most highly educated or academically inclined readers. Instead, many of the book authors regularly appear on best-seller lists and most have sold hundreds of thousands, if not millions, of copies. Although no statistical sampling of authors was carried out, an attempt was made to mix writers from a wide variety of genres.

Similarly, the sampling of titles on the MRT was deliberately biased towards popular publications. 'Highbrow' academic and low-circulation small press publications which would be known by only the most highly educated or academically inclined readers were avoided. The publications on the MRT almost all have circulations in the hundreds of thousands – in many cases, millions. The foil items on the MRT do not appear in the 60,000 listings in *The Standard Periodical Directory* (Manning, 1988) and the foil names on the ART were drawn from lists of editorial board members of psychological and educational journals.

This checklist method has several advantages. First, it is immune to the social desirability effects that may contaminate responses to subjective self-estimates of socially valued activities such as reading. Guessing is not an advantageous strategy because it is easily detected and corrected for by an examination of the number of foils checked. Further, the cognitive demands of the task are quite low. The task does not necessitate frequency judgements as do most question-naire measures of print exposure, nor does it require retrospective time judgements as does the use of daily activity diaries. Finally, the measures can be administered in a matter of a few minutes.

These checklist tasks are of course proxy indicators of someone's print exposure rather than measures of absolute amounts of reading in terms of minutes or estimated words (Anderson *et al.*, 1988). The fact that the measures are very indirect proxy indicators is problematic in some contexts, but it is also sometimes a strength. Clearly, hearing about a magazine or author on television without having been exposed to the actual written work is problematic. The occurrence of this type of situation obviously reduces the validity of the tasks. However, a post-experimental comment sometimes made by adult subjects in our studies is worth noting: some subjects said they knew a certain name was that of an author, but had never read anything that the author had written. When questioned about how they knew that the name was a writer, the subjects often replied that they had seen one of the author's books in a bookshop, had seen an author's book in the 'new fiction' section of the library, had read a review of the author's work in *Newsweek*, had seen an advertisement in the newspaper, etc. In short, knowledge of that author's name was a proxy for reading activities, despite the fact that the particular author had not actually been read. Thus, although some ways of gaining familiarity with author names would reduce validity (TV, radio), most behaviours leading to familiarity with the author names are probably reflections of immersion in a literate environment.

The Title Recognition Test (TRT) is a measure that has the same signal detection logic as the adult ART and MRT, but involves children's book titles rather than authors or magazines as items. This children's measure shares the same advantages of immunity from socially desirable responding, objective assessment of response bias, low cognitive load and lack of necessity for retrospective time judgements. The TRT consists of an intermixed list of actual children's book titles and foils for book names. The titles utilized were selected from a sample of book titles generated in pilot investigations by groups of children aged 6–8 years, by examining various lists of children's titles, and by consulting teachers and reading education professionals knowledgeable about current trends in children's literature. In selecting the items to appear on the TRTs used in our investigations, we attempted to choose titles that were not prominent parts of classroom reading activities in the schools in which our studies were to be conducted. Because we wanted the TRT to reflect out-of-school rather than school-directed reading, we attempted to avoid books that were used in the school curriculum. Thus, if the test is used for this purpose, versions of it will necessarily differ somewhat in item content from classroom to classroom and from school to school.

The score on all of these checklists – both child and adult versions – was the proportion of correct items checked minus the proportion of foils checked. This is the discrimination index from the two-high threshold model of recognition performance (Snodgrass and Corwin, 1988). Other corrections for guessing and differential criterion effects (*ibid.*) produce virtually identical correlational results.

Early literacy environment and the development of orthographic and phonological skills

With the exception of the seminal work of Maclean *et al.* (1987) on knowledge of nursery rhymes, there has been very little work on the experiential correlates of early phonological and orthographic processing skill. We addressed this issue in the present investigation by examining whether children's phonological and orthographic processing skill is differentially related to our index of children's home literacy environment – an index that is probably an indirect indicator of individual differences in exposure to print.

In a study of 26 first-grade (6–7 years) readers, we relied primarily on three tasks to partial out phonological processing variance. The first was a deletion task which required the children to delete the initial consonant from a monosyllabic word and pronounce the embedded word. In the second deletion task, the children were required to delete the initial phoneme from a series of ten beginning consonant blends and pronounce the remaining embedded word or word-like segment. The second part of this task required the children to delete the final phoneme from a series of ten final consonant blend words and provide the remaining sounds. Our third measure was a phoneme transposition task. Essentially, the children were required to switch the beginning and ending phoneme of a monosyllabic word to create a new word (e.g. top – pot).

In addition to the spelling subtest of the Stanford Achievement Test (Primary 1, Form E), two other tasks served as measures of orthographic processing skill. The first task was taken in part from Mann *et al.*'s spelling study (1987). Target words contained at least one of the following attributes: a letter name within the word, a short vowel, a nasal, a liquid or a consonant represented with a digraph. The words were chosen to 'increase the likelihood that subjects would invent preconventional spellings that could easily be distinguished from conventional spellings' (Mann *et al.*, 1987, p. 126). To spell these items conventionally, an orthographic representation must be consulted, so that accuracy on the items becomes, at least in part, a measure of the quality of the early developing orthographic lexicon.

The third orthographic processing measure was a letter-string choice task. Stimuli were kindly provided by Rebecca Treiman. The children were presented with sixteen pairs of 3–7 letter-strings on a sheet of paper and instructed to circle the one word that looked most like it could be a real word. The children are told that neither string is an actual word, but that one letter-string is more *like* a word. One member of each pair contained an orthographic sequence that either never occurs in English or that occurs with extremely low frequency. The subject's score is the number of times that the nonword without the illegitimate or low-frequency letter-string was chosen. Although this task undoubtedly implicates phonological coding to some extent, the coding of frequent and infrequent orthographic sequences in memory should be a substantial contributor to performance. Stimuli were: beff–ffeb, ddaled–dalled, yikk–yinn, vadding–vayying, nuck–ckun, ckader–dacker, vadd–vaad, muun–munt, ist–iit, moyi–moil, aut–awt, bey–bei, dau–daw, gri–gry, chim–chym and yb–ib.

Finally, a standardized reading achievement test, the Stanford Achievement Test (Primary 1, Form E), was employed to assess children's word reading and spelling performance.

As described earlier, the Title Recognition Test (TRT) was designed as an analog of recognition measures that had previously been used to assess amount of exposure to print in adults and primary school children. In the present study employing much younger children, the measure could be viewed as a proxy for the general literacy environment in the home or, alternatively, as a measure of the child's own print exposure. The TRT was group-administered within the classroom. The title of each book was read to children and they were instructed to underline only the names of books they knew were actual books. The children were told that guessing could easily be detected because some of the titles were not the names of actual books.

Can orthographic processing ability account for unique variance in word recognition?

By utilizing the logic of hierarchical multiple regression we addressed the question of whether there is variance in word recognition that can be reliably linked to orthographic processing skill once variance due to phonological processing has been partialled out. Table 5.1 presents the results of two such analyses. The three phonological processing tasks were entered first and collectively achieved a multiple R with Stanford Word Reading of 0.504. However, when the letter-string choice task was entered fourth, it accounted for a substantial proportion of additional variance (30.1 per cent). Similarly, when the score on the experimental spelling test was entered as the fourth variable in the equation, it accounted for 29.1 per cent of the variance in Word Reading scores.

Table 5.1 Intercorrelations among variables in the study

Variable	1	2	3	4	5	6	7	8
1. Title Recognition Test Derived								
2. SAT Word Reading	0.64							
3. SAT Spelling	0.69	0.71						
4. Phoneme Deletion1	0.01	0.40	0.22					
5. Phoneme Deletion2	0.16	0.39	0.10	0.30				
6. Phoneme Transposition	− 0.04	0.20	− 0.11	0.50	0.50			
7. Letter-string Choice	0.39	0.63	0.57	0.02	0.42	0.01		
8. Experimental Spelling	0.50	0.70	0.43	0.43	0.50	0.47	0.40	

Note:
Correlations greater than 0.33 are significant at the 0.05 level (two-tailed).

Thus, there does seem to be variation in orthographic processing skill, which is linked to word recognition ability and is independent of phonological processes. The analyses reported here are at least a tentative indication that phonological and orthographic processing skills are separable components of variance in word recognition during the very earliest stages of reading acquisition. The development of print-specific knowledge is not entirely parasitic on phonological processing skill among beginning readers.

Can variance in orthographic processing ability be linked to print exposure differences that are independent of phonological processing skill?

The latter conclusion shifts attention to the question of what factors determine variation in orthographic processing abilities and, in particular, whether print exposure is related to orthographic processing skill. In exploring this relationship it is important to partial out phonological processing ability because even if differences in orthographic processing abilities had as their proximal cause differences in exposure to print, reading practice may simply be determined by how skilled the child is at phonological processing. If this is the case, then print exposure would not serve as a unique source of orthographic variance once phonological processing skill was partialled out.

The hierarchical regression analyses presented in Table 5.2 address this question. The criterion variable in the first analysis is the score on the letter-string choice task. Entered first are the three phonological processing tasks which attain a multiple R of 0.480. Entered last is the score on the TRT and it accounts for an additional 8.5 per cent of the variance. However, probably due to the modest size of the sample, this unique proportion of variance explained did not reach statistical significance ($F(1, 21) = 2.63$). The second hierarchical regression was conducted with the experimental spelling test performance as the criterion variable. The three phonological tasks attained a multiple R of 0.595

Table 5.2 Unique print exposure variance after phonological and orthographic processing variance is partialled out

Dependent variable	Predictors	Multiple R	R² change
Letter-string Choice	Phoneme Deletion1	0.020	0.020
	Phoneme Deletion2	0.435	0.169*
	Phoneme Transposition	0.480	0.042
	Title Recognition Test	0.563	0.085
Experimental Spelling	Phoneme Deletion1	0.432	0.432*
	Phoneme Deletion2	0.576	0.245*
	Phoneme Transposition	0.595	0.042
	Title Recognition Test	0.753	0.212*
Stanford Spelling	Phoneme Deletion1	0.224	0.224*
	Phoneme Deletion2	0.227	0.001
	Phoneme Transposition	0.365	0.083
	Title Recognition Test	0.753	0.432*
Stanford Word Reading	Phoneme Deletion1	0.401	0.401*
	Phoneme Deletion2	0.490	0.079
	Phoneme Transposition	0.504	0.010
	Title Recognition Test	0.777	0.349*

Note:
* $p < 0.01$.

when entered as the first three steps. When entered as the last step, the TRT accounted for a statistically significant 21.2 per cent of the variance.

The third hierarchical regression was conducted with Stanford Spelling subtest scores as the criterion variable. This task was assumed to contain substantial orthographic processing variance because it is a spelling recognition test and because it displayed substantial correlations with performance on the letter-string choice task and the experimental spelling test (see Table 5.1). The three phonological tasks had a multiple R of 0.365 with performance on the Spelling subtest. When entered as the fourth step, the TRT accounted for a substantial 43.2 per cent of additional variance. Thus, in two of the three analyses reported here, exposure to print (as measured by the TRT) accounted for significant variance in orthographic processing variance once individual differences in phonological processes had been statistically controlled. The orthographic processing knowledge or processing skill that is separable from phonological processes appears to be linked to individual differences in the children's experiential history of literacy activities.

The final hierarchical regression shown in Table 5.2 simply illustrates that performance on the TRT also accounts for significant variance in Stanford Word Reading scores after phonological abilities have been partialled out.

In summary, this study demonstrates that it is possible to separate variance in orthographic processing skill from variance in phonological processing ability very early in the reading acquisition process. The findings converge with investigations of older children and adults (e.g. Treiman, 1984; Bryant and Impey, 1986;

Freebody and Byrne, 1988; Stanovich and West, 1989; Cunningham and Stanovich, 1990).

There is a substantial body of evidence on the importance of phonological processing in early reading, but less is known about how orthographic processing skill and/or the buildup of an orthographic lexicon interacts with the early stages of reading acquisition. This study has linked at least part of this variance in orthographic structures and/or processes to variation in children's literacy environments which can be measured with a very simple indicator. The study has demonstrated, in the orthographic domain, how reading might itself develop skills and knowledge bases which then serve to enable more efficient subsequent reading. We are just beginning to understand the mechanisms by which print exposure differences act to create rich get richer and poor get poorer effects in educational achievement (Stanovich, 1986, 1993). Our second study sheds further light on the relation between early literacy environment and the development of children's cognitive skills and more general knowledge bases.

A longitudinal investigation of print exposure and the development of cognitive skills

In a study of 56 first-grade readers (6–7 years) we administered a battery of tasks, which included measures of intelligence (Otis-Lennon School Ability Test and Raven Progressive Coloured Matrices, 1962), vocabulary (Peabody Picture Vocabulary Test, PPVT) and reading achievement (Metropolitan Reading Achievement Test, 1978). The cognitive performance of the children was tracked during the subsequent ten-year period. In the latter part of this study, we assessed a variety of declarative knowledge bases and verbal skills as well as the students' level of print exposure. Twenty-seven eleventh-grade (16–17 years) students remained from our earlier sample. The variables we report in this chapter are two measures of vocabulary (the Peabody Picture Vocabulary Test and the Nelson–Denny Reading Test: Vocabulary, Form F), two measures of general knowledge (National Assessment of Educational Progress Test of History and Literature, Ravitch and Finn, 1987, and Cultural Literacy Test, Riverside Publishing, 1989), a measure of reading comprehension (Nelson–Denny Reading Test: Comprehension, Form F) and secondary school versions of the ART and MRT.

Print exposure as a predictor of ten years of cognitive growth

A primary purpose of this study was to track the relation between children's literacy environment and their subsequent cognitive skill level. A composite z score of the ART and MRT was created for the following analyses (ARTMRTZ).

Table 5.3 Print exposure as a predictor of increase in reading ability (first to third grade) after differences in general ability are partialled out

Criterion variable = Third-grade Metropolitan Achievement Test, Elementary		
Step	Multiple R	R^2 change
1. First-grade Raven	0.119	0.013
2. First-grade PPVT	0.245	0.047
3. First-grade WRAT	0.595	0.294*
4. ARTMRTZ	0.734	0.185*
1. First-grade Raven	0.119	0.014
2. First-grade PPVT	0.308	0.081
3. First-grade MAT	0.789	0.528*
4. ARTMRTZ	0.833	0.071**

Notes:
 * $p < 0.01$.
 ** $p < 0.05$.

In some of these analyses, we interpreted the print exposure measures as cumulative indicators of variance in reading volume which had taken place many years earlier. Although we did not measure the literacy environment directly in the early years of our study, presumably the variance in the indicators reflects not just variance at the time of testing but also variance occurring during early years as well. Thus, we view the measures as in some sense retrospective indicators, tapping the cumulative experiences and habits of the children during the entire time-period.

In our first set of longitudinal analyses, we addressed the question of whether our retrospective index of exposure to print (ARTMRTZ) could predict growth in reading ability from the first to the third grade. To control for differences in general ability, first-grade performance on the Raven Progressive Matrices and the Peabody Picture Vocabulary Test were entered first into the regression equation predicting third-grade performance on the Metropolitan Achievement Test, Elementary. Collectively, the Raven and PPVT accounted for just 6.0 per cent of the variance in third-grade reading ability as measured by the Metropolitan Achievement Test, Elementary. When first-grade performance on the Reading subtest of the Wide Range Achievement Test was entered as the third step, it accounted for a substantial 29.4 per cent additional variance ($F (1,22) = 9.95$). However, when our measure of print exposure was entered as the fourth step, it still accounted for a sizeable 18.5 per cent additional variance in third-grade reading ability ($F (1,22) = 6.95$). When first-grade performance on the Metropolitan Achievement Test, Primary was substituted for the WRAT in a parallel analysis, the MAT accounted for 53.1 per cent additional variance and print exposure accounted for a smaller but still significant 7.1 per cent additional variance ($F (1,22) = 4.43$).

Table 5.4 Print exposure as a predictor of increase in reading ability (first to eighth grade) after differences in general ability are partialled out

Criterion variable = Eighth-grade Metropolitan Achievement Test, Intermediate		
Step	Multiple R	R^2 change
1. First-grade Raven	0.009	−0.048
2. First-grade PPVT	0.158	0.025
3. First-grade WRAT	0.687	0.276*
4. ARTMRTZ	0.745	0.183*
1. First-grade Raven	0.009	0.048
2. First-grade PPVT	0.158	0.025
3. First-grade MAT	0.687	0.447*
4. ARTMRTZ	0.745	0.083*

Note:
* $p < 0.01$.

A similar pattern was observed across a broader age range (see Table 5.4). In a second set of hierarchical regression analyses, our criterion variable was performance on the eighth-grade Metropolitan Achievement Test, Intermediate and the predictor variables were first-grade Raven, PPVT, MAT, WRAT and print exposure. Parallel to the previous analysis, this analysis addresses the question of whether print exposure can predict first- to eighth-grade growth in reading ability after general ability differences in the first grade are partialled. Collectively, the Raven and PPVT attained a non-significant multiple R of 0.158 (F (1,22) = 0.507). When the WRAT was entered at the third step, it accounted for 27.6 per cent additional variance. Entered last was the print exposure composite (ARTMRTZ), which accounted for a statistically significant 18.3 per cent of the variance (F (1,22) = 6.39). In a similar sequence, the MAT was entered after the Raven and PPVT and contributed 44.7 per cent additional variance. Entered next, print exposure accounted for 8.3 per cent additional variance (F (1,22) = 4.32). The results of these analyses demonstrate that print exposure accounted for significant variance in later reading ability once individual differences in general ability and first-grade reading ability were statistically controlled.

Table 5.5 displays a third hierarchical regression employing eleventh-grade reading comprehension ability (Nelson–Denny Reading Comprehension) as the criterion variable. Fifth-grade MAT performance was entered first and attained a multiple R of 0.625. Scores on the Raven matrices administered in the eleventh grade were entered next and accounted for a non-significant 2.2 per cent of the variance (F (1,23) = 0.80). When entered as the last step, the ARTMRTZ composite accounted for a statistically significant 5.8 per cent of the variance (F (1,23) = 5.92) – thus demonstrating that an indicator of exposure to print can

Table 5.5 Print exposure as a predictor of increase in reading ability (fifth to eleventh grade)

Criterion variable = Nelson–Denny Reading Test: Comprehension		
Step	Multiple R	R^2 change
1. Fifth-grade MAT	0.625	0.390*
2. Eleventh-grade Raven	0.642	0.022
3. ARTMRTZ	0.696	0.058**

Notes:
  * $p < 0.01$.
  ** $p < 0.05$.

predict individual differences in growth in reading comprehension from the fifth to the eleventh grade.

These are just a sampling of numerous analyzers, which demonstrate basically the same thing: that growth in reading comprehension ability between any two grades between the first and the eleventh grade is predicted by an index of print exposure administered in the eleventh year.

First-grade cognitive skills as predictors of subsequent print exposure

Our next set of analyses explored the relation between children's early cognitive skill levels and subsequent exposure to print. These analyses explore – correlationally, of course – the relative contributions of general abilities and early reading comprehension skill in explaining individual differences in children's literacy environments. Any indication that early comprehension ability plays a significant role in determining individual differences in subsequent print exposure would be consistent with the existence of Matthew effects in reading development.

Table 5.6 displays a hierarchical analysis in which the performance on the first-grade administration of the Raven matrices was entered as step 1 and attained a multiple R of 0.328 with the criterion variable (ARTMRTZ score). Performance on the Peabody Picture Vocabulary Test was entered second and predicted 23.4 per cent additional variance in subsequent print exposure. Performance on the first-grade administration of the WRAT predicted a sizeable 38.5 per cent of the variance (F (1,23) = 8.55). Performance on the first-grade Metropolitan was also entered in this same sequence and contributed a smaller but still significant 21.9 per cent additional variance (F (1,23) = 9.76). Although correlational, these results lend further support to the hypothesis that early reading ability plays a significant role in shaping one's later literacy environments. The rich appear to get richer, not only in terms of absolute levels of reading ability, but in their levels of print exposure as well.

Table 5.6 Cognitive skills (first grade) as a predictor of print exposure

Criterion variable = ARTMRTZ Step	Multiple R	R^2 change
1. Raven	0.328	0.107
2. PPVT	0.584	0.234*
3. WRAT	0.726	0.385*
1. Raven	0.328	0.107
2. PPVT	0.584	0.234*
3. MAT	0.748	0.219*

Note:
* $p < 0.01$.

Print exposure as a predictor of knowledge and vocabulary

One mechanism by which print exposure might lead to cognitive change is as a builder of an individual's knowledge base. Very little attention has focused on this form of reciprocal causation – that is, on the possibility that differences in exposure to print affect the development of declarative knowledge bases (see, however, Stanovich and Cunningham, 1993). Thus, our next set of analyses were structured to address the issue of whether measures of print exposure can account for variance in declarative knowledge after variance in relevant prior abilities has been partialled out.

In our first set of analyses, the criterion variable was eleventh-grade vocabulary scores on the Nelson–Denny Reading Test: Vocabulary. The first hierarchical regression displayed in Table 5.7 partialled fifth-grade reading ability (Metropolitan Reading Achievement Test, Elementary) and performance on the eleventh-grade Raven matrices before entering the index of print exposure. Fifth-grade MAT attained a multiple R of 0.431 and eleventh-grade Raven contributed 23.3 per cent additional variance. Print exposure accounted for a sizeable 33 per cent additional variance in vocabulary knowledge ($F (1,23) = 17.37$).

Because it could be argued that partialling reading comprehension ability from these analyses is unduly conservative (see Stanovich, 1993; Stanovich and Cunningham, 1993), we conducted a further analysis, which partialled two tests of general ability, one administered in the fifth grade and the other in the eleventh grade. Fifth-grade performance on the Otis–Lennon School Ability Test was partialled, followed by eleventh-grade Raven performance and then the print exposure composite. The combined multiple R of the two ability measures was 0.397. Print exposure was entered last and accounted for 51 per cent additional variance. Print exposure is thus the dominant predictor of vocabulary knowledge in these analyses.

In a parallel set of analyses, we examined the relative contribution of print exposure towards general knowledge as measured by National Assessment of

Table 5.7 Variance in declarative knowledge as predicted by print exposure (eleventh grade)

Step	Multiple R	R^2 change
Criterion variable = Nelson–Denny Reading Test: Vocabulary – Eleventh-grade		
1. Fifth-grade MAT	0.431	0.186*
2. Eleventh-grade Raven	0.647	0.233*
3. ARTMRTZ	0.866	0.331*
1. Fifth-grade Otis–Lennon	0.172	0.030
2. Eleventh-grade Raven	0.397	0.128
3. ARTMRTZ	0.817	0.509*
Criterion variable = General Knowledge – Eleventh Grade		
Step		
1. Fifth-grade MAT	0.503	0.253*
2. Eleventh-grade Raven	0.531	0.029
3. ARTMRTZ – Eleventh-grade	0.674	0.172*
1. Fifth-grade Otis–Lennon	0.244	0.060
2. Eleventh-grade Raven	0.482	0.172*
3. ARTMRTZ	0.676	0.225*

Note:
* $p < 0.01$.

Educational Progress Test of History and Literature (Ravitch and Finn, 1987) and Cultural Literacy Test (Riverside Publishing, 1989). As displayed in the bottom half of Table 5.7, print exposure explained a significant 17.2 per cent additional variance in general knowledge after fifth-grade MAT and eleventh-grade Raven were partialled. When just the nonverbal ability measures of fifth-grade Otis–Lennon and eleventh-grade Raven were entered, print exposure subsequently explained 22.5 per cent additional variance.

The results displayed in Table 5.8 examine print exposure as a concurrent predictor of declarative knowledge. In these analyses, we entered eleventh-grade Raven and Nelson–Denny reading comprehension prior to our print exposure measure. Each variable accounted for significant additional variance when entered in this order, and as a set resulted in a multiple correlation of 0.632. This particular conservative regression analysis, by entering concurrent reading comprehension ability, attempts to 'stack the deck', so to speak, against our index of literacy experience. We do not, of course, mean to imply by structuring the analyses in this way that print exposure is not a determinant of reading comprehension ability. Our intention is merely to bias the analyses against our print exposure measure, thereby controlling for any spurious relation with ability. None the less, we found that print exposure accounted for 35 per cent additional variance in vocabulary knowledge. Print exposure accounted for a significant, but much smaller, amount of the variance in general knowledge (7 per cent). Despite the conservative structuring of the analyses, print exposure appears to be a

Table 5.8 Print exposure as a concurrent predictor of knowledge and vocabulary

Criterion variable = Nelson–Denny Reading Test: Vocabulary – Eleventh-grade		
Step	Multiple R	R^2 change
1. Eleventh-grade Raven	0.552	0.305*
2. Eleventh-grade Nelson–Denny Comprehension	0.632	0.095*
3. ARTMRTZ	0.864	0.346*
Criterion variable = General Knowledge – Eleventh Grade		
Step		
1. Eleventh-grade Raven	0.402	0.161*
2. Eleventh-grade Nelson–Denny Comprehension	0.744	0.393*
3. ARTMRTZ	0.787	0.065*

Note:
* $p < 0.01$.

powerfully unique predictor of the declarative knowledge bases of secondary school pupils.

Conclusions

The results of these analyses suggest that print exposure, although clearly a consequence of developed reading ability, is probably a significant contributor to the development of other aspects of verbal intelligence. Such rich-get-richer and their converse (poor-get-poorer) effects are becoming of increasing concern to educational practitioners (Chall, 1989; Adams, 1990) and are playing an increasingly prominent role in theories of individual differences (Nagy and Anderson, 1984; Stanovich, 1986, 1988, 1993; Anderson *et al.*, 1988; Hayes, 1988; Hayes and Ahrens, 1988; Juel, 1988; Siegel, 1989; van den Bos, 1989; Chall *et al.*, 1990). Several authors have emphasized that both in and out of school, readers of higher ability are progressively exposed to more print than their less skilled peers, thus leading to an increasing divergence in the performance of skilled and less skilled readers (Biemiller, 1977–8; Allington, 1980, 1983, 1984; Nagy and Anderson, 1984; Nagy, Herman and Anderson, 1985; Stanovich, 1986; Anderson *et al.*, 1988; Juel, 1988).

Our longitudinal analyses have provided us with a window on the past literacy experiences of our first-grade sample and provided some clues as to the cause of their subsequent divergences in reading ability and vocabulary. It is likely that our check-list measures of print exposure tap into individual differences in exposure to print outside the classroom (Allen *et al.*, 1992; Stanovich, 1993; West *et al.*, 1993) and our results indicate that such print exposure differences are uniquely predictive of certain cognitive outcomes. These results, along with earlier work (Anderson *et al.*, 1988; Hayes, 1988; Cunningham and Stanovich, 1990, 1991;

Guthrie, Schafer and Hutchinson, 1991; West and Stanovich, 1991; Stanovich and Cunningham, 1992, 1993), strengthen the case for expanding our models of reading development and general theories of cognitive development to include a more prominent role for exposure to print. We propose a more complex causal model than is common in individual differences research – one that views individual differences in basic cognitive processes and knowledge bases as at least in part resulting from the experience of reading itself (see Stanovich, 1986, 1993; Stanovich and Cunningham, 1993). Given that cognitive and developmental psychologists continue to emphasize the importance of domain knowledge in determining processing efficiency (Keil, 1984; Chi, Hutchinson and Robin, 1989; Ceci, 1990), it may pay to focus further research attention on reading as a mechanism that builds knowledge bases and that exercises verbal talents.

Our studies, of course, do not say anything about how the differential exposure to print comes about. We have only demonstrated that variance in general ability is not completely coextensive with variance in amount of reading. Certainly, environmental differences such as cultural opportunities, parental modelling and quality of schooling may be a contributing factor. Active as well as passive organism/environment correlations (see Scarr and McCartney, 1983) may be an important factor in determining individual differences in print exposure. Children who exhibit high interest often have greater access to print, are read to more often and watch less television (e.g. Morrow, 1983). Additionally, personality dispositions towards literacy activities may also play a role, and the environmental and genetic determinants (see Plomin *et al.*, 1990) of such behavioural propensities are completely unknown.

References

Adams, M.J. (1990), *Beginning to Read: Thinking and learning about print*, Cambridge, MA: MIT Press.

Allen, L., Cipielewski, J. and Stanovich, K.E. (1992), 'Multiple indicators of children's reading habits and attitudes: construct validity and cognitive correlates', *Journal of Educational Psychology*, *84*, 489–503.

Allington, R.L. (1980), 'Poor readers don't get to read much in reading groups', *Language Arts*, *57*, 872–6.

Allington, R.L. (1983), 'The reading instruction provided readers of differing reading abilities', *The Elementary School Journal*, *83*, 548–59.

Allington, R.L. (1984), 'Content coverage and contextual reading in reading groups', *Journal of Reading Behavior*, *16*, 85–6.

Alwin, D.F. and Thornton, A. (1984), 'Family origins and the schooling process: early versus late influence of parental characteristics', *American Sociological Review*, *49*, 784–802.

Anderson, R.C., Wilson, P.T. and Fielding, L.G. (1988), 'Growth in reading and how children spend their time outside of school', *Reading Research Quarterly*, *23*, 285–303.

Biemiller, A. (1977–8), 'Relationships between oral reading rates for letters, words, and simple text in the development of reading achievement', *Reading Research Quarterly*, *13*, 223–53.

Bryant, P. and Impey, L. (1986), 'The similarities between normal readers and developmental and acquired dyslexics', *Cognition*, *24*, 121–7.

Cahan, S. and Cohen, N. (1989), 'Age versus schooling effects on intelligence development', *Child Development*, *60*, 1239–49.

Ceci, S.J. (1990), *On Intelligence . . . More or Less: A bio-ecological treatise on intellectual development*, Englewood Cliffs, NJ: Prentice-Hall.

Ceci, S.J. (1991), 'How much does schooling influence general intelligence and its cognitive components? A reassessment of the evidence', *Developmental Psychology*, *27*, 703–22.

Chall, J.S. (1989), 'Learning to read: the great debate 20 years later', *Phi Delta, Kappa*, *70*, 521–38.

Chall, J.S., Jacobs, V.A. and Baldwin, L.E. (1990), *The Reading Crisis: Why poor children fall behind*, Cambridge, MA: Harvard University Press.

Chi, M.T.H., Hutchinson, J.E. and Robin, A.F. (1989), 'How inferences about novel domain-related concepts can be constrained by structured knowledge', *Merrill-Palmer Quarterly*, *35*, 27–62.

Chomsky, C. (1972), 'Stages in language development and reading exposure', *Harvard Educational Review*, *42*, 1–33.

Cipielewski, J. and Stanovich, K.E. (1992), 'Predicting growth in reading ability from children's exposure to print', *Journal of Experimental Child Psychology*, *54*, 74–89.

Cunningham, A.E. and Stanovich, K.E. (1990), 'Assessing print exposure and orthographic processing skill in children: a quick measure of reading experience', *Journal of Educational Psychology*, *82*, 733–40.

Cunningham, A.E. and Stanovich, K.E. (1991), 'Tracking the unique effects of print exposure in children: associations with vocabulary, general knowledge, and spelling', *Journal of Educational Psychology*, *83*, 264–74.

Ennis, P.H. (1965), *Adult Book Reading in the United States*, National Opinion Research Center Report No. 105, Chicago: University of Chicago.

Estes, T.H. (1971), 'A scale to measure attitudes toward reading', *Journal of Reading*, *15*, 135–8.

Fielding, L., Wilson, P. and Anderson, P. (1986), 'A new focus on free reading: the role of trade books in reading instruction', in T. Raphael and R. Reynolds (eds), *Contexts of Literacy*, New York: Longman.

Fielding, L.S., Jenkins, J.R. and Pany, D. (1979), 'Effects on poor readers' comprehension of training in rapid decoding', *Reading Research Quarterly*, *15*, 30–48.

Freebody, P. and Bryne, B. (1988), 'Word-reading strategies in elementary school children: relations to comprehension, reading time, and phonemic awareness', *Reading Research Quarterly*, *23*, 441–53.

Furnham, A. (1986), 'Response bias, social desirability and dissimulation', *Personality & Individual Differences*, *7*, 385–400.

Gathercole, S.E. and Baddeley, A.D. (1989), 'Evaluation of the role of phonological STM in the development of vocabulary in children: a longitudinal study', *Journal of Memory and Language*, *28*, 200–13.

Greaney, V. (1980), 'Factors related to amount and time of leisure time reading', *Reading Research Quarterly*, *15*, 337–57.

Greaney, V. and Hegarty, M. (1987), 'Correlates of leisure-time reading', *Journal of Research in Reading*, *10*, 3–20.

Guthrie, J.T. (1981), 'Reading in New Zealand: achievement and volume', *Reading Research Quarterly*, *17*, 6–27.

Guthrie, J.T. and Greaney, V. (1991), 'Literacy acts'. In R. Barr, M.L. Kamil, P. Mosenthal and P.D. Pearson (eds.) *Handbook of Reading Research*, Vol. 2, New York: Longman, pp. 68–96.

Guthrie, J.T., Schafer, W.D. and Hutchinson, S.R. (1991), 'Relations of document literacy and prose literacy to occupational and societal characteristics of young black and white adults', *Reading Research Quarterly*, *26*, 30–48.

Guthrie, J.T. and Seifert, M. (1983), 'Profiles of reading activity in a community', *Journal of Reading*, *26*, 498–508.

Hayes, D.P. (1988), 'Speaking and writing: distinct patterns of word choice', *Journal of Memory and Language*, *27*, 572–85.

Hayes, D.P. and Ahrens, M. (1988), 'Vocabulary simplification for children: a special case of "motherese"?', *Journal of Child Language*, *15*, 395–410.

Hess, R.D., Holloway, R.D., Dickson, W.P. and Price, G.P. (1984), 'Maternal variables as predictors of children's school readiness and later achievement in vocabulary and mathematics in sixth grade', *Child Development*, *55*, 1902–12.

Hewison, J. and Tizard, J. (1980), 'Parental involvement and reading attainment', *British Journal of Educational Psychology*, *50*, 209–15.

Iverson, B.K. and Walberg, H.J. (1984), 'Home environment and learning: a quantitative synthesis', *Journal of Experimental Education*, 144–51.

Juel, C. (1988), 'Learning to read and write: a longitudinal study of 54 children from first through fourth grades', *Journal of Educational Psychology*, *80*, 437–47.

Keil, F.C. (1984), 'Mechanisms of cognitive development and the structure of knowledge'. In R. Sternberg (ed.) *Mechanisms of Cognitive Development*, New York: W.H. Freeman, pp. 81–99.

Lewis, R. and Teale, W.H. (1980), 'Another look at secondary school students' attitudes toward reading', *Journal of Reading Behavior*, *12*, 187–201.

Maclean, M., Bryant, P. and Bradley, L. (1987), 'Rhymes, nursery rhymes and reading in early childhood', *Merrill-Palmer Quarterly*, *33* (3), 255–81.

Mann, V.A., Tobin, P. and Wilson, R. (1987), 'Measuring phonological awareness through the invented spelling of kindergarten children', *Merrill-Palmer Quarterly*, *33* (3), 365–91.

Manning, M. (1988), *The Standard Periodical Directory*, 11th edition, New York: Oxbridge Communications, Inc.

Morrison, F.J. (1987), *The '5–7' Shift Revisited: A natural experiment*, Paper presented at the meeting of the Psychonomic Society, Seattle, WA.

Morrow, L.M. (1983), 'Home and school correlates of early interest', *Journal of Educational Research*, *76*, 221–31.

Nagy, W.E. and Anderson, R.C. (1984), 'How many words are there in printed school English?' *Reading Research Quarterly*, *19*, 304–30.

Nagy, W.E., Herman, P.A. and Anderson, R.C. (1985), 'Learning words from context', *Reading Research Quarterly*, *20*, 233–53.

Paulhus, D.L. (1984), 'Two-component models of socially desirable responding', *Journal of Personality and Social Psychology*, *46*, 598–609.

Plomin, R., Corley, R., DeFries, J.C. and Fulker, D.W. (1990), 'Individual differences in television viewing in early childhood: nature as well as nurture', *Psychological Science*, *1*, 371–7.

Ravitch, D. and Finn, C.E. (1987), *What Do Our 17-year-olds Know?* New York: Harper & Row.

Scarr, S. and McCartney, K. (1983), 'How people make their own environments', *Child Development*, *54*, 424–35.

Share, D.L., McGee, R. and Silva, P. (1989), 'IQ and reading progress: a test of the capacity notion of IQ', *Journal of the American Academy of Child and Adolescent Psychiatry*, *28*, 97–100.

Share, D.L. and Silva, P.A. (1987), 'Language deficits and specific reading retardation: cause or effect?' *British Journal of Disorders of Communication*, *22*, 219–26.

Sharon, A.T. (1973–4), 'What do adults read?' *Reading Research Quarterly*, *9*, 148–69.

Siegel, L.S. (1989), 'IQ is irrelevant to the definition of learning disabilities', *Journal of Learning Disabilities*, *22*, 469–78.

Snodgrass, J.G. and Corwin, J. (1988), 'Pragmatics of measuring recognition memory: applications to dementia and amnesia', *Journal of Experimental Psychology: General*, *117*, 34–50.

Stanovich, K.E. (1986), 'Matthew effects in reading: some consequences of individual differences in the acquisition of literacy', *Reading Research Quarterly*, *21*, 360–407.

Stanovich, K.E. (1988), 'The right and wrong places to look for the cognitive locus of reading disability', *Annals of Dyslexia*, *38*, 154–77.

Stanovich, K.E. (1992), 'Are we overselling literacy?' In C. Temple and P. Collins (eds.) *Stories and Readers: New perspectives on literature in the elementary classroom*, Norwood, MA: Christopher-Gordon, pp. 209–31.

Stanovich, K.E. (1993), 'Does reading make you smarter? Literacy and the development of verbal intelligence'. In H. Reese (ed.) *Advances in Child Development and Behavior*, Vol. 24, Orlando, FL: Academic Press, pp. 133–80.

Stanovich, K.E. and Cunningham, A.E. (1992), 'Studying the consequences of literacy within a literate society: the cognitive correlates of print exposure', *Memory & Cognition*, *20*, 51–68.

Stanovich, K.E. and Cunningham, A.E. (1993), 'Where does knowledge come from? Specific associations between print exposure and information acquisition', *Journal of Educational Psychology*, *85*, 211–29.

Stanovich, K.E. and West, R.F. (1989), 'Exposure to print and orthographic processing', *Reading Research Quarterly*, *24*, 402–33.

Sternberg, R.J. (1985), *Beyond IQ: A triarchic theory of human intelligence*, Cambridge: Cambridge University Press.

Taylor, B.M., Frye, B.J. and Maruyama, G.M. (1990), 'Time spent reading and reading growth', *American Educational Research Journal*, *27*, 351–62.

Treiman, R. (1984), 'Individual differences among children in reading and spelling styles', *Journal of Experimental Child Psychology*, *37*, 463–77.

van den Bos, K.P. (1989), 'Relationship between cognitive development, decoding skill, and reading comprehension in learning disabled Dutch children'. In P. Aaron and M. Joshi (eds.) *Reading and Writing Disorders in Different Orthographic Systems*, Dordrecht: Kluwer Academic, pp. 75–86.

Walberg, H.J. and Tsai, S. (1983), 'Matthew effects in education', *American Educational Research Journal*, *20*, 359–73.

West, R.F. and Stanovich, K.E. (1991), 'The incidental acquisition of information from reading', *Psychological Science*, *2*, 325–30.

West, R.F., Stanovich, K.E. and Mitchell, H.R. (1993), 'Reading in the real world and its correlates', *Reading Research Quarterly*, *28*, 34–50.

6

Basic mechanisms in learning to read

Egbert M.H. Assink and Göran Kattenberg
Department of Psychology, Utrecht University

Introduction

This chapter deals with the mechanisms of visual word identification. The focus will be on reading difficulties experienced by developing readers. Their problems will be contrasted with normally reading peers and skilled performance observed in adults. It is impossible to present a complete overview of the research literature here. Rather, we shall focus on just one aspect in this chapter. Our purpose is to present a set of our own experiments comparing normal and poor readers in their use of word identification mechanisms. This comparison will be made at various processing levels involved in word identification. We do *not* deal with the development of word identification in early reading.

Our focus will be on word identification skills emerging after the child has mastered the basics of reading. This period is completed when the child has learned the sound–spelling correspondences and has progressed from decoding words on an individual letter basis to fluent reading by automatic word recognition. This is normally achieved at the age of about 8 or 9 years.

When the child identifies a string of letters as a word, he or she performs an amazingly complex skill. Word identification is concerned not only with discriminating single letters, it also involves extracting information beyond the single letter level. In this chapter we shall discuss mechanisms involved at various processing levels in a bottom-up fashion.

We start our excursion with the mechanisms working at the *letter feature level*, followed by a discussion of processes affecting the *individual letter level*. Then, the *letter cluster level*, the intermediate stage between the single letter and the *whole word level*, will be dealt with. Next we present research focusing on identification mechanisms working at the sentence context level. Finally, a general discussion evaluating the presented results concludes the chapter.

Research strategies

There is a vast amount of literature on which method is most appropriate for conducting research into reading problems. Roughly speaking, three types of approach have been used. The earliest investigations in reading disabilities compared dyslexics and normal readers *matched on chronological age*. A problem with this kind of comparison is that established differences are not readily interpretable.

In order to overcome the criticisms on the age match comparison dyslexics and normal readers were matched on their *reading age level*. This type of design (normally referred to as RL-design) has become popular in the last decade, in particular after the publications of Bryant and his associates (Bradley and Bryant, 1983). This work also provoked heated debates on the strengths and weaknesses of RL-designs (Backman *et al.*, 1984; Goswami and Bryant, 1989; Jackson and Butterfield, 1989; Vellutino and Scanlon, 1989). In their review article on phonological deficits and reading disability, Rack *et al.*, (1992) note that RL-designs have certain characteristic problems. One of these is that the poor readers or dyslexics participating in an RL-type experiment are, by definition, much older, and they may therefore have some additional skills at their disposal which are absent in matched younger normals. Age-related differences in familiarity with printed texts is a good example of this.

The third research method for investigating differences in reading ability has been to look at peculiarities of poor readers' and dyslexics' reading skills in the *individual case study approach*. This kind of approach is useful for generating hypotheses about the reading processes involved. Case studies and group studies are complementary methods for studying similar issues.

Although RL-design studies certainly do not provide solutions to all research design problems, they are a promising instrument for penetrating deeper into the complexities of reading disability. Rack *et al.* (1992) selected RL-design studies for their literature review. One of the reasons for doing this was that RL-designs provide a good opportunity for addressing a number of theoretically interesting issues.

In the discussion of the roots of reading problems two hypotheses are highlighted. Both hypotheses are specifications of the more general issue of the role of processes other than phonological ones in reading ability. A substantial part of the research on reading disability and the development of word identification skills has been concerned with the question of how the interrelation between the use of phonemic and graphemic information changes as a function of developing reading skill. Two accounts have been posited.

On the one hand, the *phonological deficit hypothesis* suggests that chronic reading failure results from inefficient phonological processes which impede both acquiring phoneme awareness and processing spoken and written language (Fowler, 1991; Rack *et al.*, 1992). Alternatively, the *orthographic hypothesis* (Ehri, 1989) suggests that phoneme awareness tasks, and potentially other phonological measures associated with reading failure, depend not on underlying phonological representations, but on orthographic representations derived as a function of reading experience.

We shall present a series of RL-design experiments comparing normal and poor readers' word identification mechanisms. We focused on subjects who were well beyond the initial stages of reading; that is, children from about 9 years onwards. The experiments were designed to study word identification mechanisms at various levels of processing.

The presentation sequence is bottom-up. The processing levels addressed in this chapter are respectively:

1. the sub-letter or letter feature level;
2. the letter level;
3. the letter cluster level;
4. the single word level;
5. the sentence context level.

We start with a study on the mechanisms working at the letter feature level. The central hypothesis is that reading problems may arise at several levels of processing. A more detailed account of the problems associated with these levels will provide a better understanding of the roots and causes of reading disability.

Identification mechanisms operating at the sub-letter or letter feature level

A first step in learning to read is letter recognition, and in learning to recognize letters, children must be able to discriminate one letter from another. Older children scan distinctive letter feature information more effectively than beginning readers (Nodine and Simmons, 1974). Skilled readers can only accomplish their task by attending to essential letter information and by ignoring coincidental cues, such as letter case, typeface, and so on.

A generally accepted implication is that normal, skilled reading proceeds largely through case- and font-independent *abstract letter identities* (Besner *et al.*, 1984). It also leads to the conclusion that general word shape is not an important cue for word identification in normal readers (Paap *et al.*, 1984). Whether this is also the case with poor readers is still under discussion. In order to clarify this point further we decided to conduct an experiment focusing on letter processing by normal and poor readers. We wanted to investigate whether normal and poor readers,[1] matched on reading level, show differences in their capacity to process letters in words and pseudowords automatically.

The basic premiss was straightforward: we simply assigned the letters of the alphabet to two categories – letters with congruent shapes in uppercase and lowercase (e.g. O/o, S/s) and letters with incongruent upper/lowercase shapes (E/e, R/r). The next step was constructing two lists of words, the first containing exclusively congruent letters, the other containing only incongruent letters.

We designed an experiment in which subjects were presented with pairs of words. The subjects were asked in a same–different task to decide whether a pair contained identical letter-strings or not. We were interested to see if extra time was needed to evaluate case-incongruent pairs, e.g. *BEAR – bear*, as compared to congruent pairs, e.g. *LOOK – look*. A second point of interest was what the effect of eliminating word meaning would be. This was done by presenting the same task with pseudowords, non-existent analogous pairs (e.g. compare *FAB – fab* with *pos – POS*).

Experiment 1

Method

Subjects   Two groups of normal and poor readers ($n = 21$ in each group) matched on reading level participated in the experiment. The poor readers attended a school for children with learning difficulties in order to improve their reading skills. Poor readers were defined as subjects scoring at least 2 years below their age norm, as measured by a standard Dutch reading ability test[2] (Brus and Voeten, 1972). Poor readers (mean age 12.7 years) were matched with a group of normal readers (mean age 9.4 years).

Materials   The task consisted of comparing the identity of two strings of letters presented on a computer screen. The elements of an item were either real words or pseudowords. The other manipulated factor was the shape, or more precisely the uppercase/lowercase congruence, of the individual letters of the presented strings. Letters were divided into uppercase/lowercase congruent (e.g. the letters *o/O, s/S, p/P*) or incongruent (e.g. *a/A, b/B, r/R*). Examples are: *koop – KOOP* and *BEER – beer* (real words, congruent and incongruent case) versus *JOUK – jouk* and *frad – FRAD* (pseudowords, congruent and incongruent case). In addition to identical strings ('yes' items) there was an equal number of controls ('no items'). These items contained a letter-string in which the first and the last letter were transposed (e.g. *luik – KUIL* (congruent case, control item) and *BRET – treb* (incongruent case). Sample items are listed in Table 6.1.

Procedure and design   Presentation of items was computer-controlled. An IBM personal computer with a monochrome cathode-ray tube (CRT) display was used. Subjects were instructed by the experimenter in person. After initial instruction the subjects could ask for additional explanation, and then they were given a few practice items. A 2 (groups) × 2 (string types) x 2 (case congruence) mixed factorial repeated measures design was used.

Table 6.1 Sample pairs used in Experiment 1

Experimental ('Same') – items

Words/Congruent shape	*Pseudowords/Congruent shape*
KUS – kus	suk – SUK
vis – VIS	ZIP – zip
POL – pol	pos – POS

Words/Incongruent shape	*Pseudowords/Incongruent shape*
heg – HEG	FAB – fab
DAG – dag	ret – RET
rat – RAT	TAG – tag

Control ('Different') – items

Words/Congruent shape	*Pseudowords/Congruent shape*
SUK – kus	SUK – kus
siv – VIS	zip – PIZ
LOP – pol	POS – sop

Words/Incongruent shape	*Pseudowords/Incongruent shape*
GEH – heg	baf – FAB
gad – DAG	TER – ret
TAR – rat	gat – TAG

Table 6.2 Mean decision latencies* on words and pseudowords, Experiment 1

	Intraword location	
	Congruent	Incongruent
Words		
Poor readers	2,049 (630)	2,160 (717)
Normal readers	1,730 (426)	1,676 (356)
Pseudowords		
Poor readers	2,396 (747)	3,285 (658)
Normal readers	2,140 (626)	2,319 (496)

Note:
* Decision times in milliseconds. Standard deviations in parentheses; performance data on the experimental items ('yes' items).

Results

The results are represented in Table 6.2 and Figure 6.1. MANOVAs with both subject and item means as units were used to process the data. The analyses showed three main effects: one for group ($F1(1,40) = 7.01$, $p < 0.012$) for subjects and ($F2(1,32) = 94.52$, $p < 0.001$) for the items, one for congruence ($F1(1,40) = 18.60$, $p < 0.001$) for subjects and ($F2(1,32) = 4.08$, $p < 0.05$) for

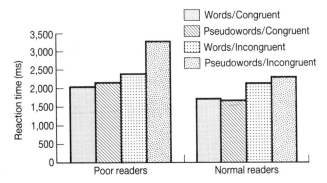

Figure 6.1 Letter congruence in words and pseudowords.

items, and one for string type ($F1(1,40) = 106.01$, $p < 0.001$) for subjects and ($F2(1,32) = 20.53$, $p < 0.001$) for items. There were first-order interactions of group × congruence ($F1(1,40) = 11.27$, $p < 0.002$) for subjects and ($F2(1,32) = 17.71$, $p < 0.001$) for items. Finally, there was a second-order interaction of group × congruence × string type ($F1(1,40) = 7.38$, $p < 0.01$) for subjects and ($F2(1,32) = 6.85$, $p < 0.013$) for items.

Figure 6.1 shows that the poor readers needed more decision time in this experiment. As expected, evaluating pseudoword letter-strings took more decision time than real words. The overall conclusion from the data is that uppercase/lowercase letter congruence appears to influence word recognition speed. Poor readers proved to be especially vulnerable to incongruent uppercase/lowercase shifts, in particular in meaningless, pronounceable, word-like letter-strings.

An additional analysis of the results on the control items ('no' decisions) showed a main effect of group ($F1(1,40) = 6.31$, $p < 0.016$; $F2(1,32) = 83.6$, $p < 0.001$), and a first-order congruence × string type interaction ($F1(1,40) = 9.96$, $p < 0.003$; $F2(1,32) = 3.13$, $p < 0.086$). Poor readers had more difficulty in identifying differences between the two elements of an item. This problem manifested itself in particular when pseudowords were involved. This pattern of results parallels the results on the experimental items ('yes' decisions).

Discussion
The data suggest that poor readers who are well beyond the initial phase of learning to read continue to have problems with basic mechanisms in perceiving letter information during word identification. It demonstrates that they show insufficient competence in the automatized processing of letter features during speeded word matching.

There is empirical evidence that for normal readers the case of letters appears to be largely irrelevant to the perception of words (Smith *et al.*, 1969). Our data suggest that this does not seem to apply to poor readers, even if they have several years' reading experience. In accordance with other sources of evidence (Coltheart and Freeman, 1974), letters appear to be relevant to the perception of words for poor and developing readers.

The emerging picture is that there may be nothing intrinsically wrong with poor readers' letter identification abilities, but adding orthographic complexity strains their processing system. The results collected in Experiment 1 suggest that one obstacle facing poor readers is the automatized processing of abstract letter identities, causing an overload of their cognitive system in the initial stage of the identification process.

Investigating identification mechanisms operating at the single letter level

A central question in reading research is which mechanisms of the reading process enable or facilitate automatized word identification. Although word recognition in skilled reading is assumed to be a holistic process, there is a growing body of evidence suggesting that automatized processing of sub-lexical orthographic units is critically involved in skilled reading (Treiman and Zukowski, 1988). In a study by Rayner (1988), the relative importance of various cues in word recognition, such as graphemic cues, orthographic[3] cues and grapheme–phoneme correspondence rules, is emphasized. It should be realized that our alphabetic writing system contains a set of system-inherent features. Subjects at various developmental stages of reading skill probably differ in their capabilities to exploit the variety of (ortho)graphic and linguistic information coded in text.

Skilled word identification is accelerated by letter cluster units which, as a result of their frequency in text, operate as autonomous orthographic cues (Healy and Drewnowski, 1983; Seidenberg, 1987). In order to get a clearer view on the functional role of these types of cues in a sentence reading task, we examined the role of *intraword position* and *positional bigram frequency* (PBF) (Young-Loveridge, 1985). Experiments 2 and 3 were designed to test our hypothesis that normal and poor readers differ in their use of graphemic and phonemic cues in printed words. In a reading level design two groups of normal and poor readers, matched for reading performance on a standardized reading test, were presented with a computer-controlled reading task.

Experiment 2

In Experiment 2 the subjects were presented with words containing an *e/c* letter substitution, e.g. the word 'lett*c*r'. Subjects were asked to identify these substitutions. Positional bigram frequency[4] was manipulated in combination with e/c-type substitutions. In congruence with previous research (van Rijnsoever,

Table 6.3 Sample items, Experiment 2

1. *e/c substitutions* (experimental items)	
First part/high PBF	*First part/low PBF*
gcbak	kctting
gcmist	bcnde
Second part/high PBF	*Second part/low PBF*
vadcr	adrcs
middcn	agcnt
2. *n/m substitutions* (distracter items)	
First part	*Second part*
steempuist	zwemmem
staamplaats	wordem
3. *d/t substitutions* (distracter items)	
First part	*Second part*
spoetgeval	schoonheit
grontverf	achtergront

1988) we expected to find that detecting a target letter in high-frequency letter clusters is more difficult than in low-frequency letter clusters. High-frequency letter clusters are processed automatically, and consequently the constituent individual letters are more difficult to access. Our prediction was that this, in particular, would occur in the second part of the word.

Method

Subjects   Participating subjects were two matched groups of primary school children. Twenty third-graders (mean age 9.4 years), classified by their class teacher as good readers, were matched with the twenty poor readers from the fifth grade (mean age 11.6 years) on a standard Dutch reading ability test (Brus and Voeten, 1972). Both groups had been taught to read with comparable instruction materials; and there were no differences in teaching methods employed.

Materials   Three types of letter substitution were used. Experimental sentences contained e/c-type substitutions, e.g. *bcgin* for *begin*. There were two types of control sentences: (1) completely correct sentences, and (2) sentences containing distracter letter substitutions, such as *d/t* substitutions in words where a final *-d* sounded as [t] in Dutch, as in *paart* for *paard* [pa:rt] ('horse'), and *n/m*-type substitutions, like *buitem* for *buiten* ('outside'). Sample items are listed in Table 6.3.

Design   The *e/c* substitutions were factorially manipulated with intraword position (initial or final) and with PBF.[5] Target words were presented in sentence frames, focusing the attention on semantic evaluation. Experimental sentences

Table 6.4 Mean correction detection scores* on e/c-type
substitutions, Experiment 2

	Intraword location	
	First part	Second part
High PBF		
Poor readers	1.60 (1.79)	1.35 (1.50)
Normal readers	2.30 (1.90)	1.90 (1.97)
Low PBF		
Poor readers	2.80 (2.31)	1.90 (1.83)
Normal readers	2.85 (2.30)	2.40 (2.16)

Note:
* Maximum score is 6; standard deviations in parentheses.

contained an *e/c* misspelled target word. Sentences with control items (see
'Materials' above) were added to control for preference effects. The number of
sentences containing a letter substitution equalled the number of control
sentences.

Procedure and apparatus   Presentation of the reading materials was computer-
controlled. An IBM personal computer was used with a sixteen-colour display
monitor. Subjects were instructed to respond orally. The experimental session
started with a letter encoding memory test introduced to control for encoding
random letter-strings. Ten 5-letter-strings were displayed on the screen for the
duration of 1 second. Subjects were asked to reproduce these strings. Finally, the
reading task was presented. All sentences were projected on the screen for a fixed
period of 4 seconds. Subsequently two probe words were presented. The
subject's task was to select the contextually best fitting probe. Before this
response could be given, a secondary task had to be completed. This secondary
task was checking for the presence of incorrectly spelled words. Subjects
responded orally, with the experimenter entering responses with keyboard
strokes. Presentation of the subsequent sentence was subject-controlled. Presentation order of the sentences was random. The session concluded with a spelling
test with same types of words. These were included to control for memory and
spelling ability.

Results
Our main interest was to find differences in the number of misspellings detected
by the two groups. Detections following an incorrect semantic decision were very
sporadic in both groups and were excluded from the data. Analyses of covariance
for repeated measures with letter encoding memory and spelling ability as
covariates were used in the data analysis. The results obtained in the *e/c*-type
letter substitution task are presented in Table 6.4.

A MANOVA on these data with reader group, position and PBF as factors and with letter encoding memory and spelling ability as covariates showed two main effects, one for position ($F(1,37)=9.41$, $p < 0.004$) and one for PBF ($F(1,37) =$ 15.07, $p < 0.000$). The e/c-type substitutions that were located in the initial part of the word were detected more often than in the final position. Moreover, detection of e/c substitutions proved to be more difficult when the letter was situated in a high PBF cluster. Notably, there was no main effect for group, nor were there any interactions.

Significant and theoretically interesting was the finding that PBF and position did not interact. Both normal and poor readers found it harder to detect e/c substitutions in high PBF clusters, irrespective of word position. There was no effect of the covariates (letter encoding memory and spelling ability).

Discussion

The results allow us to draw two general conclusions. First, e/c-type substitutions produced only main effects for position and letter cluster frequency (PBF). This type of substitution, which represents shape-preserving, orthographically illegitimate word reading options, did not differentiate between the two groups of subjects. The two groups were equally sensitive to both factors, which suggests that this type of letter substitution does not differentially influence word identification.

Second, the expected interaction between letter cluster frequency and intra-word position (PBF) was not found. The present data suggest that frequency effects on a subword level, as defined by PBF, operate quite independently of intraword location. That is to say, this conclusion holds for the e/c-type substitutions employed in our experiment.

The foregoing should not be interpreted to suggest that the final letter clusters of a word are always redundant and therefore more difficult to identify. On the contrary, there is empirical evidence to show that particularly the first characters of a word, but also the final characters, are better perceived than the letters located in the middle (Mason, 1975; Scheerer-Neumann, 1981). The initial and final letters often provide more information about the identity of a word than the middle letters, possibly because of the orthographic, phonological and morpho-logical constraints (Barron, 1981).

Experiment 3

To get a more complete picture of the mechanisms involved in speeded word identification we decided to study the effect of reducing semantic context. For this reason we designed an experiment focusing on the identification of isolated words.

Method

Subjects   Subjects were two groups of normal and poor readers matched on reading age. Normal readers were third-graders (mean age 8.6 yrs) classified by

Table 6.5 Sample items used in Experiment 3

Misspelled words	Correct words	Nonwords	Misspelled words	Correct words	Nonwords
e/c substitutions, High PBF, 1st syllable			*e/c* substitutions, Low PBF, 1st syllable		
g*c*vecht	g*e*luid	gucveht	*d*ftal	k*e*nnis	cftzal
b*c*hang	g*e*zicht	bcpnag	l*c*kker	c*e*ntrum	lkckir
e/c substitutions, High PBF, 2nd syllable			*e/c* substitutions, Low PBF, 2nd syllable		
knikk*c*r	grot*e*r	knifnkcr	best*c*k	adr*e*s	bsotck
vark*c*n	donk*e*r	vagrcn	tromp*c*t	mod*e*rn	tormnct
d/t substitutions, 1st syllable (distracters)			*d/t* substitutions, 2nd syllable (distracters)		
ron*t*reis	wan*d*klok	ronetkris	werel*t*	dakran*d*	wearlt
han*t*bal	noor*d*pool	hnatoal	avon*t*	nieman*d*	vaomt
n/m substitutions, 1st syllable (distracters)			*n/m* substitutions, 2nd syllable (distracters)		
ko*m*den	sto*n*den	omsden	fietst*e*m	blijv*e*n	fitbsem
la*m*den	ke*n*den	lkemdn	kocht*e*m	dacht*e*n	khactem

their class teacher as good readers. They were matched on a standard Dutch reading ability test (Brus and Voeten, 1972) with 18 poor readers (mean age 11.4 years) from a school for learning disabilities. Both groups had been taught reading with comparable instruction materials; there were no differences in teaching methods employed.

Materials   The same types of letter substitution as used in Experiment 2 were inserted in the set of stimuli. Only *e/c*-type substitutions, such as *bcgin* for *begin*, were considered for the data analysis. Sample items are listed in Table 6.5.

Design   In *e/c*-type substitutions PBF and intraword position (initial/final) were manipulated factorially. Target words were presented in isolation.

Procedure and apparatus   The reading materials were presented on an IBM personal computer with a sixteen-colour cathode-ray tube (CRT) display monitor. Subjects were asked to respond by pressing buttons on a panel. This panel controlled a screen synchronization program enabling registration of reaction times (RT) with a precision of 1 ms. The experimental session started with a letter discrimination test, assessing the subject's visual discrimination performance. Following this test, the main reading task was presented. Subjects were told that their task was to evaluate letter-strings appearing on the screen. They were urged to combine speed with accuracy. There were three classification options: (1) correct words, (2) misspelled words, and (3) nonsense. These options could be entered on the button panel by pressing the green, red or yellow buttons, respectively. Presentation of the next item was subject-controlled. Presentation order of the stimuli was random. The session ended with a spelling

Table 6.6 Mean detection scores* on e/c-type substitutions, Experiment 3

	Intraword location	
	First part	Second part
High PBF		
Poor readers	3.94 (2.10)	3.56 (1.92)
Normal readers	5.33 (0.69)	5.06 (1.21)
Low PBF		
Poor readers	3.06 (1.89)	3.50 (1.86)
Normal readers	4.94 (0.87)	4.33 (1.28)

Note:
* Maximum score is 6; standard deviations in parentheses.

test presenting the same types of words, included to control for differences in spelling ability.

Results

Of primary interest was whether there were systematic differences in the amount of correctly classified misspelled words. Analyses of covariance for repeated measures were used in the data analysis. The results obtained for e/c-type letter substitutions are presented in Table 6.6. A MANOVA on accuracy scores showed two main effects, one for group ($F(1,34) = 10.48, p = 0.003$) and one for PBF ($F(1,34) = 12.59, p \leqslant 0.001$). The e/c-type substitutions located within high-frequency clusters were detected better than in low-frequency clusters. Normal readers performed better than poor readers matched on reading age level. At the accuracy level, there was no position effect or interactions.

A MANOVA on reaction time scores showed a similar pattern (see Table 6.7). There were main effects for group ($F(1,34) = 5.77, p < 0.002$), for PBF ($F(1,34) = 15.57, p < 0.000$) and for position ($F(1,34) = 14.70, p < 0.001$). Both normal and poor readers needed more time to detect e/c-type substitutions in low PBF clusters, irrespective of word position. Decisions were faster when the substitution was located in the initial part of the word. There was no effect of covariates (STM for random letter-strings and spelling ability). Figure 6.2 summarizes the results from Experiments 2 and 3 on detection accuracy. Figure 6.3 presents the latency results obtained in Experiment 3.

A MANOVA of performance on the control words (trials with correctly spelled words) showed no main group effect for accuracy (per cent of correct decisions). At the latency level, however, there were significant group differences ($F(1,34) = 11.99, p < 0.001$). There was also a main effect for cluster frequency (PBF) ($F(1,34) = 4.27, p < 0.047$). These results are presented in Table 6.8. Words containing a high frequency cluster were classified faster. These trends are similar to those found on the detection of misspellings. Overall latencies for evaluating misspelled words were longer.

Table 6.7 Mean decision latencies* on e/c-type substitutions, Experiment 3

	Intraword location	
	First part	Second part
High PBF		
Poor readers	3,350 (1,224)	3,679 (1,030)
Normal readers	2,690 (659)	2,891 (800)
Low PBF		
Poor readers	3,659 (1,211)	4,172 (1,487)
Normal readers	3,076 (841)	3,180 (808)

Note:
* Reaction times in milliseconds; standard deviations in parentheses.

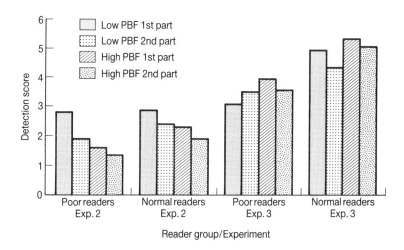

Figure 6.2 Accuracy data in Experiments 1 and 2.

Discussion

Compared with Experiment 1, Experiment 3 shows some interesting parallels and divergences. A major parallel present in both studies is that no interactions between group membership and the other manipulated factors were found. Another striking parallel is the absence of interaction between position and letter cluster frequency (PBF).

There are also some marked differences. First, between-group differences were only found in Experiment 3. These group differences were present at both the level of accuracy and decision speed. The most plausible explanation for

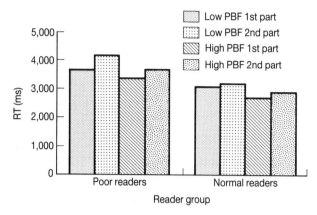

Figure 6.3 Decisions latencies, Experiment 3.

Table 6.8 Mean latency scores* on correct words (e/c type), Experiment 3

	Intraword location	
	First part	Second part
High PBF		
Poor readers	2,633 (1,129)	2,981 (1,456)
Normal readers	1,998 (504)	1,890 (444)
Low PBF		
Poor readers	3,026 (1,380)	3,749 (1,229)
Normal readers	2,161 (411)	2,518 (727)

Note:
* Reaction times in milliseconds; standard deviations in parentheses.

finding only group effects in Experiment 3 is that response registration procedure was more sensitive. The most striking difference in the outcomes of the experiments is related to the role of high-frequency letter clusters in automatized word identification. The combined results of both experiments suggest that the role of high-frequency letter clusters in word identification is dependent on task demands. If the focus of attention is orthographic processing (Experiment 3) high-frequency letter clusters facilitate the process of scanning the word for letter information. If attention is directed to sentence comprehension with orthographic processing as a subsidiary task, high-frequency clusters are units that are more difficult to penetrate.

General discussion of Experiments 2 and 3

In Experiment 3 normal readers aged 8 outperformed poor readers three years older, matched on a standardized test for reading level. This outcome can be explained if we presume that during speeded word identification readers scan parts of the visual and orthographic[6] information present in printed words. Poor readers are probably less successful in extracting full orthographic cues from printed words. They scan the word's orthographic contents more superficially.

In this respect a question of interest is whether the poor readers' identification strategy is only characterized by inaccurate word scanning or by superficial scanning as a result of poor orthographic representations at the mental level. Our results, as well as other research (Reitsma, 1983; Horn and Manis 1987) suggest that the second option is more probable. The implication is that reading instruction for poor readers should be focused more on acquiring knowledge of intraword orthographic structure.

A striking result of Experiments 2 and 3 was the opposite effect of high redundancy clusters in the reading tasks used. This finding should not be interpreted as contradictory. In Experiment 2 subjects were asked to search for misspelled words as part of the main task of evaluating sentences semantically. This task required a more global, whole-word orientation. Experiment 3 differed in this respect. Subjects were asked to classify words as misspellings, correct items or nonsense words. This task demands an analytic technique, breaking up words into their component orthographic parts. When they are faced with this task, subjects make use of intraword redundancy. Words are scanned for high-frequency letter clusters, serving as flags or slots in the identification process.

No group effects were found in Experiment 2. We have argued that this may be attributed to differences in task setting. An additional factor is the possibility that both groups differentially invested mental effort in the main task of sentence evaluation. This may have levelled out potentially existing differences at the individual word identification level.

An obvious obstacle when studying word identification mechanisms in sentence contexts is that it does not allow us to specify the amount of effort invested in the two task components of semantic integration and orthographic processing. For this reason experiments using single-word reading tasks are probably more sensitive for establishing between-group differences. We think that we are likely to uncover poor readers' inherent deficiencies if the compensating support of sentence context is removed.

Investigating identification mechanisms operating at the letter cluster level

Do normal and poor readers differ in their strategic use of intraword structure? This question has stimulated research of experimental, developmental and educational psychologists for the last decades. We were interested in exploring differences in the use of onsets and rimes as functional units during word identification. Recent research suggests that onsets and rimes are critically involved as functional units in word identification (Treiman and Chafetz, 1987; Goswami, 1988; Kirtley *et al.*, 1989; Treiman and Zukowski, 1989; Bowey, 1990; Bruck and Treiman, 1990). Experimental evidence for this has been presented by Bowey (1990). In three experiments using a partial identity priming paradigm she showed that orthographic onsets and rimes serve as functional units in visual word recognition.

Linguists view the syllable as having an ordered and hierarchical internal structure, being composed of an onset unit and a rime unit. The onset unit consists of the (optional) consonant group at the beginning of a syllable (e.g. /b/ in *book*, or /sk/ in *sky*); the rime unit consists of the vowel and the (optional) final consonant group (e.g. /uk/ in *book* and /aI/ in *sky*). Although initially introduced as purely linguistic concepts, there is now a growing body of evidence concerning syllable onset and rime as psychological units in processing words (Claxton, 1974; Cutler *et al.*, 1987).

We wanted to study these phenomena in greater depth by raising two main questions: (1) How is the functional use of onsets and rimes related to developmental aspects of reading skill? And (2) How do onsets and rimes interact with other possible sub-lexical units for word recognition, such as high-frequency letter clusters?

As to the first question, it is worth noting that although the issue of functional units in reading is theoretically important, empirical research focusing on developmental aspects of reading ability is relatively scarce. Bowey's (1990) results were obtained with fluent readers (university students). Our goal was to find out whether normal and poor readers show strategy differences in their use of onsets and rimes as reading units. There is evidence that poor readers have difficulty with the efficient use of intraword letter structure (Scheerer-Neumann, 1981), which suggests that poor readers are less sensitive to onset and rime units as a mode to accelerate their word identification routines.

As to the second question, it should be realized that in addition to onsets and rimes, other potential identification units are present in printed words. The psychological status of these units, such as high-frequency letter clusters, syllables, morphemes and basic orthographic syllabic structures (Taft, 1979), is still open to debate. Presumably, one of the conclusions will be that there is no single sub-lexical unit, but multiple sub-lexical units, which are processed in parallel. Huey (1908) argued that the unit may vary with the purpose (task at hand).

As we were interested in the psychological status of onsets and rimes as identification units, we decided to manipulate them in high- and low-frequency letter clusters. Previous research showed that effects of partial priming are more robust in low-frequency words (Seidenberg *et al.*, 1985). Since we were using subjects still improving and automatizing their reading skills, we expected to obtain effects of orthographic priming primarily in high-frequency orthographic clusters, in contrast with the results obtained in experiments with skilled readers as subjects.

Experiments 4A and 4B

Method

Subjects Two matched groups of normal and poor readers participated in two separately conducted experiments, Experiments 4A and 4B. The poor readers attended a school for children with learning difficulties to improve their reading skills. Poor readers were defined as subjects scoring at least 2 years below their chronological age norm, as measured by a standard Dutch reading ability test (Brus and Voeten, 1972). These subjects (N = 20; mean age 12.6 years) were matched with a group of normal readers (N = 20; mean age 9.4 years). There was one additional control group, consisting of proficiently reading adults (N = 20; mean age 19 years). All subjects were native Dutch speakers.

Materials Two sets of stimuli were prepared. For Experiment 4A (*onset experiment*) the set consisted of forty low-frequency (Dutch) words containing a consonant or consonant group onset. Half of these words were randomly selected for priming on the complete onset. In the other half the prime, always consisting of two letters, did not coincide with the onset. Thus, these non-coinciding items were words with either a one- or a three-letter onset. The stimuli were additionally controlled for letter cluster frequency. Half the onsets had a high positional bigram frequency (HPBF), the other half of the onsets were part of a low positional bigram frequency (LPBF) letter cluster.

For Experiment 4B (*rime experiment*) the set consisted of forty low-frequency words containing a vowel plus consonant group rime. Half these words were randomly assigned for priming on the complete rime, the other half was used for partial rime priming. The stimuli were controlled for letter cluster frequency. Half the rimes were part of a high positional bigram frequency (HPBF), the remaining half of the rimes comprised a low positional bigram frequency (LPBF) letter cluster.

Procedure and design All subjects were tested individually in a computer-controlled task setting. The stimuli were presented in lowercase on a mono-chrome high-resolution IBM-type personal computer screen. Subjects were asked to read aloud the projected words. Primes were always followed by a visual mask. Non-primed items were preceded by a row of asterisks. Registration of the subject's responses was computer-controlled. Accuracy and response latency (in ms) were the dependent variables of interest. Primes were shown for a period of 120 ms, followed by the target. Target words disappeared after activation of the voice key by the subject, or after 5 seconds had elapsed. An experimental session

Egbert M.H. Assink and Göran Kattenberg

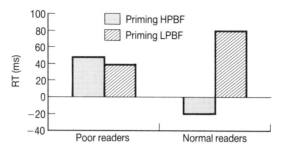

Figure 6.4 Group × prime × PBF interaction: rime data.

was preceded by six test trials. The materials were prepared and presented using the Micro Experimental Laboratory (MEL) program. Experiments 4A and 4B both used a 2 (group) × 2 (prime) × 2 (PBF) × 2 (cluster priming congruence) factorial design.

Results
The data analysis focused primarily on the comparison of the two matched groups. As expected, the adult controls were superior in both experiments. Their response patterns most resembled those of the normal readers.

Onset experiment Onset data were analyzed with MANOVAs. Only correct responses were included in the analysis. Altogether 4.8 per cent trials were discarded as invalid, due to failure to trigger the voice key. Three-way analyses of variance were computed with both subject and item means as units. Main effects in the subjects analysis were obtained for prime ($F(1,34) = 14.78, p < 0.001$) and for PBF ($F(1,34) = 5.45, p < 0.026$). There was no main effect for group and there were also no interaction effects. The items analysis produced essentially the same results. There was an overall facilitation of priming. Generally, high PBF targets were processed faster.

Rime experiment A MANOVA on the rime data showed main effects for prime ($F(1,36) = 6.18, p < 0.018$), congruence ($F(1,36) = 10.78, p < 0.002$) and a marginally significant effect for group ($F(1,36) = 3.64, p < 0.064$). There were first-order interactions for PBF by prime ($F(1,34) = 4.28, p < 0.046$), and for prime by congruence ($F(1,36) = 4.77, p < 0.036$). Significantly, there was also a second-order group by prime by PBF interaction ($F(1,36) = 6.02, p < 0.019$). This interaction is presented in Figure 6.4.

Normal readers showed significantly more priming facilitation in low-frequency rime units. The items analysis produced essentially the same results.

Discussion Comparison of the onset and rime experiments enables us to draw some conclusions. First, the onset experiment showed that, in addition to the expected facilitating effects of priming and letter cluster frequency, there was also an overall performance difference between the two matched groups. There was also difference of priming on onset congruent and incongruent letter clusters. In accordance with Bowey (1990), an additional facilitating effect of onset priming could be established in the current experiment. This suggests that onsets and rimes are used functionally as identification units by readers approaching the level of fluent reading. Second, high PBF clusters facilitated identification. This suggests a general positive effect of high-frequency letter groups as chunks in word recognition. However, this process does not differ between the two reader groups. This suggests that the groups exploited the orthographic information present in the initial part of the word equally effectively.

In several respects the rime experiment shows a complementary picture. First, the main effect of congruence indicates that primed rimes were more effective. This also holds for the group of readers studied in our two experiments. Secondly, the first-order interactions are in agreement with the expectations. Priming proved to be more effective in high-frequency letter clusters, especially if the prime coincided with the rime unit of the word.

Theoretically, the most interesting finding was the differential effect of priming for both groups in low-frequency clusters. Normal readers were more sensitive for priming in low-frequency rime units. This suggests that these subjects scan letter information in the low redundant, apparently more informative, final part of the word, more effectively.

This interaction effect generates some interesting questions regarding further investigations in the development of effective identification strategies. First, our findings suggest that at the sub-lexical level, normal readers can focus their attention on low redundant, less predictable final parts of words. This finding needs to be analyzed further in experiments using multi-syllabic words. Similar differential focusing effects should be found. Second, by adding different ability groups (adding more selected groups, varying in reading skill) it should be possible to get a better and more complete picture of developing word identification skill. Third, if our results are supported in subsequent verification studies, it should be possible to design intervention studies aimed at the acceleration of poor readers' word identification skill by explicit training in the processing of the sub-lexical units involved (see Goswami, Chapter 4, this volume). The most promising perspective from these training experiments, aimed at processing sub-lexical units, is that potentially they are capable of producing transfer in word identification.

Investigating identification mechanisms operating at the whole word level

In order to test the hypothesis that poor readers have a deficit in processing both phonemic and orthographic information at the whole word level, we employed a semantic decision task. This consisted of comparing the meanings of singular–plural pairs of nouns. Essential for the experiment were the various classes of singular–plural pairs, as defined by the degree of similarity, or congruence, in phonological and/or orthographic structure of the stem morphemes occurring in the singular–plural pair.

The pairs of nouns were presented on a computer monitor screen. Subjects were native Dutch speakers.[7] A pair always consisted of a singular and a plural form. The subject was encouraged to decide as quickly as possible if the members of the pair had identical stem morphemes (roots) or not (e.g. compare *book–books* versus *brook–books* in English). Of special interest was the comparison of decisions relating to congruent pairs with decisions concerning pairs showing intraword phonologic and/or orthographic variations. To illustrate, consider the pairs *boek–boeken* ('book–books') and *doos–dozen* ('box–boxes'). The first pair represents a perfect phonological correspondence, as well as congruence in orthographic structure, whereas *doos–dozen* exemplifies orthographic as well as phonological incongruence: the *oo* of the singular changes into *o*, and /*do:s*/ of the singular stem alters into /*do:z*/ in the plural.

We wanted to assess differential phonemic and/or orthographic processing by normal and poor readers by utilizing the described semantic decision task. In agreement with the phonological deficit hypothesis, we expected that poor readers would have more difficulty in processing phonologically incongruent pairs. Our second prediction was that poor readers would also have more problems evaluating orthographically incongruent pairs.

Experiment 5

Method

Subjects Two matched groups of normal and poor readers participated in the experiment. The poor readers attended a school for children with learning difficulties to improve their reading skills. Poor readers were defined as subjects scoring at least 2 years below the age norm, as measured by a standard Dutch reading ability test (Brus and Voeten, 1972). These subjects (N = 11; mean age 12.6 years) were matched on reading level on this test with a group of normal readers (N = 11; mean age 9.4 years).

Materials The following types of singular–plural pairs[8] were used as items:

1. Pairs representing perfect sound–spelling correspondence, e.g. *boek–boeken* (type O+/P+).
2. Orthographically congruent, phonologically incongruent[9] pairs, e.g. *paard–paarden* [pa:rt/pa:rdən] (type O+/P−).
3. Orthographically and phonologically incongruent pairs, e.g. *huis–huizen* (type O−/P−).
4. Similar to type C, but with additional alternating vowel orthography, e.g. *baas–bazen* [ba:s/ba:zən] (type O−/P−).

5. Orthographically and phonologically congruent pairs, showing reduplication of the final stem consonant in the plural, e.g. *fles–flessen* (type O+/P+).
6. Orthographically incongruent, phonologically congruent pairs, e.g. *droom–dromen* [dro:m/dro:mən] (type O−/P+).
7. Pairs with a strong[10] plural formation, e.g. *stad–steden* (type O−/P−).

In addition to these seven types of experimental items there were three types of control items:

8. Semantically unrelated pairs, e.g. *bloem–bomen*.
9. Semantically unrelated, but phonologically similar items, e.g. *boek–boeren*.
10. Semantically unrelated, but orthographically interfering items, e.g. *bom–bomen* [bom/bo:mən].

Experimental pairs were selected and matched on word frequency (Uit den Boogaart, 1975). Each type was represented by four different pairs. In the experiment each pair was presented twice, once with the singular form as the left member of the pair, and once vice versa. The sequence of this repeated left–right presentation was random. Moreover, experimental and control pairs were never presented more than three times in succession. The same held for singular–plural presentation order. In order to control for possibly confounding effects of response bias the number of experimental ('yes') and control ('no') trials was practically equal ($2 \times 7 \times 4 = 56$ and $2 \times 3 \times 9 = 54$, respectively).

Procedure and apparatus Presentation of the items was computer-controlled. An IBM personal computer with a monochrome cathode-ray tube (CRT) display was used. Subjects were told that they would be shown pairs of nouns, one in the singular and one in the plural. They had to check whether the pairs contained identical stem morphemes or not. After instruction the subjects were presented five practice items. All items were presented in capital letters. Subjects responded by pushing one of two buttons, a green one for 'yes' (semantically related) and a red one for 'no' responses. Response registration was effected by the computer program. A specially designed screen synchronization program enabled registration of reaction times (RT) with a precision of 1 ms.

Results
The main results are presented in Table 6.9. To locate the independent contributions of phonemic and orthographic cues in the semantic decision task used, we ran a 2 (groups) × 2 (phonological congruence) × 2 (orthographic congruence) MANOVA on predefined groupings of the various types of pairs used. In order to avoid inflated between-group differences, the strong plural type O−/P− (*stad–steden*) was not included in this analysis. Thus, the six remaining types were assigned according to phonological and orthographic congruence. This resulted in a 2 (reader groups) × 2 (phonological congruence) × 2 (orthographic congruence) design. The corresponding MANOVA showed two main effects, one for phonological congruence ($F1(1,20) = 15.42$, $p < 0.001$; $F2(1,44) = 3.70$, $p < 0.05$) and one for repetition ($F1(1,20) = 7.28$, $p < 0.014$; $F2(1,40) = 6.41$,

Table 6.9 Semantic decision and
phonological congruence, Experiment 5

Phonologically congruent	
Poor readers	2,074*
Normal readers	2,051
Phonologically incongruent	
Poor readers	2,269
Normal readers	2,095

Note:
* Mean latency scores; reaction times in
milliseconds.

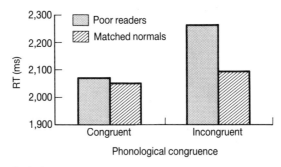

Figure 6.5 Phonological congruence by group interaction.

$p < 0.015$), respectively. Phonologically congruent pairs, (type O+/P+, *broek–broeken*; type O+/P+, *bril–brillen* and type O−/P+, *droom–dromen*) were processed faster than phonologically incongruent pairs (type O+/P−, *bord–borden*; type O−/P−, *buis–buizen* and type O−/P−, *baas–bazen*). Second trials elicited shorter decision times. This repetition effect also interacted with group membership, poor readers being less sensitive to repetition ($F1(1,20) = 6.03$, $p < 0.023$; $F2(1,40) = 5.48$, $p < 0.024$). Finally, there was an interesting group by phonology interaction (see Figure 6.5). As the figure shows, poor readers turned out to have particular problems in processing phonologically incongruent pairs ($F1(1,20) = 7.42$, $p < 0.013$; $F2(1,44) = 2.83$, $p < 0.10$).

Discussion   The results suggest that poor readers who are well beyond the initial stage of instruction encounter specific problems in assessing the lexical identity of singular–plural pairs. These problems were shown to be related to the automatized processing of phonological incongruencies in singular–plural transformations. The poor readers also proved to be less sensitive to the repeated presentation of the test items.

In normal readers, word identification is accelerated by speeded access to intraword letter clusters. In other words, the automatic processing of words is at least partially dependent on identification routines working at the subword level. The results obtained in Experiment 5 are clearly in accordance with the phonological deficit hypothesis. However, our data provide additional evidence for deficits in orthographic processing. Experiment 5 does not allow us to specify the precise contribution of both types of cue.

Identification mechanisms operating at the sentence context level

Do normal and poor readers differ in their use of context during processing orthographic information? Reading research conducted more than a decade ago (West and Stanovich, 1978; Stanovich, 1980; Perfetti and Roth, 1981) has provided evidence for the hypothesis that in word identification poor readers are more context-dependent than normal readers. A similar effect was found for younger readers compared with more experienced readers. Context dependency and reading ability have been a topic on the research agenda ever since the interactive-compensatory hypothesis (Stanovich, 1980) was launched.

Research on context use has produced inconsistent results. This can be attributed in part to insufficient clarity in the use of the term 'context effect'. Context may be used to facilitate comprehension of text, but it may also be used to accelerate ongoing word recognition. In this chapter we define context as the semantic/syntactic sentence structure affecting orthographic processing of a given target word. Discrepancies in findings across studies may also partly be attributed to the divergency in the tasks (e.g. naming, lexical decision) used. Findings that conflict with the interactive-compensatory hypothesis come largely from natural-istic studies using oral reading analysis (Bowey, 1985). The present study diverges in this respect. Emphasizing the importance of a naturalistic task setting, it focuses on orthographic processing in silent reading.

Context effects have been reported in a number of studies using oral reading measures (Juel, 1980; Goldsmith-Phillips, 1989). Our first aim was to provide a more complete view of reading ability and context use in orthographic processing during silent reading. A second goal was to examine the role of sub-lexical high-frequency letter clusters (Young-Loveridge, 1985). This was accomplished by presenting normal and poor readers with target words containing letter sub-stitutions in two contrasting context conditions. We expected that presenting a word in a highly predictable context would induce subjects to proceed to the next segment of text without completing the processing of units at lower levels in the hierarchy (e.g. constituent letters). The letter substitutions we used affected orthographic structure in one of three ways, similar to the response alternatives used in a study by Rayner (1988), labelled '*sound*' (e.g. *cote* for *coat*), '*shape-legal*' (e.g. *coet* for *coat*) and '*shape-illegal*' (e.g. *bcok* for *book*), respectively. These three letter substitution types were manipulated in compound target words, at well-specified intraword locations. The reading materials were presented in a computer-controlled experiment.

The interactive-compensatory hypothesis enables us to make two predictions. First, highly predictable contexts will facilitate semantic processing, and consequently inhibit the detection of letter substitutions. Second, poor readers will be more affected by this general context inhibition effect than normals.

Complementary to the interactive-compensatory hypothesis, specifying mechanisms beyond the word level, we were interested in relating reading ability to orthographic processing mechanisms at the intra- or subword level (Young-Loveridge, 1985). These include: (1) differential processing sensitivity dependent on intraword position; (2) processing differences of high-frequency intraword letter clusters; and (3) sensitivity differences for detecting orthographically illegal letter-strings. To summarize, our question of interest was to assess the relative magnitude of mechanisms working at the word context level as well as at the intra-word level.

Experiment 6

Method

Subjects Two matched groups of normal and poor readers participated in the experiment. The poor readers attended a school for children with learning difficulties to improve their reading skills. Poor readers were defined as subjects scoring at least 2 years below the age norm, as measured by a standard Dutch reading ability test (Brus and Voeten, 1972). These subjects (N = 20; mean age 12.1 years) were matched on reading level on this test with a group of normal readers (N = 20; mean age 8.9 years). Both groups had been taught reading with comparable instruction materials; there were no differences in teaching methods employed.

Materials The subjects were presented a sentence/random word-string reading task. Experimental sentences contained a misspelled word (the target). These targets were Dutch bisyllabic words (e.g. Dutch *schoolbord*, 'blackboard'). All words with a misspelling were constructed by substituting one letter. Three types of letter substitution were used: e/c-type substitutions, e.g. *vcrfpot* for *verfpot* (shape-illegal type), d/t-type substitutions, in words where a final -*d* is sounded as [t] in Dutch, e.g. *raspaart* for *raspaard* (sound type), and n/m-type substitutions, e.g. *buitemhuis* for *buitenhuis* (shape-legal type).

Design All substitutions were manipulated factorially with intraword position (first/second part). Letter cluster frequency effects were investigated by manipulating e/c-type substitutions factorially with positional bigram frequency (high/low PBF; Young-Loveridge, 1985). Targets were presented in a coherent sentence context and in a scrambled word order context. Experimental sentences contained a misspelled target word. Each cell in the design contained six replications. Control sentences, added to control for accuracy and preference effects, consisted of equivalent, correctly spelled words. In total there were 128 trials, including the control trials.

Procedure and apparatus Presentation of the reading materials was computer-controlled. Subjects were instructed to respond orally. An experimental session started with a performance test for memory of random letter-strings, then the main reading task was presented. Subjects were told that they were participating in a reading comprehension experiment, and that their comprehension ability would be tested by evaluating on line their choice between two probe words presented after the sentence (or random word-string) had disappeared from the screen. Their task was to select the probe fitting in the semantic content of the sentence (word-string) presented just before. They were told that, in order to make this main task of semantic evaluation harder, a supplementary task would be inserted just before the semantic evaluation response could be given. Subjects were asked to report any spelling irregularities, if present, in the previously displayed sentence (word-string). The orthographic irregularities detected had to be located exactly. Subjects responded orally, with the experimenter recording the responses by keyboard. Presentation duration was subject-controlled. Presentation order was randomly controlled by the program and distributed over two working sessions. Subjects received online feedback on their semantic evaluation responses. The second session concluded with a spelling test containing a sample of words equivalent to the experimental targets.

Results
MANOVAs were used for data analysis. The predicted overall context effect was found $(F(1,35) = 12.04, p < 0.001)$. Letter substitution detection in context was 51 per cent versus 56 per cent in the scrambled context condition. There was also a strong main position effect $(F(1,80) = 6.55, p < 0.01)$. Detection in initial position was 84 per cent versus 70 per cent in final position. The predicted context by group interaction was not found.

The three substitution types were further analyzed separately. The shape-illegal type (e/c) showed main effects for group $(F(1,33) = 5.64, p < 0.024)$ (better detection by the normals), for PBF $(F(1,35) = 4.09, p < 0.05)$ (letters in high PBF clusters more often missed) and a strong position effect $(F(1,35) = 27.07, p < 0.001)$ (84 per cent detections in initial versus 70 per cent in final position). The orthographically legal substitution types (m/n and t/d) showed no group or context main or interaction effects.

Substitution-type effects were established by comparing the low PBF trials in all conditions. This analysis showed a strong main type effect (77 per cent detections for the illegal type, versus 38 per cent for legal and 22 per cent for sound) $(F(1,35) = 153.02, p < 0.001$; and $F2(1,70) = 186.6, p < 0.001)$ for items.

In 9 per cent of the trials a correctly identified word was followed by an incorrect letter identification. These inaccuracies were also analyzed separately. There was a strong session (learning) effect ($F(1,35) = 31.68$, $p < 0.001$). More interesting, however, was the main effect of group: poor readers were less accurate in locating the substitutions (11 per cent incorrect versus 7 per cent for normals) ($F1(1,33) = 4.88$, $p < 0.03$; $F2(1,80) = 14.6$, $p < 0.001$) for items. Shape-illegal substitutions (e/c) were the exclusive source of this effect.

Discussion

The main effect of context was found. The context by ability interaction, predicted by the interactive-compensatory hypothesis, however, could not be established. The poor readers participating in our experiment did not encounter more difficulty in detecting letter substitutions in semantically coherent contexts. There are several possible explanations for this outcome. One possibility is that our task was not sensitive enough to assess the interaction of interest. That orthographic effects were found, in particular the accuracy and learning effects, however, does not support this option.

We think the most plausible and straightforward interpretation is that in this type of task the interactive-compensatory hypothesis appears not to apply. Our task was focused on context use during orthographic processing of word or word-like structures. The implication of our findings would be that normal and poor readers do not differ primarily in their use of context, but in the way they process letter information at the intraword level. The main group difference found in the accuracy analysis reported here confirms this. It is also in agreement with recent research with beginning and disabled readers (Ehri and Saltmarsh, 1992). The use of context, presumably, is a post-lexical access mechanism.

The implication is that poor readers' problems should be tackled primarily at their central locus: processing letter information at the word and subword levels. Our theorizing about the remediation of reading problems has long been biased by a stress on the primacy of context use and syntactic processing. Today research is reorienting towards the word and intraword level. The challenge will be how educational psychologists and instructional designers deal with this issue.

General discussion and conclusion

The results of the experiments reported in this chapter may be summarized under three headings:

(1) Between-group differences were found in the experiments addressing decoding skills at the letter feature level, the single letter level and the letter cluster level (Experiments 1, 3 and 4, respectively). There were no differences at the sentence context level. This suggests that the poor readers participating in our experiments experienced problems at processing levels operating in the initial stages of the identification process.

(2) Group-specific differences were found for decoding skills at the letter feature level, the letter cluster level and the whole word level (Experiments 1, 4 and 5, respectively). These interactions are specially informative, since they enable us to specify in more detail the sources of reading problems. The interaction effects suggest that the 12-year-old poor readers participating in our studies differed from their two years younger matched peers in the automatized processing of letter information at the word level and at the subword level.

(3) The fact that no ability differences were found in the experiments addressing skills at the sentence context level (Experiments 6 and 2) is also informative, in combination with the differences described under (1) and (2) above. This is in line with other research on the role of context in word identification (Stanovich, 1986). Taken together, these three main trends in our data suggest that poor readers' identification strategies differ from normal readers in their deficient use of decoding skills at the subword level.

The pattern of the results presented in this chapter can be related to two central issues in reading research. The first issue is concerned with the *role of orthographic and phonological information in reading*. The controversy has been outlined in the introduction of this chapter: Does reading disability primarily originate from a phonological deficit, or is it the result of an orthographic processing deficit? Is poor reading primarily a 'hardware' problem, caused by dysfunctioning brain systems, or is it a failure in the acquisition of a culturally mediated cognitive skill, normally developing as a result of prolonged reading experience? Or is it perhaps a combination of both accounts of poor reading?

Our findings suggest that both accounts of poor reading are true, but incomplete. Our poor readers showed processing deficits of phonological and orthographic information. Evidence for a phonological deficit was found in Experiment 5. Poor readers had more difficulty in dealing with phonologically incongruent singular–plural pairs. Experiment 1 demonstrated that poor readers had more difficulty in dealing with orthographic codes.

The second issue addressed by our data is concerned with the question of whether poor readers show *qualitative differences in reading* strategy. An alternative to the phonological deficit hypothesis is the developmental lag or delay hypothesis (Treiman and Hirsh-Pasek, 1985). According to the phonological deficit hypothesis poor readers face a specific problem. The delay hypothesis denies this specificity aspect by claiming that poor readers do exactly what normally developing readers do in learning to read, only they do so more slowly.

Stated in terms of the reading level design: the developmental lag hypothesis predicts comparable performance profiles in reading level matched groups of normal and poor readers, whereas the deficit hypothesis predicts group-related specific differences. Our data provides support for the deficit hypothesis, since it can explain the first-order interactions between group membership (normal or poor reader) and task variables established in Experiments 1, 4 and 5. Experiments 1 and 5 further indicate that this deficit is not confined to phonological skills, but also applies to orthographic skills.

We have argued that it is incorrect to conclude that poor readers do no more than lag behind their reading matched peers. Poor readers not only differ quantitatively; their strategies are also qualitatively different. A model of reading development recently proposed by Ehri (1992) may be helpful to make this clear. According to Ehri's model, there are three stages in the development of sight word reading. Each phase is defined by the kinds of connection that are formed between visual cues seen in print and information about a specific word stored in memory. During the first phase, salient visual cues seen in or around a word are linked to the meaning and pronunciation of the word in memory, but this link is not phonemic. This is the *visual cue reading* or *logographic* stage.

In the second phase systematic visual–phonological connections between letters in a word and sounds detected in their pronunciations are established. This is the *phonetic cue reading* stage. In the final phase, students continue to use the alphabetic principle, but in a more mature way. Individual letters are linked to individual phonemes, but also sequences of letters are connected to the blend of phonemes. In Ehri (1992) this stage is called *cipher sightword reading*, to indicate that spellings are fully analyzed as visual symbols for phonemic constituents in pronunciations.

Evaluating our data through Ehri's model generates a characterization of reading disability which can be summarized as follows. Poor readers experience problems with phonological and with orthographic coding. At the orthographic level the following problems are manifest: (1) the letter feature, (2) the single letter, and (3) at the letter cluster levels. Poor readers are also less competent in the use of orthographic structure, in particular if word meanings are excluded (i.e. in pseudowords). Finally, they do not appear to make a different use of sentence context in order to compensate for their problems present at a more basic level of processing.

In terms of Ehri's (1992) model the emerging picture is that the poor readers' performance profile corresponds best with the second (or phonetic cue reading) stage. However, if the deficit account of reading is true this would imply that this transitional stage could be the final stage for most of these subjects. This is exactly the reason why it is both theoretically and practically challenging to design and test scientifically well-founded training programmes in order to establish the limits of improvement in reading instruction. Chapter 8 below discusses this topic in more detail. The concluding point we would emphasize here is that effective remedial reading instruction must be rooted in a solid body of knowledge concerning the malfunctioning mechanisms involved.

Notes

1. The authors would like to thank pupils and teaching staff of the Paulusschool in Utrecht, the Albert Schweitzer school (Utrecht), The Kohnstamm school (Utrecht), De Wegwijzer, Putten (Gld.), and the Utrechtse Heuvelrug school, located in Zeist,

for their cooperation in the experiments reported in this chapter. They also want to thank Charlotte Wortmann, Alex Bos and Wytse de Jong for their participation in conducting the experiments reported in this chapter.

2. A combined speed and accuracy reading test, containing words of increasing phonemic and orthographic complexity.

3. These cues provide information beyond the single-letter level, thus enabling the reader to evaluate the orthographic status, in terms of legality of letter-strings.

4. As a measure for letter cluster frequency we adopted mean positional bigram frequency (PBF). The PBF value of a letter is calculated by taking the arithmetic mean of the frequencies of the two bigrams that include the target letter (in initial or final position, respectively).

5. Positional bigram frequency values were derived from the positional bigram frequency list for Dutch (Rolf and Van Rijnsoever, 1984). This method is described in Van Rijnsoever (1988). The list of selected words has been controlled for differences in positional letter frequency (Mason, 1975).

6. Visual cues refer to gross aspects of words that are independent of specific letters (e.g. word shape and word length). Orthographic cues refer to the orthographic legality of letter-strings.

7. In this study the focus is on the effect of orthographic structure on word identification. Related studies using Dutch words as stimulus materials are Bergman (1988), Bergman *et al.* (1988), on the role of morphological factors in word processing, and De Groot (1983, 1985) on lexical-context effects in visual word recognition.

8. O+ means orthographically congruent, P− means phonologically incongruent, etc.

9. The term congruence refers to singular–plural correspondence here.

10. Change of vowel in the root, comparable to cases like 'goose–geese' in English.

References

Backman, J.E., Mamen, M. and Ferguson, H.B. (1984), 'Reading level design: conceptual and methodological issues in reading research', *Psychological Bulletin*, *96*, 560–8.

Barron, R.W. (1981), 'Development of visual word recognition: a review'. In G.E. MacKinnon and T. Gary Waller (eds.) *Reading Research. Advances in theory and practice*, Vol. 3. New York, etc.: Academic Press.

Bergman, M.W. (1988), *The Visual Recognition of Word Structure. Left-to-right Processing of Derivational Morphology*. Unpublished Ph.D. Dissertation, Catholic University of Nijmegen.

Bergman, M.W., Hudson, P.T.W. and Eling, P.A.T.M. (1988), 'How simple complex words can be: morphological processing and word representations', *The Quarterly Journal of Experimental Psychology*, *40A*, 41–72.

Besner, D., Coltheart, M. and Davelaar, E. (1984), 'Basic processes in reading: computation of abstract letter identities', *Canadian Journal of Psychology*, *38*, 126–34.

Bowey, J.A. (1985), 'Contextual facilitation in children's oral reading in relation to grade and decoding skill', *Journal of Experimental Child Psychology*, *40*, 23–48.

Bowey, J.A. (1990), 'Orthographic onsets and rimes as functional units of reading', *Memory & Cognition*, *18*, 419–27.

Bradley, L. and Bryant, P.E. (1983), 'Categorizing sounds and learning to read – a causal connection', *Nature*, *301*, 419–21.

Bruck, M. and Treiman, R. (1990), 'Phonological awareness and spelling in normal children and dyslexics: the case of initial consonant clusters', *Journal of Experimental Child Psychology*, *45*, 157–78.

Brus, B.Th. and Voeten, M. (1972), *Eén minuut test* [One-minute Test], Nijmegen: Berkhout.

Claxton, G.L. (1974), 'Initial consonant groups function as units in word production', *Language & Speech, 17*, 271–7.

Coltheart, M. and Freeman, R. (1974), 'Case alternation impairs word recognition', *Bulletin of the Psychonomic Society, 3*, 102–4.

Cutler, A., Butterfield, S. and Williams, J.N. (1987), 'The perceptual integrity of syllabic onsets', *Journal of Memory & Language, 26*, 406–18.

De Groot, A.M.B. (1983), *Lexical-context Effects in Visual Word Recognition*. Unpublished Ph.D. Dissertation, Catholic University of Nijmegen.

De Groot, A.M.B. (1985), 'Word-context effects in word naming and lexical decision', *The Quarterly Journal of Experimental Psychology, 37A*, 281–97.

Ehri, L.C. (1980), 'The role of orthographic images in learning printed words.' In J. Kavanagh and R. Venezky (eds.) *Orthography, Reading and Dyslexia*, Baltimore, MD: University Park Press, pp. 155–70.

Ehri, L.C. (1989), 'The development of spelling skill and its role in reading acquisition and reading disability', *Journal of Learning Disabilities, 22*, 356–65.

Ehri, L.C. (1992), 'Reconceptualizing the development of sight word reading and its relationship to recoding.' In P.B. Gough, L.C. Ehri and R. Treiman (eds.) *Reading Acquisition*, Hillsdale, NJ: Lawrence Erlbaum.

Ehri, L.C. and J. Saltmarsh (1992), *Do Beginning and Disabled Readers Detect Letter Alterations in Words They have Learned to Read?* Paper presented at the 1992 AERA Meeting, San Francisco, CA.

Fowler, A.E. (1991), 'How early phonological development might set the stage for phoneme awareness.' In S.A. Brady and D.P. Shankweiler (eds.) *Phonological Processes in Literacy*, Hillsdale, NJ: Lawrence Erlbaum.

Goldsmith-Phillips, J. (1989), 'Word and context in reading development: a test of the interactive-compensatory hypothesis', *Journal of Educational Psychology, 81*, 299–305.

Goswami, U. (1988), 'Orthographic analogies and reading development', *The Quarterly Journal of Experimental Psychology, 40A*, 239–68.

Goswami, U. (1990), *Onset and Rime Units and Transfer In Reading*, Paper presented at the AERA Annual Meeting, Boston, MA. (Also submitted to *Child Development*.)

Goswami, U. and Bryant, P. (1989), 'The interpretation of studies using the reading level design', *Journal of Reading Behavior, 21*, 413–24.

Healy, A.F. and Drewnowski, A. (1983), 'Investigating the boundaries of reading units: letter detection in misspelled words', *Journal of Experimental Psychology: Human perception and performance, 9*, 413–26.

Horn, C.C. and Manis, F.R. (1987), 'Development of automatic and speeded reading of printed words', *Journal of Experimental Child Psychology, 44*, 92–108.

Huey, E.B. (1908), *The Psychology and Pedagogy of Reading*, New York: Macmillan. (Republished: Cambridge, MA: MIT Press, 1968.)

Jackson, N.E. and Butterfield, E.C. (1989), 'Reading-level-match designs: myths and realities', *Journal of Reading Behavior, 21*, 387–412.

Juel, C. (1980), 'Comparison of word identification strategies with varying context, word type, and reader skill', *Reading Research Quarterly, 15*, 358–76.

Kirtley, C., Bryant, P., Maclean, M. and Bradley, L. (1989), 'Rhyme, rime, and the onset of reading', *Journal of Experimental Child Psychology, 48*, 224–45.

Mason, M. (1975), 'Reading ability and letter search time: effects of orthographic structure defined by single-letter positional frequency', *Journal of Experimental Psychology: General, 104* (2), 146–66.

Nodine, C.F. and Simmons, F.G. (1974), 'Processing distinctive features in the differentiation of letterlike features', *Journal of Experimental Psychology, 103*, 21–8.

Paap, K.R., Newsome, S.L. and Noel, R.W. (1984), 'Word shape's in poor shape for the race to the lexicon', *Journal of Experimental Psychology: Human performance and perception*, *10*, 413–28.
Perfetti, C.A. and Roth, S. (1981), 'Some of the interactive processes in reading and their role in reading skill.' In A.M. Lesgold and C.A. Perfetti (eds.) *Interactive Processes in Reading*, Hillsdale, NJ: Lawrence Erlbaum.
Rack, J.P., Snowling, M.J. and Olson, R.K. (1992), 'The nonword reading deficit in developmental dyslexia: a review', *Reading Research Quarterly*, *27*, 28–53.
Rayner, K. (1988), 'Word recognition cues in children: the relative use of graphemic cues, orthographic cues, and grapheme–phoneme correspondence rules', *Journal of Educational Psychology*, *80*, 473–9.
Reitsma, P. (1983), 'Printed word learning in beginning readers', *Journal of Experimental Child Psychology*, *36*, 321–39.
Rolf, P.C. and van Rijnsoever, R.J. (1984), *Positionele letter frequenties in het Nederlands* [Positional Letter Frequencies in Dutch], Lisse: Swets & Zeitlinger.
Scheerer-Neumann, G. (1981), 'The utilization of intra word structure in poor readers: experimental evidence and a training program', *Psychological Research*, *43*, 155–78.
Seidenberg, M.S. (1987), 'Sublexical structures in visual word recognition: access units or orthographic redundancy?' In M. Coltheart (ed.), *Attention and Performance*, Vol. XII: *Reading*, Hillsdale, NJ: Lawrence Erlbaum.
Smith, F., Lott, D. and Cronnell, B. (1969), 'The effect of type size and case alternation on word identification', *American Journal of Psychology*, *82*, 248–53.
Stanovich, K.E. (1980), 'Towards an interactive compensatory model of individual differences in the development of reading fluency', *Reading Research Quarterly*, *16*, 32–71.
Stanovich, K.E. (1986), 'Cognitive processes and the reading problems of learning-disabled children: evaluating the assumption of specificity.' In J. Torgeson and B. Wong (eds.), *Psychological and Educational Perspectives on Learning Disabilities*. London, etc.: Academic Press.
Taft, M. (1979), 'Lexical access via an orthographic code: the basic orthographic syllabic structure (BOSS), *Journal of Verbal Learning and Verbal Behaviour*, *18*, 21–39.
Treiman, R. and Chafetz, J. (1987), 'Are there onset and rime-like units in written words?' In M. Coltheart (ed.) *Attention and Performance*, Vol. XII. London: Lawrence Erlbaum.
Treiman, R. and Hirsh-Pasek, K. (1985), 'Are there qualitative differences in reading behavior between dyslexics and normal readers?' *Memory & Cognition*, *13*, 357–64.
Treiman, R. and Zukowski, A. (1988), 'Units in reading and spelling, *Journal of Memory and Language*, *27*, 466–77.
Uit den Boogart, P.C. (ed.) (1975), *Woordfrequenties van geschreven en gesproken Netherlands* [Word frequencies of written and oral Dutch], Utrecht: Oosthoek, Scheltema and Holkema.
Van Rijnsoever, R.J. (1988), *Spelling en leren lezen* [Spelling and Learning to Read], unpublished PhD thesis, University of Nijmegen.
Vellutino, F.R. and Scanlon, D.M. (1989), 'Some prerequisites for interpreting results from reading level matched designs', *Journal of Reading Behavior*, *21*, 361–85.
West, R.F. and Stanovich, K.E. (1978), 'Automatic contextual facilitation in readers of three ages', *Child Development*, *49*, 717–27.
Young-Loveridge, J.M. (1985), 'Use of orthographic structure and reading ability. What relationship?' *Journal of Experimental Child Psychology*, *40*, 439–49.

7

Grammatical awareness and learning to read: a critique

Judith A. Bowey
Department of Psychology, University of Queensland

Beginning in the mid-1970s, there was a decade of intense interest in the development of children's metalinguistic abilities, culminating in the publication of several books (e.g. Sinclair *et al.*, 1978; Hakes, 1980; Tunmer *et al.*, 1984). This included the study of children's ability to reflect on grammaticality. By the late 1970s, research in the development of grammatical awareness began to merge with two other streams of research, one investigating the association between phonological sensitivity and reading achievement, and the other, the development of metacognition.

With the case for the contribution of phonological awareness to reading success receiving consistent support, it was not long before speculation began concerning the potential contribution of other aspects of metalinguistic skill to the reading process. For instance, kindergarten children's ability to segment spoken sequences into word units was found to predict subsequent reading achievement (McNinch, 1974). Ehri (1979) wondered whether word awareness allowed children to acquire a sight vocabulary by associating printed forms with word units, and Tunmer and Bowey (1984) similarly argued that word awareness was required before children could begin to acquire the letter–sound correspondences necessary to develop efficient decoding skills.

In a similar vein, it was argued that grammatical awareness contributed to reading comprehension. For instance, Tunmer and Bowey (1984) argued that grammatical awareness contributed to children's ability to reassemble decoded words into meaningful syntactic groups which can be more easily recalled. This process may be particularly important in comprehending written language, where

This work was supported by the Australian Research Council. I would like to thank Julie Hansen for her helpful comments on an earlier version of this chapter.

punctuation provides only minimal prosodic cues and when situational cues are all but absent. The ability to reflect on grammaticality may also assist children in detecting and correcting reading errors, thus enhancing comprehension monitoring (Tunmer and Bowey, 1984). Sensitivity to grammatical well-formedness may even facilitate the development of word recognition processes. The ability to detach sentence meaning from sentence structure may be a prerequisite for word awareness (Ehri, 1979).

Relative to the enormous literature investigating the association between phonological awareness and reading, there has been comparatively little work on grammatical awareness and reading. Nevertheless, sufficient evidence has accumulated for strong claims to emerge regarding the contribution of grammatical awareness to beginning reading achievement. The time has come to take stock of the available literature and critically assess these claims.

With this aim in mind, this chapter provides a critique of research on this topic. It adopts a conservative methodological stance, with the aim of suggesting avenues for further research that will elucidate the role of grammatical awareness in beginning reading. In particular, it argues that much of the available literature has used grammatical awareness tasks that are confounded by semantic processing.

The chapter begins with a critical examination of the tasks most frequently used to assess grammatical awareness, pointing to the difficulties involved in obtaining relatively pure estimates of this ability in beginning readers and the widespread contamination of experimental measures of grammatical awareness by semantic and other cognitive processes. Suggestions are made for the design of grammatical awareness tasks that minimize the utility and thus the contribution of semantic processing strategies. The second section reviews the literature examining the association between grammatical awareness and reading. It is argued that, although the available evidence is consistent with the hypothesis that grammatical awareness contributes directly to reading ability, most studies permit alternative interpretations. For instance, it has not yet been clearly demonstrated that poor readers show any deficit in grammatical awareness that is independent of more general delays in language development or other skills. Similarly, training studies are typically confounded by teaching children active semantic processing and comprehension monitoring strategies. Later sections critically examine the potential contribution of grammatical awareness to reading comprehension and word recognition processes, offering both alternative interpretations of existing studies and suggestions for further work.

Assessing grammatical awareness in children

What is metalinguistic ability?

Metalinguistic ability is generally defined as the ability to reflect on and manipulate language structure. In normal language use, the speaker and hearer use their tacit knowledge of language structure to produce and comprehend meaningful utterances. Attention is focused on the meaning of the linguistic message; language structure is the vehicle used to encode meaning. Language structure is thus transparent, with both the speaker and the listener focusing on meaning. Minor articulation errors, pauses and grammatical errors pass unnoticed. It is usually only when structural difficulties impair communication that attention focuses on language structure. At this point, language structure becomes the opaque object of reflection.

Metalinguistic performance differs from language comprehension and production in that metalinguistic performance requires the language system (rather than meaning) to be treated as the object of thought. The central feature of metalinguistic functioning is an attention shift from content to form (Lundberg, 1978; see also Bowey, 1988).

There is nothing in this view of metalinguistic ability that implies that, to be classified as metalinguistic, the attention shift from meaning to structure must be under intentional ('attentional') control. Rather, any activity in which attention is focused primarily on any aspect of language structure is metalinguistic in nature (see Bowey, 1988). Signs of metalinguistic reflection can sometimes be observed in very young children (see Clark, 1978; Bowey, 1988; Grieve, 1990).

From a very early age children do reflect on grammatical form, as is obvious from both spontaneous speech repairs and occasional comments about grammatical structure. Some researchers (e.g. Tunmer and Herriman, 1984) interpret speech repairs as revealing the operation of automatic speech-editing processes. While it is difficult to rule out such an explanation for many grammatical speech repairs (e.g. sentence 1, below), other instances, particularly those including contrastive stress or negative forms, are less easily eliminated (see sentences 2–5, below). These examples demonstrate that from time to time very young children may focus attention on grammatical acceptability. (For other arguments against the automatic speech-editing account, see Bowey, 1988.)

1. KATE (2;8 years):   It's – it's – he's too big. (Clark and Anderson, 1979)
2. HEIDA (3;2 years):   It's watching we cutting – our cutting – we cutting – It's watching our's cutting. (Slobin, 1978)
3. SVETA (2;9 years):   Ja sam cuo da se srusio [I heard it collapse].
   MILETA (2;9 years):   [Correcting her twin, and using contrastive stress for emphasis] Da se srusi*lo*. (Savic, 1982).
4. FRANS (2;9 years):   Sma haender hedder det – lille hand – sma haender – lille haender – nae sma haender[1] [They are called small hands – lille hand – small hands – lille hand – no small hands]. (Jesperson, 1922)
5. HILDEGARD (4;3 years): If there is one you say *Schuh*; if there are two you have to say *Schuhe*. (Leopold, 1949)

Although spontaneous speech repairs and occasional metalinguistic comments imply that young children do sometimes contemplate grammatical structure, such observations do not lend themselves to statistical analysis – hence the need for experimental metalinguistic tasks.

Experimental metalinguistic tasks are often presented in disembedded contexts; essentially, they presuppose that children can control their attentional processes by focusing on language structure at the whim of the investigator. Grammatical awareness then becomes operationalized as the ability of children, on demand, to focus attention on grammatical structure.[2] In that sense, experimental metalinguistic tasks incorporate a cognitive (or 'attentional') control component (see also Bialystok and Ryan, 1985). The attentional control component is the essential feature underlying the effective and flexible use of cognitive strategies, which develops in children at about the same time as they show the ability to perform a wide range of experimental metalinguistic tasks (see Ryan and Ledger, 1984; Tunmer and Bowey, 1984; Bialystok and Ryan, 1985). With increasing cognitive development comes the ability to use cognitive strategies (see Flavell, 1985). Performance on metalinguistic tasks is strongly correlated with cognitive development (Hakes, 1980; Tunmer *et al.*, 1988; Tunmer, 1989) and scalogram analysis of performance on a series of experimental metalinguistic and cognitive tasks suggests that these tasks reflect a single underlying ability (Hakes, 1980).

The extension of cognitive control processes to the metalinguistic domain represents an extremely important achievement and one that is clearly associated with beginning reading achievement. However, we must not confuse metalinguistic functioning *per se* with the ability to perform experimental metalinguistic tasks. Performance on experimental metalinguistic tasks inescapably incorporates a cognitive control component, but this does not imply that younger children do not engage in metalinguistic activity. To overlook the cognitive control component of experimental metalinguistic tasks may produce a fundamental misunderstanding of the nature of the association between abilities like grammatical awareness and beginning reading.

Because of the disembedded nature of most experimental metalinguistic tasks, it is often difficult to design tasks that children can understand. This is particularly true with young children, who have extremely limited metalinguistic vocabularies. If we overlook the problem of task comprehension, we can completely misrepresent children's metalinguistic capacities. Ehri (1979) reviewed several studies in which children who at first appeared to lack particular metalinguistic skills showed abrupt and dramatic increases in performance after short periods of training. In those studies, the training component sometimes appeared to act as an extended series of instructions (see also Bowey *et al.*, 1984). When sufficient care is taken in task design, substantial numbers of 3-year-olds perform well above chance on some experimental metalinguistic tasks (Smith and Tager-Flusberg, 1982; MacLean *et al.*, 1987; Chaney, 1992).

The use of puppets and game formats does not ensure that metalinguistic tasks lose their disembedded quality. For instance, I have observed that very simple changes in the format of grammatical error correction task instructions can produce dramatic performance increases in 5-year-olds. Both sets of instructions related to a game format error correction task using puppets as props, but the children could not comprehend task requirements until the instructions were modified. Similarly, the word-order discrimination task used by Bohannon (1975) is presented in game format. Yet if we are to believe Bohannon, many 5-year-olds cannot discriminate between well-ordered and randomly ordered sentences! (See Bowey, 1986a, for a further discussion of Bohannon's task.)

Assessing grammatical awareness

Linguists base their theoretical descriptions of grammar on adult informants' intuitions concerning the acceptability of various sentences. It has long been acknowledged that adult intuitions concerning grammatical structure are not independent of semantic considerations (e.g. Schlesinger, 1968; Levelt *et al.*, 1977). It is hardly surprising, then, that semantic factors strongly affect young children's grammaticality judgements. The influence of these factors is probably exacerbated by the use of ambiguous tasks which include semantically anomalous sentences as well as grammatically deviant sentences and by requiring children to judge whether sentences are 'good' or 'silly' (see Bowey, 1988; Fowler, 1988). Children with the capacity to reflect on sentence form often experience difficulty in understanding the sentence judgement task, as excerpt 6 (from Gleitman *et al.*, 1972) shows:

6. EXPERIMENTER: How about this one? *Boy is at the door.*
   CHILD (aged 5): Good.
   EXPERIMENTER: Good? Is that the way you would say it?
   CHILD: No. *A boy is at the door. Boy is at the door* isn't a good sentence.

Because of the difficulty of interpreting the outcomes of sentence judgement tasks, researchers have increasingly relied on the sentence correction task, in which children are told that the sentences they will hear are 'wrong' and are asked to 'fix them up'. This task is often presented in the context of a game in which children are introduced to puppets who have not yet learned to talk properly. Following a series of practice examples in which feedback is supplied, children are given the test trials.

Using this procedure, Pratt *et al.* (1984) found that both 5- and 6-year-olds performed virtually at ceiling (90 per cent correct) when asked to correct morphologically deviant sentences. On this task, there was no age difference. However, on a second task in which children were asked to correct word-order violations, performance was much lower, particularly in the 5-year-olds (about 50 per cent correct). The different levels of performance across the two correction tasks demonstrates the task-dependent nature of any attribution of 'grammatical awareness' to a child (see also Chaney, 1992).

Pratt *et al.* interpreted the higher level of morphological error correction performance as primarily reflecting the fact that word-order violations produced more fundamental changes in the underlying syntactic representations than morphological errors, thus requiring greater efforts to return the test sentences to an acceptable form. Since word-order violations are essentially solved using a strategy of juggling constituents until a meaningful utterance results, the correction of word-order errors relies more heavily on verbal working memory and semantic processing strategies than does morphological error correction, in which the intended meaning of the sentence is usually obvious (see below).

It is possible that some morphological error corrections may reflect the operation of automatic speech-editing processes. Pratt *et al.* argued against this view, partly on the grounds that some children used contrastive stress to emphasize their morphological corrections. Bowey (1986a) investigated the role of 'spontaneous' corrections by incorporating an error imitation task. She found that 5-year-olds did indeed spontaneously correct grammatically deviant sentences, even when explicitly reminded not to and when reminded of this requirement whenever they spontaneously corrected two successive test sentences. The rate of spontaneous corrections dropped markedly between 5;1 and 5;8 years, although resistance to spontaneous corrections nevertheless maintained a consistent association with the Revised Peabody Picture Vocabulary Test (PPVT-R) vocabulary age. It is thus likely that the high rate of morphological error corrections noted by Pratt *et al.* in their sample (aged 5;5) did include some spontaneous corrections. Thus, the difference in performance on the word-order and morphological error correction tasks probably reflects both the genuinely greater difficulty of the word-order correction task and the inflation of morphological correction rates by spontaneous corrections.

The probable confounding of word-order correction tasks by working memory and semantic processing strategies cautions against a direct interpretation of any association between word-order correction performance and reading achievement. Although it is difficult to eliminate semantic processing completely from grammatical awareness tasks, the contribution of these processes can be reduced by changing the nature of the items. For instance, nonsense word materials (sentence 7, below) or semantically reversible materials can be developed in which word-order errors can be corrected only by focusing on grammatical agreement (e.g. sentences 8–11, below). These items appear much harder than the items traditionally used in word-order correction tasks (sentences 12 and 13, below), but this reinforces the suggestion that word-order correction tasks frequently rely heavily on semantic processing:

7. * A cartoshes visted all the blan.
8. * The dog chasing were the boys.
9. * I visit Jane me to asked.
10. * She me read to.
11. * Them dogs those ate.

12. * Rode Susan bike the (from Tunmer *et al.*, 1987).
13. * Clapped his hands Mark (from Tunmer *et al.*, 1987).

An alternative method of reducing the contribution of semantic strategies is to use items in which the intended meaning of the deviant sentence is transparent (see Bowey and Patel, 1988; Fowler, 1988). Bowey and Patel asked 6-year-old children to correct grammatical and morphological errors in sentences in which the error minimally distorted intended sentence meaning (sentences 14 and 15, below). All these errors were 'natural', having been observed in the speech of younger children. Bowey and Patel controlled for spontaneous correction tendencies by requiring children to repeat verbatim deviant sentences, leaving the grammatical error intact. The number of spontaneous corrections was subtracted from children's scores on the correction task (see also Bowey, 1986a, 1986b). In this task, children need to expend minimal mental resources in recovering intended meaning, and thus their performance reflects more accurately their ability to reflect on and correct grammatical form. This grammatical error correction task appears much easier than the word-order correction task, although, since 6-year-olds' performance on this task was 63.9 per cent after allowance was made for spontaneous error corrections, this task is suitable for predictive work with school entrants.

14. * What you are doing? (from Bowey and Patel, 1988).
15. * Last week he drop a glass (from Bowey and Patel, 1988).

Tasks employing nonsense word items or semantically reversible items may be more suitable for assessing deficits difficulties in grammatical awareness performance in older reading disabled children for whom the Bowey and Patel task is probably too easy. However, findings that older poor readers can perform the Bowey and Patel task while still encountering difficulty with nonsense word items or semantically reversible items would imply that the primary difficulty for poor readers is not an inability to focus on grammatical form *per se*, but rather inefficiencies in this process. Such a pattern of results would parallel findings that, while younger reading-level controls score higher, less skilled fourth-grade readers still score above chance on tests of phonological sensitivity (Bradley and Bryant, 1978; Bowey *et al.*, 1992).

Care must also be taken to ensure that the grammatical structures chosen for testing are not unduly difficult; in such cases the grammatical awareness test becomes a *de facto* measure of grammatical development. It may be that children *can* focus on grammatical structure *per se*, but are uncertain as to the correct form of particular, more difficult, grammatical structures. Where the grammatical awareness task is based on late-acquired grammatical structures, poor performance may reflect a general language delay, rather than a metalinguistic deficit. This difficulty applies particularly to the use of grammatical proficiency tests using oral cloze procedures, such as the Grammatic Closure subtest of the

Illinois Test of Psycholinguistic Abilities (ITPA; Kirk *et al.*, 1968), to estimate grammatical awareness. This test was designed as a measure of morphological development, not grammatical awareness. In such tasks, it is possible that in supplying a grammatical completion, the child has focused primarily on meaning. The use of the correct morphological form certainly implies mastery of that form, but this is not equivalent to grammatical awareness.

Even if we assume that the cloze task does assess grammatical awareness, performance on standardized tests that were originally designed as tests of morphological development is difficult to interpret. Success on the first few items demonstrates that the child can indeed perform the cloze component of the task and thus that the child *can* reflect on grammatical form. Failure on later items probably indicates delayed grammatical development rather than an impaired ability to reflect on grammatical well-formedness *per se*. For instance, Chaney (1992) found that 3-year-olds could judge the grammaticality of the agentive *-er* form, but could not perform an oral cloze task requiring them to supply this form. This was interpreted as 'indicating a later acquisition of the agent "er" form in their dialect rather than a metalinguistic deficiency' (Chaney, 1992, p. 500).

There are other difficulties with the oral cloze test. The cloze procedure forms the basis of several reading comprehension tests (e.g. McLeod, 1967; Woodcock, 1987). Oral cloze tasks have also been used to assess grammatical awareness in relation to reading. However, cloze tasks involving content word deletions clearly require sensitivity to both grammatical *and* semantic constraints (Tunmer and Bowey, 1984, p. 164). Cloze tasks restricted to function word deletions may be more safely interpreted as indices of grammatical awareness.

This brief discussion of the assessment of grammatical awareness provides the implicit background of the remainder of this chapter. Several conclusions should be highlighted. First, experimental metalinguistic tasks inevitably incorporate a cognitive control component. Second, metalinguistic ability requires attention to be focused primarily on structure rather than meaning. From this, it follows that the semantic processing component of grammatical awareness tasks must be actively minimized. To the extent that grammatical awareness tasks can be successfully completed using semantic processing strategies, their interpretation is compromised. Third, care must also be taken to ensure that the grammatical structures chosen for testing are not unduly difficult. Finally, verbal working memory and other processing demands should be reduced as far as is practically possible.

This overview of the tasks most commonly used to assess grammatical awareness suggests that the grammatical error correction task is most readily comprehended by young children. This task most effectively assesses grammatical awareness when the intended meaning of the sentence is obvious, but where the grammatical means used to express that meaning is deviant. In such cases, error correction reflects children's capacity to reflect on and manipulate grammatical well-formedness.

The association between grammatical awareness and reading

Correlational studies

This section focuses mainly on research carried out in the 1980s. Earlier studies had tended to use tasks which children may have had difficulty in understanding. These studies have been comprehensively reviewed by Ryan and Ledger (1984). The conclusions drawn in this section do not differ from those that would be drawn from a fuller review.

Vogel (1975) reported a major study of the association between grammatical proficiency and reading achievement. She compared the performance on a range of language tasks of dyslexic boys with boys with age-appropriate reading ability. To avoid problems associated with dialect differences, the sample was restricted to monolingual Caucasians ranging in age from 7;4 to 8;5 years, with both groups having a mean age of 7;9 years. The two groups were equivalent in terms of socioeconomic status and Peabody Picture Vocabulary Test (PPVT) receptive vocabulary. No child scored more than 1 standard deviation below the mean on an intelligence test; in fact, all scored above the 20th percentile.

Vogel compared the two groups' performance on a series of grammar tests. Four tests involved the use of cloze procedures, including two oral cloze tests in which function words were deleted, and two tests of morphological development, the Berry–Talbott Language Test of Comprehension (Berry and Talbott, 1966) and the ITPA Grammatic Closure subtest. The latter two tests were included as measures of morphological development, not grammatical awareness (see p. 129 above).

Other grammatical tests included the receptive section of the Northwestern Syntax Screening Test, a sentence repetition test, the Developmental Sentence Scoring analysis of spontaneous speech (Lee and Canter, 1971), and two clearly metalinguistic tasks. The first of the metalinguistic tests required the child to use prosodic cues to judge whether a sentence was 'telling him something or asking a question' (Vogel, 1975, p. 18). The second required children to judge grammatical well-formedness. Before each sentence in the grammaticality judgement task, children were given a cue word and asked to listen for that particular word and to judge whether it was used correctly so that the sentence sounded right, or whether the word was used incorrectly so that the sentence sounded wrong. Each word, and each sentence, was presented twice and was repeated on request. The boys were also given two verbal memory span measures, the Forward Digit Span subtest from the Wechsler Intelligence Scale for Children (WISC; Wechsler, 1949) and the Auditory Attention Span for Unrelated Words subtest from the Detroit Tests of Learning Aptitude (Baker and Leland, 1959).

Overall, Vogel (1975) found that the normal readers scored significantly higher than the dyslexics on grammar. Univariate analyses showed that these differences were significant for all but the Northwestern Syntax Screening Test and the grammaticality judgement task. On the latter task, both groups performed just better than chance (67 per cent cf. 50 per cent correct). It is possible that many of the children did not understand this task. The no difference finding should thus be conservatively interpreted.

Shankweiler and Crain (1986) argued that the association between grammatical proficiency and reading performance is partly mediated by differences in verbal working memory span. However, when Vogel (1975) analyzed her data using verbal memory span measures as covariates, the normal readers still scored higher overall on grammar than the dyslexics, although univariate analyses indicated that this difference was significant for only five of the nine measures: the prosody judgement task, the sentence repetition test, the Developmental Sentence Scoring of spontaneous speech, the Berry-Talbott Test and the Grammatic Closure test. The latter two morphology cloze tests assess grammatical development as well as grammatical awareness (see p. 129 above). On the other two cloze tasks with function word deletions, no difference remained after verbal memory span effects were controlled. Thus, Vogel's study is probably best interpreted as revealing a clear-cut general grammatical delay on the part of the dyslexic boys. Recent work has indicated that verbal span measures may not be the most appropriate measures of verbal working memory in children of this age (e.g. Hansen and Bowey, 1994). It is thus possible that the grammatical delay observed by Vogel (1975) at least partially reflects a verbal working memory deficit (Shankweiler and Crain, 1986).

The same type of conclusion may also be true of studies reporting concurrent associations between reading and grammatical awareness, as measured using grammatical error correction tasks (Ryan and Ledger, 1979; Bowey, 1986a, 1986b; Tunmer *et al.*, 1987; Bowey and Patel, 1988; Tunmer *et al.*, 1988; Tunmer, 1989; Bentin *et al.*, 1990) and oral cloze tasks (Willows and Ryan, 1986; Siegel and Ryan, 1989; So and Siegel, 1992). Both word-order correction and oral cloze tasks incorporate substantial semantic processing components, compromising the interpretation of many of these studies. In addition, several of these studies also reported generalized grammatical delays in less skilled readers (Bowey, 1986a; Willows and Ryan, 1986; Bowey and Patel, 1988; Siegel and Ryan, 1988, 1989; So and Siegel, 1992). Thus, in these studies, group differences in performance, even on valid experimental measures of grammatical awareness, may reflect underlying differences in grammatical development and/ or verbal working memory.

Willows and Ryan (1986) examined performance on a range of language-related measures in a sample of 88 first-, second- and third-grade children. With the effects of age, PPVT receptive vocabulary, Digit Span (from the WISC-R), and Raven's matrices performance effects statistically controlled, Willows and Ryan found that oral cloze was the only 'grammatical' task that reliably accounted for significant variation in reading performance. Error location, error correction and sentence repetition did not account for additional variation in written cloze, reading comprehension or word recognition performance, although they did explain variation in reading fluency. However, the finding that oral cloze was the only 'grammatical' variable to account consistently for variation in reading performance is difficult to interpret. On the one hand, since the oral cloze task assessed content word deletions, it assesses not only grammatical awareness but also semantic processing, as Willows and Ryan implicitly acknowledged by using a written cloze test as a reading comprehension measure. On the other hand, it can be argued that correlational studies, such as that reported by Willows and Ryan, are too conservative. Although, given the wide age range of their sample, it was clearly necessary to control for age effects, it is most unlikely that grammatical awareness is developmentally independent of general language and cognitive development. Thus, while possibly contributing directly to reading achievement, grammatical awareness may not account for unique variation in children's reading achievement when the effects of general language and cognitive development are statistically controlled (see Bowey and Patel, 1988).

All the studies investigating simple correlations between grammatical awareness and reading achievement are susceptible to the alternative interpretation that progress in reading enhances grammatical awareness. It is quite likely that reading instruction and practice in reading teaches children to treat language as an object of thought and thus enhances their performance across a wide range of metalinguistic tasks. In particular, reading teaches children to monitor and correct the semantic and grammatical acceptability of their rendition of the text. Few studies have used designs permitting stronger interpretation, and even in these studies, alternative accounts are possible.

Tunmer *et al.* (1987) embedded a reading level comparison of poor fourth-grade readers and good second-grade readers, performing at the same level on a series of reading tests, within a cross-sectional study. These groups were equivalent on a range of reading measures, minimizing statistical regression effects (see Rack *et al.*, 1992). Although these groups were equivalent in age-adjusted PPVT-R receptive vocabulary, the fourth-graders had wider vocabulary knowledge than the second-graders. However, the good second-grade readers did better than the poor fourth-grade readers on a grammatical error correction task in which two-thirds of the items involved word-order errors. The younger good readers also performed better on an oral cloze test which included content words and thus incorporated a semantic processing component.

Although Tunmer *et al.* (1987) used a reading-level design, their data do not unambiguously implicate grammatical awareness as a cause of reading problems. First, both grammatical awareness tasks incorporated substantial semantic components. Second, despite their advantages over same-age comparisons of groups varying in reading ability (Backman *et al.*, 1984), reading-level designs remain essentially correlational in nature. For instance, superior grammatical awareness in a younger reading-level sample may indirectly reflect the contribution of a third variable strongly related to both grammatical awareness and reading, such as phonological awareness or even general grammatical development. Although the reading-level matched groups were equivalent in age-adjusted vocabulary, the PPVT-R shows a fairly weak relationship with grammatical development. Vogel's (1975) dyslexic and control samples were statistically equivalent in PPVT performance, while differing dramatically in grammatical development (see p. 130 above).

The outcomes of reading-level designs can be confidently interpreted only when the experimental tasks represent relatively pure tests of abilities (such as pseudoword reading) or when significant differences favouring younger reading level controls are obtained alongside nonsignificant differences in other skills thought to be closely related to both the target experimental skill and reading achievement. Future reading level studies of grammatical awareness should include sensitive tests of grammatical development, phonological awareness and verbal working memory, in addition to tests of grammatical awareness that minimize the contribution of semantic processing strategies.

The few studies using grammatical awareness as a predictor of later reading success are susceptible to similar interpretative difficulties. In these studies, it is not always clear that grammatical awareness explains unique variation in subsequent reading achievement. However, as Bowey and Patel (1988) noted, it is possible for a skill to contribute directly to reading achievement without necessarily explaining unique variation. Thus, it may not be possible for predictive studies relying on multiple regression techniques to demonstrate unambiguously that grammatical awareness contributes directly to reading achievement. This limitation should be noted throughout the following discussion of predictive studies involving grammatical awareness.

Tunmer *et al.* (1988) gave children commencing school a battery of tests, including PPVT-R receptive vocabulary, operativity (assessing the attainment of concrete operational thought), word-order correction, phonemic segmentation and 'pragmatic awareness'. Incidentally, the last test, requiring children to detect inconsistencies in orally presented stories, should not be considered a meta-linguistic task. It involves the careful monitoring of language meaning, not the structural features of the message. Word-order correction performance predicted both first- and second-grade pseudoword reading and reading comprehension achievement. Word-order corrections involve semantic and verbal working memory processes, in addition to grammatical awareness. Furthermore, these simple predictive correlations were not substantially higher than those obtained for pragmatic awareness, which, according to Tunmer *et al.* (1988), does not contribute to early reading achievement.

Tunmer *et al.* (1988) did not report any analyses of the predictive association between word-order correction performance and reading in which the effects of vocabulary, operativity and phonological awareness were controlled.[3] It is thus possible that the predictive association between word-order correction perform-ance and reading incorporated contributions from other variables.

In a second predictive study (Tunmer, 1989), path analyses, including verbal intelligence (estimated from the PPVT-R) and operativity, indicated that word-order correction performance and phonemic segmentation in children at the end of the first year of schooling each contributed directly to second-grade pseudoword reading and indirectly to reading comprehension. However, no attempt was made in this study to control for end of first-grade reading achievement. This omission is surprising in view of Tunmer *et al.*'s acknowledgement that failure to control for reading ability within predictive studies can 'result in artifactually high predictive correlations' (1988, p. 140).

Bryant *et al.* (1990) attempted to control for the effects of general language and cognitive abilities in their predictive study. At 4 years of age, their sample of 65 children was administered a twelve-item error correction task based on Tunmer *et al.* (1987), with six items involving word-order corrections. A series of hierarchical multiple regression analyses indicated that word-order correction performance predicted subsequent reading ability, even with the effects of general language ability statistically controlled, although this was no longer true when full-scale IQ effects were also controlled. Bowey (1990) reported a path analysis of Bryant *et al.*'s (1990) data, showing that word-order correction contributed independently of phonological awareness to reading achievement. Her analysis effectively controlled the effects of general language and cognitive abilities, as assessed by the Reynell Expressive Language subtest (Reynell and Huntley, 1987) and the Wechsler Preschool and Primary Scale of Intelligence (Wechsler, 1967), although she noted some problems with the choice of general language measure. It is fair to say that studies claiming to show independent effects of grammatical awareness have not used particularly good measures of general language ability.

The work using reading level and predictive designs provides a strong *prima facie* case that word-order correction performance contributes to reading performance. However, only one of these studies (Bowey, 1990; Bryant *et al.*, 1990) has attempted to control for the influence of other variables and there are some minor difficulties even with this study (Bowey, 1990). Furthermore, all these studies have assessed grammatical awareness by means of the word-order correction task, where success can be achieved using semantic processing strategies. We must therefore turn to training studies for evidence that grammatical awareness contributes directly to reading skill.

Training studies

Training studies relevant to the question of whether grammatical awareness contributes directly to reading are few and far between. Furthermore, they are notoriously difficult to interpret. Negative transfer effects may indicate only that the training programme was insufficient to demonstrate the effects of grammatical awareness on reading, particularly where the training effect is itself fairly small. For this reason, training studies should probably be interpreted fairly leniently, especially when the results from a number of studies converge. Nevertheless, our conclusions must be limited by our confidence that experimental grammatical awareness training programmes are not unduly confounded by the inclusion of training in semantic processing strategies or other reading-related skills.

Weaver (1979) examined the effects on reading of teaching third-grade children performing at or above grade level a 'word grouping' strategy to solve sentence anagram tasks that are essentially equivalent to the word-order correction task frequently used to assess grammatical awareness. As noted above, this task inescapably involves semantic processing. Furthermore, the training programme taught children to use fairly sophisticated semantic and comprehension monitoring strategies to solve the anagrams. The experimental group was taught to form phrases ('word groups') by first identifying the verb ('action word') and then asking a series of Wh-questions to group the remaining words and to determine how the phrases related to the verb. The children were taught to check their answers by asking *Is the order sensible?* and *Does it make sense both semantically and syntactically?* Training produced significant gains in the number of sentence anagrams solved and in anagram solution time by the experimental group relative to the control group.

Transfer effects were assessed using four measures: (1) prompted sentence recall, (2) a passage comprehension test from the Metropolitan Achievement Test, (3) a written cloze comprehension test in which every fifth word was deleted, and (4) a speeded sentence meaningfulness judgement task, in which children had to judge whether or not sentences were meaningful, or either false or nonsensical. Overall, sentence anagram training produced significant transfer. However, univariate tests revealed that the experimental group performed better than the no treatment control group only on the prompted recall test and the cloze test. There was no difference between the groups on a follow-the-dots test included to check for the possible effects of experimental novelty. Although there are numerous possible explanations for the weakness of the transfer of sentence anagram training to reading comprehension, the facts remain that the word grouping strategy involves teaching children semantic strategies to help them actively to monitor comprehension by attending to both semantic and grammatical acceptability and that, even so, transfer effects were not strong. It would be unwise to rely on Weaver's study for evidence concerning the direct contribution of grammatical awareness to reading comprehension.

White *et al.* (1981) reported a study teaching learning disabled children (mean age 11.73 years) to use Weaver's word grouping strategy to solve sentence anagrams. The experimental group receiving the sentence anagram training was contrasted with a control group receiving 'more traditional' sentence study training. This study pre-dates theoretical concerns with the effects of grammatical awareness on reading and the grammatical emphasis of the control training programme was freely conceded by White *et al.* (1981, p. 699).[4] The two training programmes also differed in the amount of individual interaction between the teacher and the students. Children in both groups were regularly reminded that the training activities would help them become better readers. Although both treatments produced gains in sentence anagram solution tasks and in a transfer written cloze test, the gains were significantly larger for the experimental treatment group.

This study presents several interpretative difficulties. First, as was argued above in relation to Weaver's study, the sentence anagram treatment did not train grammatical awareness alone. White *et al.* interpreted their programme as 'teaching children to manipulate elements within sentences *on the basis of sentence meaning*' (1981, p. 703; emphasis added). For instance, the children were taught to apply the criterion of checking that regrouped phrases and sentences '*made sense*' (p. 699; emphasis added). Second, as White *et al.* pointed out,

> because the control condition also included a syntactic treatment, the results suggest that the *mode* of presentation of syntax may be an important consideration in accounting for comprehension gains. In short, *the mere presence or absence of syntactic training may not be sufficient to produce comprehension gains such as these. Rather, it seems that the process by which syntactic understanding is acquired and applied may independently influence comprehension achievement* (p. 703; emphasis added)

Ironically, the fact that the *control* sentence study treatment appeared to produce gains in anagram and written cloze performance suggests that grammatical awareness training may boost comprehension.

Milton (1990) reported the effects of thirty sessions of a grammatical awareness training programme extending over 10 weeks. Groups of three first-grade children were equivalent in PPVT receptive vocabulary, verbal memory span and pre-test word-order correction performance. Members of the groups were then randomly allocated to an experimental grammatical awareness training group, or either a vocabulary extension control group or a no treatment control group. The post-test word-order correction performance of the experimental training group was markedly superior to both control groups. Transfer of grammatical awareness gains to later listening and reading skills was somewhat inconsistent. The experimental group scored higher than both control groups on listening comprehension when tested midway through the school year. The experimental training group did better than the vocabulary training group on mid-year word recognition but the difference between the experimental group and the no treatment control group on this measure was not significant. All groups performed at the same level on a test of pseudoword reading accuracy, although, because few children had yet developed phonological recoding skills, few of the pseudowords were accurately read. By the end of the year, there were no between-group differences in reading performance.

Had Milton's study produced more robust effects, it may have been easier to interpret. It is notable that the experimental training transferred to listening comprehension and showed some evidence of transfer to reading. These transfer effects are relatively strong, in view of the fact that the control groups also showed marked gains in word-order correction performance. As Milton concluded, it is possible that a longer training study would have produced stronger transfer effects.

However, a more fundamental difficulty with Milton's study concerns the degree to which her programme can be interpreted as a pure grammatical awareness training programme. Milton states that the tasks used in her lessons included sentence-making, sentence comparison and listening comprehension. The lessons were designed to maintain children's interest, and the focus of some of them was clearly grammatical. For instance, in one lesson, children were taught to use the conjunctions *and* and *but* to conjoin sentences. However, it may not be possible to teach children about grammar in the absence of meaning, especially when the use of grammatical terminology is avoided. Thus, the lesson on identifying verbs required children to use a sentence to describe what people or animals represented in pictures were doing and what they were doing yesterday. In this lesson, children were taught to answer in whole sentences rather than words or phrases. Other exercises included word substitutions within sentences and the use of adjectives and adverbs.

In addition, Milton's programme included direct instruction on sentence anagrams, using an enjoyable game in which several children were asked to remember one word each. These words were given in random order. Children then had to rearrange themselves, saying their one word each, and continue to rearrange themselves '*until the sentence made sense*' (emphasis added).

Although Milton's programme is in most respects exemplary, it is not clear that her results can be interpreted as reflecting the direct effects of grammatical awareness training *per se*. Indeed, it is doubtful whether it is possible to design a purely grammatical programme which would sustain the interest of young children. Although one of Milton's control groups was given a vocabulary extension programme, this programme appeared to involve less active involvement and focused primarily on naming activities. It may thus be argued that differences between the programmes reflected differences other than the relative emphasis on grammar (see also White *et al.*, 1981).

Finally, studies finding that training on oral cloze transfers to comprehension (e.g. Kennedy and Weener, 1973; Sampson *et al.*, 1982) have sometimes been cited as evidence that grammatical awareness facilitates reading. However, studies investigating cloze as an instructional procedure have yielded highly inconsistent results (see Sampson *et al.*, 1982). In addition, the cloze procedure requires attention to be focused on both semantic and grammatical constraints. Furthermore, studies finding positive effects of cloze have often emphasized comprehension monitoring strategies. In one study, the strategy of asking whether the completion made a 'good sentence' (Kennedy and Weener, 1973, p. 531) was suggested whenever children made inappropriate responses. Similarly, Sampson *et al.* encouraged children to consider both semantic and syntactic constraints when discussing answers.

The most parsimonious interpretation to emerge from this review of training studies is that all the experimental treatment programmes emphasized strategies of checking whether or not language makes sense, and of revising it until it does. These strategies teach children to process language actively and emphasize both comprehension and comprehension monitoring. It is doubtful whether these programmes can be accurately characterized as truly metalinguistic.

Future work using a training methodology must ensure that, while maintaining student interest, the training programme focuses primarily on grammatical awareness. Training studies should either minimize the teaching of semantic processing strategies or include control groups receiving comparable levels of active semantic processing training, including a comprehension strategy training group. This would allow an assessment of effects attributable to grammatical awareness training, over and above those due to training in active semantic processing. Without selective teaching, it is difficult to avoid the conclusion that, to date, grammatical awareness training programmes have achieved their effects through enhancing motivation and strategic comprehension processes (see Paris and Oka, 1989).

Conclusions

The studies reviewed so far have demonstrated a strong association between reading achievement and performance on experimental tests of grammatical awareness. However, most of the studies are susceptible to different interpretations. Most studies have used tests of grammatical awareness in which the experimental task may be solved using semantic strategies. In many studies it is also unclear whether poor readers' difficulties were independent of underlying delays in grammatical development. Finally, the review of training studies has indicated that most experimental training programmes have been confounded by teaching children semantically oriented comprehension monitoring strategies. The strongest evidence for the contribution of grammatical awareness to the reading process comes from the control 'sentence study' treatment group in White *et al.*'s training study, although this form of training was less effective than a more active and more semantically oriented training programme.

The sections that follow critically examine the possible contribution of grammatical awareness to children's reading, along with alternative views of the association between grammatical awareness and reading and suggestions for further research.

Grammatical awareness and reading comprehension

The argument that grammatical awareness contributes directly to reading comprehension has been made by a number of researchers (see p. 122 above).

Putting aside for the moment concerns regarding task validity, the available evidence indicates that children's performance on experimental grammatical awareness measures is indeed correlated with reading comprehension (Bowey,

1986b; Bialystok, 1988; Bowey and Patel, 1988; Tunmer *et al.*, 1988; Siegel and Ryan, 1989; Tunmer, 1989; Bentin *et al.*, 1990). However, these studies permit no causal inferences. Furthermore, since word recognition contributes directly to reading comprehension, and since scores on these two aspects of reading are strongly correlated, simple correlations between measures of grammatical awareness and reading comprehension do not necessarily imply that grammatical awareness contributes directly to reading comprehension. Rather, they simply substantiate the association between grammatical awareness and reading.

Siegel and Ryan (1989) presented children differing primarily in reading comprehension skill with a range of language tasks. In children aged from 6 to 8 years, good comprehenders did better than poor comprehenders on two grammatical error correction tasks, one task including four anomalous sentences and seventeen sentences with morphological errors (see Siegel and Ryan, 1988) and the other including twenty unspecified grammatical errors. These groups also differed on both the ITPA Grammatic Closure test (see p. 128 above) and an oral cloze test including content word deletions (see Siegel and Ryan, 1988). Thus, although Siegel and Ryan observed robust differences in error correction performance between good and poor comprehenders, it is not clear that the poor comprehenders' language processing difficulties were primarily metalinguistic in nature. Corresponding differences were not significant in children aged from 9 to 14 years.

Bentin *et al.* (1990) showed that 9-year-olds differing primarily in the ability to read meaningful materials also differed in their ability to correct grammatically deviant sentences. Both groups performed at ceiling on a sentence judgement task. However, the better readers scored higher on a grammatical error correction task. In this task, many of the grammatical errors involved word-order reversals but these involved minimal disruption to the semantic transparency of the sentence. Most errors involved either grammatical agreement or word-order errors involving a single function word. The two groups did not differ in their ability to exploit grammatical redundancy in a masked sentence repetition task, but the better readers were more likely to make errors that restored grammatical form than the poor readers, who were more likely to make 'random' errors. This finding appears to contradict Bowey's (1986a, 1986b) findings that good readers are less likely to correct deviant sentences spontaneously. However, in Bowey's task children are specifically told that all the sentences they will hear are deviant and asked to repeat them with the error intact. They are also permitted to ask for sentences to be repeated. Bentin *et al.* interpreted their results as indicating that the better comprehenders made more active use of their grammatical competence in both masked sentence repetition and error correction tasks. These findings are certainly consistent with Bowey's (1986a) in suggesting that grammatical correction performance is associated with both reading ability and ongoing language monitoring skills, but it is possible that they reflect other, more basic grammatical deficits.

Tunmer *et al.* (1988) reported a path analysis examining the possible contributions of word-order correction ability to first-grade reading achievement. Both phoneme segmentation and word-order correction performance contributed to reading comprehension performance only through their direct contribution to pseudoword reading performance. The direct paths to reading comprehension were not significant. A similar set of results was observed in a second study, using concurrent data from children tested at the end of their first school year (Tunmer, 1989). Here, word-order correction contributed directly to both pseudoword reading and to listening comprehension. Although the path from pseudoword reading to reading comprehension was significant, the path from listening comprehension to reading comprehension was not. Phoneme segmentation performance also contributed directly to pseudoword reading. In neither of these studies were data reported testing the goodness-of-fit of these *ad hoc* causal models (see Biddle and Martin, 1987) and the use of concurrent data is worrying, given the acknowledged possibility of reciprocal influence inflating correlations between metalinguistic and reading measures (Tunmer *et al.*, 1988, p. 140).

Tunmer (1989) reported predictive data showing a slightly different pattern of results. Word-order correction performance at the end of the first grade predicted second-grade pseudoword reading and listening comprehension. Both of the latter skills were directly linked to second-grade reading comprehension. Phonemic segmentation performance contributed directly to pseudoword reading skill. Again, no goodness-of-fit data were reported and no attempt was made to control for pre-existing differences in reading ability.

Although at face value the path analyses of the first-grade data sets reported by Tunmer and his colleagues (Tunmer *et al.*, 1988; Tunmer, 1989) suggest that word-order correction ability only influences reading comprehension through its direct effect on decoding skills, Tunmer's (1989) analysis of second-grade data suggests that it may also contribute through its direct effect on listening comprehension.

The different patterns of relationships obtained in predicting first- and second-grade reading comprehension suggest that we should interpret these analyses with some caution; it is unclear how reliable they are (see Biddle and Martin, 1987). However, the minor differences in the outcomes of these path analyses may be resolved if it is assumed that in the first grade children's reading comprehension primarily reflects word-level reading skills (see also Hoover and Gough, 1990; Vellutino and Scanlon, 1991). This assumption explains Tunmer's (1989) finding that listening comprehension did not contribute directly to reading comprehension in children tested at the end of the first grade but that it did contribute directly to reading comprehension when tested at the end of the second grade. It also explains why neither word-order correction performance nor the ability to detect inconsistencies within stories contributed directly to first-grade reading comprehension (Tunmer *et al.*, 1988).

With this assumption, Tunmer's (1989) observation that word-order correction performance contributes to listening comprehension becomes the key finding. This outcome is compatible with the view that grammatical awareness contributes directly to reading comprehension skills only if the word-order correction task is viewed as a valid index of grammatical awareness. If, as has been argued, this task is contaminated by semantic processing, Tunmer *et al.*'s results may actually reflect the contribution of semantic processing strategies. Furthermore, other accounts of the data are available. In particular, the analyses of the concurrent first- and the second-grade data sets are susceptible to Tunmer *et al.*'s own arguments concerning reciprocal causation causing inflated correlations among key variables.

Little insight into the contribution of grammatical awareness to reading comprehension can be gained from the training literature. As we saw earlier, the results from White *et al.*'s control condition incorporating traditional grammatical training provides the strongest evidence for the contribution of grammatical awareness to reading comprehension. This programme appeared to boost both sentence anagram and written cloze performance (White *et al.*, 1981). As concluded earlier, the interpretation of the training studies is compromised by their teaching of active semantic processing strategies.

Few studies have directly examined the linkage between grammatical awareness and process variables in reading. Bowey (1986b) found that, with PPVT-R vocabulary age effects statistically controlled, performance on a grammatical error correction test[5] was correlated with the rate of contextually obligatory oral reading self-corrections, $r(46) = 0.53$), but not with the rate of contextually optional oral reading self-corrections, ($r(46) = 0.08$), in a sample of fourth- and fifth-grade children. Although her data are consistent with the view that grammatical awareness contributes to comprehension monitoring skills, it is also possible that the association between grammatical error correction and ongoing comprehension processes reflects common variation between grammatical error correction and semantic error correction abilities. Only the former should be interpreted as metalinguistic; the latter does not depart from the normal use of language to comprehend messages. Furthermore, no causal conclusions can be drawn from her study.

Although the available evidence is consistent with the hypothesis that grammatical awareness contributes directly to comprehension processes, little of this evidence is unambiguous. The assessment of grammatical awareness has been contaminated by semantic processing, and grammatical awareness training programmes have typically taught active semantic processing strategies. There is a strong need for further research investigating specific links between grammatical awareness and comprehension process variables. Predictive work needs more careful selection of instruments for assessing both grammatical awareness and grammatical development, and care needs to be taken to control for the effects of entering reading achievement. More careful design and reporting of path analytic studies is also required (see Biddle and Martin, 1987).

Grammatical awareness and word recognition

Tunmer *et al.* (1988) argued that grammatical awareness contributes to word recognition. Following Jorm and Share (1983), they noted that beginning readers frequently rely on contextual information to provide information and feedback concerning their interpretation of unfamiliar words, and argued that grammatical awareness contributes to word recognition skills through its effect on comprehension monitoring processes. This is an interesting proposal, but in assessing it care needs to be taken to ensure that hypothesized effects can be unambiguously attributed to grammatical awareness. The purely grammatical cues present in *Jabberwocky* ('Twas brillig and the slithy toves did gyre and gimble in the wabe') do not provide much assistance in decoding component words!

Tunmer *et al.* (1988) viewed as evidence for their proposal the direct predictive association observed between word-order correction performance and both word recognition and pseudoword reading (Tunmer *et al.*, 1988) and the direct path between word-order correction performance and pseudoword reading in path analyses of both concurrent and predictive data sets (Tunmer *et al.*, 1988; Tunmer, 1989). However, there are several difficulties with the empirical evidence adduced by Tunmer and his colleagues. These primarily involve the use of the word-order correction task and problematic aspects of the path analyses, noted earlier.

Nor do the available training studies shed much light on the potential contribution of grammatical awareness to word recognition. The only study to examine this issue is Milton's (1990). Her training programme enhanced word recognition performance in beginning readers, although the effects were significant only in relation to one of the two control groups, and the degree to which her programme selectively taught grammatical awareness is questionable (see p. 137 above). Her programme enhanced comprehension skills and may thereby have increased word recognition skills through children's use of contextual information to check their reading of unfamiliar words, much as Tunmer has argued. The dubious link in this chain of argument is that these effects reflect the contribution of grammatical awareness.

Clearly, further work is required to test the hypothesis that grammatical awareness contributes to word recognition. Future research using either predictive or training methodologies should attend to the suggestions outlined in the preceding sections. To eliminate alternative accounts, it may also be worth checking whether grammatical awareness training transfers to phonological awareness.

Alternative accounts

This section briefly outlines two novel, alternative accounts of the association between grammatical awareness and beginning reading achievement. Both are based on evidence of strong correlations among experimental metalinguistic tasks from different domains (e.g. Hakes, 1980; Smith and Tager-Flusberg, 1983; Bowey and Patel, 1988; Fowler, 1988; Tunmer *et al.*, 1988; Ricciardelli *et al.*, 1989; Tunmer, 1989; Bryant *et al.*, 1990; Chaney, 1992) and Hakes's (1980) finding of a single underlying ability among experimental metalinguistic and concrete operations tasks. Both accounts would predict that any experimental metalinguistic task that was strongly correlated with other metalinguistic tasks would show a strong predictive relationship with reading, but that effective training on the aspect of metalinguistic performance assessed by that task would not necessarily transfer to reading.

The first alternative account suggests that the apparent strength of the association between grammatical awareness and reading at least partly reflects the fact that experimental grammatical awareness tasks typically assess a range of other abilities in addition to grammatical awareness. It was argued earlier that experimental metalinguistic tasks inevitably incorporate a cognitive control component; performance on experimental metalinguistic tasks reflects the extension of cognitive control to the metalinguistic domain (see also Ryan and Ledger, 1984; Bialystok and Ryan, 1985; Bowey, 1988). This achievement may be significant primarily because skills that are under attentional control are probably more amenable to instruction. In addition, though, experimental metalinguistic tasks may be powerful predictors of reading precisely because they usually reflect several component abilities, all of which may independently contribute both directly and indirectly to reading achievement. This may be especially true of experimental tests of grammatical awareness, which have typically involved cognitive control, verbal working memory, active semantic processing strategies and sometimes fairly high levels of grammatical proficiency. Performance on some grammatical awareness tests may primarily reflect metacognitive skills rather than metalinguistic skills. This may be especially true where grammatical awareness tasks include a strong semantic processing component.

Indirect support for this account comes from Tunmer *et al.*'s (1988) finding that school entrants' operativity contributed directly to performance on both a composite variable, comprising phoneme segmentation, word-order correction and the detection of inconsistencies, and a Concepts about Print test (Clay, 1979), measuring children's knowledge of the reading task and early reading ability.

A second alternative account would suggest that grammatical awareness predicts reading development at least partly because it forms part of an underlying metalinguistic orientation towards language. Performance on a range of metalinguistic tasks is strongly intercorrelated in beginning readers (e.g. Bowey and Patel, 1988; Fowler, 1988; Tunmer *et al.*, 1988; Ricciardelli *et al.*, 1989; Tunmer, 1989). Furthermore, there is some, admittedly controversial, evidence that children differ in the extent to which they adopt an analytic approach to language acquisition (e.g. Bowerman, 1982). It is possible that children who have developed a more metalinguistic orientation towards language in general are more likely to understand both the reading task and the language of reading instruction (see also Downing, 1984; Bialystok and Ryan, 1985).

Conclusions

This chapter has presented a critique of research investigating the link between grammatical awareness and children's reading. The stage for this critique has been set by the strong *prima facie* case established primarily by Tunmer and his colleagues for the contribution of grammatical awareness to beginning reading achievement.

Although available evidence is certainly consistent with the view that grammatical awareness does play a role in early reading development, stronger evidence is required before we as researchers can advocate that this aspect of metalinguistic ability be incorporated into beginning reading programmes with the same degree of confidence that we feel in recommending that phonological awareness be taught in reading readiness and early reading instruction. The bottom line is this: Can we at this point recommend that children whose reading instruction time is precious be systematically engaged in activities that focus primarily on monitoring grammatical acceptability? Or would we feel more confident in suggesting that children be taught actively to monitor comprehension?

Throughout this chapter, a conservative approach has been adopted to the interpretation of performance on experimental grammatical awareness tasks. Tasks like word-order correction and oral cloze do reflect grammatical awareness, in that grammatical considerations are involved. However, they are impure measures of grammatical awareness. Successful performance on these tasks can be accomplished largely through the use of semantic processing strategies which may contribute to both comprehension and word recognition processes. It is quite likely that tasks like word-order correction and oral cloze tap children's ability to engage in deep and flexible semantic processing that typically both relies on and itself enhances active comprehension-monitoring strategies. Such active language processing abilities are not necessarily assessed by measures such as PPVT-R receptive vocabulary that are typically used to estimate and control for the effects of general language ability or verbal intelligence. PPVT-R vocabulary age is not reliably associated with early reading achievement (Bowey and Patel, 1988; Bowey and Francis, 1991; see also Tunmer *et al.*, 1988, p. 151).

The putative contribution of grammatical awareness to the process of learning to read may actually reflect the contribution of other abilities, particularly both cognitive control and active semantic processing strategies. It may even reflect the fact that children who do well on experimental measures of grammatical awareness may have developed a more metalinguistic orientation to language in general, which enhances their understanding of both the reading task and reading instruction.

In providing alternative accounts of previous work, the intention of the current chapter has been to provide a methodological discussion designed to stimulate a 'second generation' of research which will allow a more definitive evaluation of the role of grammatical awareness in the process of learning to read. Future work in this area must attend more closely to the assessment of grammatical awareness, with the aim of minimizing the contribution of extraneous abilities.

Notes

1. In Danish, *lille* is not used with plural nouns.
2. This definition can be contrasted with an over-inclusive definition of syntactic awareness as 'the ability to understand the syntax of the language' (Siegel, in press). This definition would include under the rubric of grammatical awareness any task assessing grammatical development. In other papers, Siegel interprets error correction and oral cloze tasks as 'language tasks' (Siegel and Ryan, 1989), tests of 'understanding of syntax' (Siegel, 1988) and 'syntactic skill' (So and Siegel, 1992).
3. Tunmer *et al.* (1988) reported path analyses suggesting that operativity contributes indirectly to both pseudoword reading and reading comprehension through its direct contribution to a composite metalinguistic ability measure and children's concepts about print. Receptive vocabulary appeared not to contribute to any other skills.
4. White *et al.* (1981) described the control training programme as follows: 'The lessons entailed a variety of sentence patterning tasks. One type of sentence task consisted of practice in identifying unpunctuated sentences as either statements, questions, or commands. A second type required that participants match noun phrases and verb phrases. Replacement of nouns with appropriate pronouns was another sentence study activity, as was practice underlining prepositional phrases indicating place. In the final activity of this program, participants combined simple sentences with the conjunction *and* and deleted repeated information. Each lesson began with teacher explanation and modeling and continued with student worksheet activities' (1981, p. 699). Aspects of the latter activities involve semantic processing.
5. In Bowey's (1986b) grammatical error correction task, only 5 of the 30 test items involved word-order corrections (*The teacher the story read to the children*; *Peter goes sometimes to church*; *What the girls are doing?*; *The girl lost her money who lives across the road*; *I wonder how old is he*). The latter three items were based on grammatical errors observed in younger children's spontaneous speech.

References

Backman, J.E., Mamen, M. and Ferguson, H.B. (1984), 'Reading level design: conceptual and methodological issues in reading research', *Psychological Bulletin*, *96*, 560–8.

Baker, H.J. and Leland, B. (1959), *Detroit Tests of Learning Aptitude*, Indianapolis, IA: Bobbs-Merrill.

Bentin, S., Deutsch, A. and Liberman, I.Y. (1990), 'Syntactic competence and reading ability in children', *Journal of Experimental Child Psychology*, *48*, 147–72.

Berry, M. and Talbott, W. (1966), *Berry–Talbott Language Tests*. Vol. 1: *Comprehension of Grammar*, Rockford, IL.

Bialystok, E. (1988), 'Aspects of linguistic awareness in reading comprehension', *Applied Psycholinguistics*, *9*, 123–39.

Bialystok, E. and Ryan, E.B. (1985), 'Toward a definition of metalinguistic skill', *Merrill-Palmer Quarterly*, *31*, 229–51.

Biddle, B.J. and Martin, M.M. (1987), 'Causality, confirmation, credulity and structural equation modeling', *Child Development*, *58*, 4–17.

Bohannon, J.N. (1975), 'The relationship between syntax discrimination and sentence imitation in children', *Child Development*, *46*, 444–51.

Bowerman, M. (1982), 'Reorganizational processes in lexical and semantic development'. In E. Wanner and L.R. Gleitman (eds.) *Language Acquisition: The state of the art*, Cambridge: Cambridge University Press, pp. 319–46.

Bowey, J. A. (1986a), 'Syntactic awareness and verbal performance from preschool to fifth grade', *Journal of Psycholinguistic Research*, *15*, 285–306.

Bowey, J.A. (1986b), 'Syntactic awareness in relation to reading skill and ongoing comprehension monitoring', *Journal of Experimental Child Psychology*, *41*, 282–99.

Bowey, J.A. (1988), *Metalinguistic Functioning in Children*, Geelong, Australia: Deakin University Press.

Bowey, J.A. (1990), 'On *Rhyme, language and children's reading*', *Applied Psycholinguistics*, *11*, 439–48.

Bowey, J.A., Cain, M.T. and Ryan, S.M. (1992), 'A reading-level design study of phonological skills underlying fourth-grade children's word reading difficulties', *Child Development*, *63*, 999–1011.

Bowey, J.A. and Francis, J. (1991), 'Phonological analysis as a function of age and exposure to reading instruction', *Applied Psycholinguistics*, *12*, 91–121.

Bowey, J.A. and Patel, R.K. (1988), 'Metalinguistic ability and early reading achievement', *Applied Psycholinguistics*, *9*, 367–83.

Bowey, J.A., Tunmer, W.E. and Pratt, C. (1984), 'Development of children's understanding of the metalinguistic term *word*', *Journal of Educational Psychology*, *76*, 500–12.

Bradley, L. and Bryant, P.E. (1978), 'Difficulties in auditory organisation as a possible cause of reading backwardness', *Nature*, *271*, 746–7.

Bryant, P., MacLean, M. and Bradley, L. (1990), 'Rhyme, language and children's reading', *Applied Psycholinguistics*, *11*, 237–52.

Chaney, C. (1992), 'Language development, metalinguistic skills, and print awareness in 3-year-old children', *Applied Psycholinguistics*, *13*, 485–514.

Clark, E.V. (1978), 'Awareness of language: some evidence from what children say and do'. In A. Sinclair, J.R. Jarvella and W.J.M. Levelt (eds.) *The Child's Conception of Language*, New York: Springer, pp. 17–43.

Clark, E. and Anderson, E.S. (1979), 'Spontaneous repairs: awareness in the process of acquiring a language', *Papers and Reports on Child Language Development*, *16*, 1–12.

Clay, M. (1979), *The Early Detection of Reading Difficulties*, Auckland: Heinemann.

Downing, J. (1984), 'Task awareness in the development of reading skill'. In J. Downing and R. Valtin (eds.) *Language Awareness and Learning to Read*, New York: Springer-Verlag, pp. 27–55.

Ehri, L.C. (1979), 'Linguistic insight: threshold of reading acquisition'. In T.G. Waller and G.E. MacKinnon (eds.) *Reading Research: Advances in theory and practice*, Vol. 1, New York: Academic Press, pp. 63–114.

Flavell, J.H. (1985), *Cognitive Development*, 2nd edition, Englewood Cliffs, NJ: Prentice-Hall.

Fowler, A.E. (1988), 'Grammaticality judgements and reading skill in grade 2', *Annals of Dyslexia*, *38*, 73–94.

Gleitman, L.R., Gleitman, H. and Shipley, E.F. (1972), 'The emergence of the child as a grammarian', *Cognition*, *1*, 137–64.

Grieve, R. (1990), 'Children's awareness'. In R. Grieve and M. Hughes (eds.) *Understanding Children: Essays in honour of Margaret Donaldson*, Oxford: Basil Blackwell, pp. 156–71.

Hakes, D.T. (1980), *The Development of Metalinguistic Abilities in Children*, New York: Springer.

Hansen, J. and Bowey, J.A. (1994), 'Phonological analysis skills, verbal working memory and reading ability in second-grade children', *Child Development*, 65, 938–50.

Hoover, W. and Gough, P. (1990), 'The simple view of reading', *Reading and Writing*, 2, 127–60.

Jesperson, O. (1922), *Language: Its nature, development and origin*, London: Allen & Unwin.

Jorm, A.F. and Share, D.L. (1983), 'Phonological recoding and reading acquisition', *Applied Psycholinguistics*, 4, 103–47.

Kennedy, D.K. and Weener, P. (1973), 'Visual and auditory training with the cloze procedure to improve reading and listening comprehension', *Reading Research Quarterly*, 8, 524–43.

Kirk, S., McCarthy, J. and Kirk, W. (1968), *The Illinois Test of Psycholinguistic Abilities*, (2nd edition), Urbana, IL: University of Illinois Press.

Lee, L. and Canter, S. (1971), 'Developmental sentence scoring: a clinical procedure for estimating syntactic development in children's spontaneous speech', *Journal of Speech and Hearing Disorders*, 36, 315–40.

Leopold, W.F. (1949), *Speech Development of a Bilingual Child*, Vol. 4, Evanston, IL: Northwestern University Press.

Levelt, W.J.M., van Gent, J.A.W.M., Haans, A.F.J. and Meijers, A.J.A. (1977), 'Grammaticality, paraphrase and imagery'. In S. Greenbaum (ed.) *Acceptability in Language*. The Hague: Mouton.

Lundberg, I. (1978), 'Aspects of linguistic awareness related to reading'. In A. Sinclair, J.R. Jarvella and W.J.M. Levelt, (eds.) *The Child's Conception of Language*, New York: Springer, pp. 83–96.

MacLean, M., Bryant, P. and Bradley, L. (1987), 'Rhymes, nursery rhymes and reading in early childhood', *Merrill-Palmer Quarterly*, 33, 255–81.

McLeod, J. (1967), *Gap Reading Comprehension Manual*. 2nd edition, Melbourne: Heinemann.

McNinch, G. (1974), 'Awareness of aural and visual word boundary within a sample of first graders', *Perceptual and Motor Skills*, 38, 1127–34.

Milton, M.J. (1990), *The Development of Syntactic Awareness in Year One Children and its Relationship to Reading*, unpublished DEd thesis, University of Western Australia.

Paris, S.G. and Oka, E.R. (1989), 'Strategies for comprehending text and coping with reading difficulties', *Learning Disability Quarterly*, 12, 32–42.

Pratt, C., Tunmer, W.E. and Bowey, J.A. (1984), 'Children's capacity to correct grammatical violations in sentences', *Journal of Child Language*, 11, 129–41.

Rack, J.P., Snowling, M.J. and Olson, R.K. (1992), 'The nonword reading deficit in developmental dyslexia: a review', *Reading Research Quarterly*, 27, 28–53.

Reynell, J.K. and Huntley, M. (1987), *Developmental Language Scales*, 2nd edition. East Windsor: NFER-Nelson.

Ricciardelli, L.A., Rump, E.E. and Proske, I. (1989), 'Metalinguistic awareness as a unitary construct and its relation to general intellectual development', *Rassegna Italiana di Linguistica Applicata*, 21, 19–40.

Ryan, E.B. and Ledger, G.W. (1979), 'Grammaticality judgments, sentence repetitions, and sentence corrections of children learning to read', *International Journal of Psycholinguistics*, 6, 23–40.

Ryan, E.B. and Ledger, G.W. (1984), 'Learning to attend to sentence structure: links between metalinguistic development and reading'. In J. Downing and R. Valtin (eds.) *Language Awareness and Learning to Read*, New York: Berlin, pp. 149–71.

Sampson, M.R., Valmont, W.J. and van Allen, R. (1982), 'The effects of instructional cloze on the comprehension, vocabulary, and divergent production of third-grade students', *Reading Research Quarterly*, *17*, 389–99.

Savic, S. (1982), *How Twins Learn to Talk*. New York: Academic Press.

Schlesinger, I.M. (1968), *Sentence Structure and the Reading Process*, The Hague: Mouton.

Shankweiler, D. and Crain, S. (1986), 'Language mechanisms and reading disorder: a modular approach', *Cognition*, *24*, 139–68.

Siegel, L.S. (1988), 'Evidence that IQ scores are irrelevant to the definition and analysis of reading disability', *Canadian Journal of Psychology*, *42*, 201–15.

Siegel, L.S. (in press), 'The cognitive basis of dyslexia'. In R. Pasnak and M.L. Howe (eds.) *Emerging Theories in Cognitive Development*, Vol. 2, New York: Springer-Verlag.

Siegel, L.S. and Ryan, E.B. (1988), 'Development of grammatical-sensitivity, phonological, and short-term memory skills in normally achieving and learning disabled children', *Developmental Psychology*, *24*, 28–37.

Siegel, L.S. and Ryan, E.B. (1989), 'Subtypes of developmental dyslexia: the influence of definitional variables', *Reading and Writing*, *2*, 257–87.

Sinclair, A., Jarvella, J.R. and Levelt, W.J.M. (eds.) (1978), *The Child's Conception of Language*, New York: Springer.

Slobin, D.I. (1978), 'A case study of early language awareness'. In A. Sinclair, J.R. Jarvella and W.J.M. Levelt, (eds.) *The Child's Conception of Language*, New York: Springer, pp. 845–54.

Smith, C.L. and Tager-Flusberg, H. (1982), 'Metalinguistic awareness and language development', *Journal of Experimental Child Psychology*, *34*, 449–68.

So, D. and Siegel, L.S. (1992), *Learning to Read Chinese: Semantic, syntactic, phonological and short-term memory skills in normally achieving and poor Chinese readers*, unpublished paper, Ontario Institute for Studies in Education.

Tunmer, W.E. (1989), 'The role of language-related factors in reading disability'. In D. Shankweiler and I. Liberman (eds.) *Phonology and Reading Disability: Solving the reading puzzle*, Ann Arbor, MI: University of Michigan Press, pp. 91–131.

Tunmer, W.E. and Bowey, J.A. (1984), 'Metalinguistic awareness and reading acquisition'. In W.E. Tunmer, C. Pratt and M.L. Herriman (eds.) *Metalinguistic Awareness in Children*, New York: Springer-Verlag, pp. 144–68.

Tunmer, W.E. and Herriman, M.L. (1984), 'The development of metalinguistic awareness: a conceptual overview'. In W.E. Tunmer, C. Pratt and M.L. Herriman (eds.) *Metalinguistic Awareness in Children*, New York: Springer-Verlag, pp. 12–35.

Tunmer, W.E., Herriman, M.L. and Nesdale, A.R. (1988), 'Metalinguistic abilities and beginning reading', *Reading Research Quarterly*, *23*, 134–58.

Tunmer, W.E., Pratt, C. and Herriman, M.L. (eds.) (1984), *Metalinguistic Awareness in Children*, New York: Springer-Verlag.

Tunmer, W.E., Nesdale, A.R. and Wright, A.D. (1987), 'Syntactic awareness and reading acquisition', *British Journal of Developmental Psychology*, *5*, 25–34.

Vellutino, F.R. and Scanlon, D.M. (1991),'The preeminence of phonologically based skills in learning to read'. In S.A. Brady and D.P. Shankweiler (eds.) *Phonological Processes in Literacy: A tribute to Isabelle Y. Liberman*, Hillsdale, NJ: Lawrence Erlbaum, pp. 237–52.

Vogel, S.A. (1975), *Syntactic Abilities in Normal and Dyslexic Children*, Baltimore, MD: University Park Press.

Weaver, P.A. (1979), 'Improving reading comprehension: effects of sentence organization instruction', *Reading Research Quarterly*, *15*, 129–46.

Wechsler, D. (1949), *Wechsler Intelligence Scale for Children*, New York: The Psychological Corporation.

Wechsler, D. (1967), Manual for the Wechsler Preschool and Primary Scale of Intelligence, Cleveland, OH: The Psychological Corporation.
White, C.V., Pascarella, E.T. and Pflaum, S.W. (1981), 'Effects of training in sentence construction on the comprehension of learning disabled children', Journal of Educational Psychology, 73, 697–704.
Willows, D.M. and Ryan, E.B. (1986), 'The development of grammatical sensitivity and its relationship to early reading achievement', Reading Research Quarterly, 21, 253–66.
Woodcock, R.W. (1987), Woodcock Reading Mastery Tests, 2nd edition, Circle Pines, MN: American Guidance Service.

8

Remediation of reading problems: effects of training at word and subword levels

Wim H.J. Van Bon
Department of Special Education, University of Nijmegen

In trying to create order in the accumulating number of empirical studies on the remediation of reading problems, different approaches can be taken. Studies can be classified according to the type of instruction or training used, according to the reading level, the amount of reading backwardness, or the types of reading problem of their subjects. Ideally, one would prefer to combine these different approaches, but the space limits of this chapter necessitate making a choice. The approach I have adopted here is that of ordering the studies according to the linguistic level the remedial intervention was intended to influence and the linguistic units that were studied in effect evaluation. The reason for choosing this point of view is that most reading problems probably are rooted in defective language competence. If remedial reading instruction at a certain linguistic level gives better results, then this would suggest that language (in)competence at that level is important for the explanation of reading problems.

The review is restricted to studies at the word and subword levels, because the basic reading problems seem to reside in context-free word reading skill (e.g. Stanovich, 1986; Siegel and Faux, 1989). In successive sections, training studies with poor readers are discussed that involve decoding units of increasing size: grapheme–phoneme correspondences, sub-syllabic units consisting of more than one grapheme/phoneme, syllables and morphemes, and whole words. First, however, is a review of studies that aimed at improving the basic phonological skills of phonemic segmentation and speech–sound discrimination.

Much attention and space is devoted in this chapter to Dutch studies. This is deliberate, since some of these studies have appeared only as unpublished

I am grateful to Rob Schreuder, Jan ter Laak and Rebecca Treiman for their comments on an earlier draft of this chapter.

doctoral dissertations and others to date have not been published in English. This review offers an opportunity to bring them to the attention of a larger public.

Phonological skills

There is little doubt that reading ability is closely related to the awareness that words can be segmented into lower-level components and to segment manipulation skills. More specifically, children with reading problems have lower phonological awareness skills than normal readers of the same age or younger children of the same reading level (e.g. Liberman, 1973; Fox and Routh, 1976, 1983, 1984; Golinkoff, 1978; Tornéus, 1984; Tunmer and Nesdale, 1985; Juel *et al.*, 1986). Training studies have played an important role in verifying hypotheses about the causal relations underlying the correlation between one and the other. If phonological awareness training at pre-reading stages reduced the incidence of reading problems, or if such training remediated existing reading problems, this would corroborate the case for a phonemic awareness deficit lying at the basis of reading problems. What is more, if phonological awareness deficits are at the core of reading problems, timely intervention would prevent the gap between poor and normal readers from widening and prevent this specific deficit from becoming a generalized learning disability (Stanovich, 1986).

One way of proving the prophylactic effects of phonemic awareness training would be to show that after such training the lower end of the reading skill distribution contains fewer cases than would be found under control conditions. Studies of the effects of phonological awareness training in pre-schoolers on their later reading development, however, generally report only differences between group means (e.g. Fox and Routh, 1975, 1976; Treiman and Baron, 1983; Lundberg *et al.*, 1985; Ball and Blachman, 1991; Cunningham, 1991). Lundberg *et al.* (1988), for example, revealed higher group reading means in first- and second-grade children who at pre-school had undergone an extensive meta-linguistic training programme, than for children in the no training control condition. Such a finding is a necessary condition, but not sufficient evidence for phonological awareness training to have the supposed prophylactic effect. It is possible that the facilitating effects of training apply less to the lower region of the reading competence distribution and more to children who are already well equipped for entering reading education. Lie (1991), however, found an interaction of pre-reading intelligence and segmentation training on reading scores, with low-ability students profiting most. This provides evidence against such a Matthew ('the rich get richer') effect (cf. Stanovich, 1986).

Another way of testing for preventive effects would be to adminster phonemic awareness training programmes to pre-schoolers who are at risk of becoming reading disabled. That was the strategy taken by Bradley and Bryant (1983, 1985). They used odd word out tasks to determine whether children were able to categorize words according to their phonemic composition. Children scoring extremely low on these sound categorizing tasks were selected for training. As it was found in the same study that pre-school categorization scores are highly correlated with later reading and spelling scores, one might infer that the selected children were likely to become poor readers. Those among the selected who received sound categorization training over two years tended to be better readers and spellers than the children in a conceptual categorization control and in a no training control group, but the difference was not significant. The children who received training in which plastic letters were used in sound categorizing scored significantly better in reading, and particularly in spelling, than the children in the control groups. From this the authors concluded that sound categorization training is even more effective if it is taught with explicit connection to the alphabet.

However, because the post-test differences between the sound categoriz-ation only and the control conditions were not significant, the claim is at least equally plausible that sound categorization *only* helps if it is taught in connection with the alphabet. But even significant progress of the children in this condition would not constitute conclusive evidence for the prophylactic effects of this type of phonemic awareness training. Training started in the pre-reading stage and continued into the reading instruction stage. As effects were not evaluated until the subjects were 8 years of age on the average, any positive effects need not stem from training in the pre-reading stage, but may have originated in the period in which categorization training went together with learning to read and write.

Objections such as this show that it has not been demonstrated beyond doubt that reading problems can be prevented by preceding phonemic awareness instruction. Does phonemic segmentation training remediate existing reading problems? Williams (1980) suggests beneficial effects from including explicit segmentation and blending exercises in reading instruction for learning disabled children. The extensive training programme, however, differed also by other features – explicit teaching of phoneme–grapheme correspondence rules, for example – from the forms of instruction in the no treatment control classes. Not only those additional training elements, but also general effects of the experimental design, such as a Hawthorne effect on teachers or pupils, cannot be excluded as determinants of the effectiveness.

Vellutino and Scanlon (1986) designed an experiment to investigate whether a phonics oriented method for teaching word identification leads to reading strategies that differ from those acquired under a whole word regime. Their study is of relevance here because Vellutino and Scanlon explicitly designated their phonics condition as a phonemic segmentation training that was intended to foster an analytic attitude in word processing. After an initial stage, which differed according to the experimental condition, students learned to recognize a set of pseudowords written in a novel alphabet. The (regular) letter–sound associations were not taught explicitly, but had to be inferred by the students. In a transfer stage students were required to read new pseudowords which had not been trained before. The important finding is that students who received only phonemic segmentation training performed considerably better on the transfer task than those who received nonsense word familiarization training as a simulation of a whole word approach. The segmentation training apparently enhanced detection and application of letter–sound correspondence rules. This seems to apply to poor readers and normal readers alike, to second-grade as well as to sixth-grade pupils.

The phonics condition, however, went further than mere phonemic segmentation training. Using spoken and written words, subjects 'were taught to detect letter–sound correspondences' (Vellutino and Scanlon, 1986, p. 147). Therefore, the benefit need not be associated with the segmentation component of the phonics condition, but could possibly result from the use of letters, perhaps in conjunction with the segmentation training. Such an interpretation is suggested by the outcome of the Bradley and Bryant (1983, 1985) study.

In order to investigate possible beneficial effects of visual support in phonemic awareness training Kerstholt *et al.* (1993) selected children who were backward in reading and spelling and who were also poor at segmenting monosyllabic words. Three computer-supported training strategies were compared: the standard type of word-splitting exercise in which no visual support is given, and two types of exercise giving visual support. In one of these, the number of squares in a diagram (cf. Elkonin, 1973) indicated the number of segments that were to be produced. After naming a segment, the subject clicked on the leftmost square, which thereupon was replaced by the grapheme for the segment that should have been named. The remaining number of squares indicated the number of segments left to be produced. In the other visual support condition no such information about the number of phonemes was given beforehand. The screen just contained one square that had to be clicked on by the child when naming the next segment, thereby producing the successive graphemes of the word. No differential effects of training procedures were found. However, pooling across training groups' segmentation test scores improved from pre- to post-test, and changes in segmentation test scores were moderately correlated to changes in reading and spelling ($r = 0.40$ and 0.50, respectively). Although this outcome fits with the hypothesis that poor reading and spelling skill improves through segmentation training, it does not provide definitive proof.

An experimental design which is more adequate for showing remedial effects of phonemic awareness training is that of Sanchez and Rueda (1991). Subjects reading at least 1½ years below grade level received one of two types of phonemic awareness training or a perceptual-motor control training. Even though segmentation scores in the two experimental groups eventually reached levels similar to those of normal readers, reading gain scores were not significant; spelling scores, however, improved significantly from pre- to post-test. That there is a marked difference in effects of segmentation training on reading and spelling is not surprising. Phonemic segmentation has a much more prominent place in spelling models than in reading models (van Bon and Duighuisen, 1993).

Nevertheless, the between-training groups' *F* ratio for the critical reading test was well above unity, and probably was not significant because of the small number of subjects in the study. Although neither study provides decisive evidence for remedial effects of phonemic awareness training in case of reading problems, they do warrant further investigation.

Hurford (1990) suggested that the poor phonemic segmentation performance of backward readers is caused by their poor phonemic discrimination skill. He tested this hypothesis by training reading-disabled second- and third-grade children in phonemic discrimination. Their phonemic segmentation performance indeed improved, whereas the segmentation performance of the reading-disabled children in the no training control condition remained at the pre-test level. After training, the third-grade pupils even performed at the level of their non-disabled peers. Because reading performance after training was not examined it is not certain whether the hypothesized causal chain linking phonemic discrimination to reading was in fact present. Moreover, Hurford employed a very complex phoneme discrimination task in which children were required to judge whether two pairs of syllables presented aurally were the same or different (e.g. is /*di*/–/ *gi*/ the same as /*gi*/–/*gi*/?). This task poses heavy demands on handling verbal material in working memory, as does the phonemic segmentation task used (e.g. 'Say /*bug*/ without the /*b*/ sound'), and likewise reading. A rival explanation for training effects on phonemic segmentation – and perhaps on reading – is therefore that this discrimination training made the children more adroit in manipulating speech sounds in tasks with heavy working memory load.

Whereas the evidence that problems involving phonemic awareness are at the basis of developmental reading problems is substantive, the evidence from training studies, although in accordance with the hypothesized prophylactic and remedial effects, does not constitute proof. One of the questions that should be answered in future research is whether phonemic awareness training should better be incorporated in ongoing reading and spelling instruction, or whether it should be given in isolation. There is some evidence that linking awareness training to reading instruction is more profitable than independent training (e.g. Bradley and Bryant, 1983, 1985; Cunningham, 1991). As we have seen, Vellutino and Scanlon's (1986) results can be interpreted in the same vein. Studies by Kerstholt *et al.* (referred to above), and also with pre-reading children as the subjects, however, suggest that training phonemic segmentation using letters does not lead to better effects than independent training. Resolution of this empirical paradox is important for designing preventive and remedial programmes.

Grapheme–phoneme correspondences

Learning grapheme–phoneme correspondence rules implicates the phonological skills that were discussed in the previous section, but as they require other skills as well, they will be discussed separately here.

Letter–sound correspondences have long been thought to be critical in reading disabilities. According to one opinion, poor speech sound discrimination is fundamental to reading problems (e.g. Johnson and Myklebust, 1967); another point of view is that letter discrimination causes the problems (e.g. Bender, 1957). Both points of view lead to the expectation that reading problems would be alleviated by the discrimination learning that is involved in letter–sound training. In fact, such an orientation has led many to advocate phonics as an effective remedy. Another argument for adopting phonics instruction is that knowledge of grapheme–phoneme correspondences along with segmentation ability are among the basic requirements for learning to read (Snowling, 1987). As Chall's (1983) review suggests, this is not without empirical support. Research favours code-oriented programmes for initiation into reading, and direct code teaching rather than indirect phonics programmes in which the students themselves are supposed to infer the 'reading rules' from whole words.

As disabled readers have problems acquiring grapheme–phoneme correspondences (e.g. Siegel and Faux, 1989), it is surprising that no studies could be located in which the effects of isolated letter–sound conversion accuracy or speed training on reading performance were examined. Positive effects of such training on reading performance, apart from its practical relevance, would provide a strong argument for the causal role of letter–sound conversion problems in reading disabilities. Studies on the effect of letter–sound conversion training also included training of other reading and spelling skills which may explain any positive results. Williams (1980), for instance, examined the effects of code emphasis instruction on the decoding ability of learning disabled students. The instruction was added to their regular, eclectic basal reading programme. Beneficial effects were indeed found, but, as we have seen above, the programme comprised other elements too, such as segmentation and blending exercises. The studies by Lovett and her associates (Lovett *et al.*, 1988, 1989, 1990) used decoding training which emphasized grapheme–phoneme conversion learning, but also included other decoding and word recognition skills as well as spelling skills. Lovett *et al.* (1990), for example, taught some disabled readers to read orthographically regular words by whole word methods, and others by training the constituent grapheme–phoneme correspondences; both groups learned exception words using whole word methods. In the decoding-oriented training condition, for each regular word that was incorrectly read on an earlier occasion, the child first learned the sound values of its constituent graphemes. Next, the word was sounded out, one grapheme at a time, until the word was accurately blended. Context-dependent and morphemic reading rules relevant for the word in question were explicitly stated and rehearsed. Finally, the student was required to read words that rhymed with the one under study and had been taught earlier. The words that had been studied in this way were reviewed and practised repeatedly. The children in this condition practised spelling regular words that they misspelled on an initial attempt by first segmenting them into their component speech sounds, using the correctly written word as a model. If necessary, the relevant spelling rules were explained. Finally, the child wrote the word from memory and checked the result against the model.

As will be apparent, aside from correspondence rule learning the decoding-oriented instruction thus also included blending and segmentation training. Moreover, as the words which the children learned to read and to write stemmed from the same limited set, the chances are high that the same words were used in reading and in spelling instruction. Thereby, word spelling knowledge probably supported reading, and vice versa. Lastly, the instructional procedure can be assumed to involve a certain amount of word specific learning because of the repeated word reviewing.

After thirty-five 1-hour sessions, both the decoding and the whole word groups achieved considerably better than a problem-solving and study skill training control group. Both groups made significant gains in the recognition and spelling of the words that had been taught. Transfer was found in the spelling of words that rhyme with and are spelled similarly to words that had been taught, but not in the reading of those words. Despite the comprehensive character of the letter–sound training programme, the children in the whole word group profited more, as was evident from a standardized reading test and from their superiority in spelling regular words that had not been taught in the experimental programme. Apparently, training grapheme–phoneme conversion did not produce the expected general skills that can be used for reading and spelling new words. Especially critical in this respect is a pseudoword reading test, on which neither experimental treatment group improved significantly. Lovett *et al.* concluded that the disabled readers made their gains by acquiring word-specific knowledge, and did not profit from letter–sound training.

One of the explanations that Lovett *et al.* offer for this failure to acquire and use grapheme–phoneme conversion rules is that a different and more explicit approach to strategy training may be necessary with reading disabled children. It is suggested that the decoding strategies of their subjects had not been well enough consolidated for reliable application of the conversion skills to uninstructed words. This explanation may be correct, because even the decoding-oriented training possibly favoured the application of whole word recognition strategies. In this training condition half the words were instructed by means of whole word methods and all words were presented again in a reviewing procedure. Because of the presence of irregular words, and because children would have been aware that the words reviewed had been taught before, whole word recognition strategies may have been preferred, especially by children who probably have problems in reading by phonological strategies (e.g. Siegel, in press). If so, one may expect better effects of training that is one-sidedly phonics-oriented and that eschews whole word recognition strategies, than from training in which whole word and phonics techniques are combined.

Vellutino and Scanlon's (1986) study was designed to make this comparison. In addition to the phonics and the whole word training group, there was a group that received a combination of phonics and whole word training. As we have seen, the phonics group performed better on a new pseudoword reading test than the whole word group. Contrary to what the preceding reasoning would suggest, however, the phonics group did not do better on this transfer task than the group that received a combined training. One problem in interpreting Vellutino and Scanlon's results, however, is that the purpose of the specific whole word training component was familiarization with the spoken pseudowords. This was achieved in one task by having the subjects repeat the nonsense words said by the experimenter, and in another task by instructing them to label pictures of fantasy animals with the pseudowords. Although this kind of familiarization is part of most whole word methods, in actual learning to read these aspects of word learning are undoubtedly brought about by previous extracurricular activities for the most part, and thus cannot be considered characteristic for whole word training. On the contrary, the association learning between unanalyzed ortho-graphic items and spoken words which is essential for whole word learning was practised by all three groups. Even the children in the phonics condition were introduced to the grapheme–phoneme correspondence rules by learning associ-ations between written and spoken words according to a whole word ('look say') format. From these paired associates they were stimulated to derive the letter–sound correspondences. Therefore, the whole word as well as the phonics and the combined condition in Vellutino and Scanlon (1986) cannot be considered pure representatives of the respective reading methodologies.

Clearly, the issue of whether reading disabled children profit from explicit letter–sound conversion training – and, by implication, whether deficient letter–sound conversion skill is an impediment to their reading competence – cannot be resolved from the literature. Training studies using treatments of a less com-prehensive character are required which will permit more specific comparisons and more precise conclusions.

Grapheme–phoneme conversion training of a different type was provided by Wise (1987). In her study first- and second-grade school children with low reading scores could demand synthetic speech feedback about words that were presented on a computer screen. In one condition the speech feedback consisted of the sounds of single graphemes. The fewest words were learned in this condition. More words were learned if speech feedback was about larger units; for example, about the whole word or about its syllables. This result seems to imply that this indirect way of grapheme–phoneme training is not very profitable. The strongest and most consistent result across different subject groups was that grapheme–phoneme segmentation was least helpful for word learning (Olson *et al.*, 1990). Wise suggests that this follows from the difficulty children had in blending isolated speech sounds, a difficulty that was resolved if larger speech units were used. However, the conditions of this study may have favoured set-specific discrimination learning. The subjects may have learned to differentiate only the words that were used in the study, so that they could recognize a word from the other words in the same set. They may not have acquired a more general competence which can be transferred to new words. Only thirty-six words were studied for a number of training trials, and only those words were presented in pre- and post-testing. If speech blending was a problem for the subjects, then perhaps response learning has been facilitated for the words that were trained with speech feedback about larger units, the pronunciation of which could be assembled more easily. It remains to be shown that these words still are recognized better if they are mixed with others that are orthographically similar. Moreover, each subject participated in every training condition. Therefore, the most one can conclude is which training situation is the most profitable for learning specific word pronunciations, and not which training situation induces the most effective independent reading strategy. Finally, if the problems of poor readers lie in phonological decoding skills they may have adopted word recogition skills that operate on units above the phonemic level. Presenting feedback at these higher levels may make them persist in such idiosyncratic word recognition strategies without helping to learn the more basic decoding stategies that are difficult for them.

Another grapheme–phoneme conversion training of a more indirect kind was provided by van Bon *et al.* (1987) on the development of word naming latency under time pressure. Subjects were poor readers from special education schools. They knew the basic correspondence rules of Dutch orthography, but had difficulty in reading monosyllabic words more complex than CVs and VCs. In each session the subjects read real and pseudowords which varied from CVC to CCVCC. (Cs and Vs being defined not in terms of letters, but as graphemes.) Words were presented on a computer screen. Naming latency was measured by means of a voice key. Subjects were instructed to respond as quickly as possible. Feedback about latency was provided. Van Bon *et al.* reasoned that by using different words in all sessions no learning effects would be produced by word-specific pattern learning, but application of decoding rules would be practised. Latency diminished monotonically over sessions, for pseudowords more than for real words.

Two other findings are relevant here. First, that latency was dependent on word length. This suggests that the words were decoded in a grapheme-by-grapheme fashion. Second, and the most interesting, latency decrease for the different word structures was parallel. Whereas naming times for CVCs and CVCCs or CCVCs became shorter, the difference between these word structures remained the same. The same was found for CVCCs and CCVCs on the one hand, and CCVCCs on the other. Apparently, time pressure was effective in bringing about faster word decoding. One wonders, however, which decoding processes were affected by the training. It is unlikely that grapheme–phoneme conversion was speeded up, because then the effect should have been larger for longer words. A convergence of naming latency for longer words with that for shorter words was not found, however.

The van Bon *et al.* (1987) study was replicated in two extensive training experiments by van den Bosch (1991; van den Bosch *et al.*, submitted). In the first experiment, van den Bosch attempted to differentiate between the effects of short stimulus duration and of pressure to respond quickly in flash card-like training situations. Poor readers from special education schools were assigned to one of the four training conditions which resulted from the combination of limited versus unlimited exposure duration with pressure or no pressure to respond quickly. In each session, monosyllabic words and monosyllabic pseudo-words were randomly selected from larger sets and presented in blocks. Naming speed improved over training sessions. There was no interaction between latency development and training conditions. Collapsing latency data over training conditions, the development of the different word types (CVCs to CCVCCs) was analyzed. Naming latency was related to the number of graphemes. A response to a long (pseudo)word took more time than a response to a short one. Moreover, children became faster in naming pseudowords and words, progress again being larger for pseudowords than for words. The latter finding can be explained by assuming that it is phonological decoding that improves, and that pseudowords require complete phonological decoding, but real words do not. Comparison of CVCs with CCVCCs showed a parallel decrease of latency over sessions for pseudowords. For words a certain convergence was found that may have resulted from the fact that the mean printed frequency was higher for the real CVCs than for the CCVCCs. Some real CVCs probably were not identified by phonological decoding, but by direct recognition. Improvement of phonological decoding as a result of the training therefore affected real CVCs only to a small extent.

In a second experiment van den Bosch (1991; van den Bosch *et al.*, 1993) compared the effects of limited exposure duration with those of merely reading aloud the same words and with a no training control condition. In each session monosyllabic pseudowords with one or two consonant clusters were read by poor readers. In the first experiment, a fixed word exposure time had been determined prior to the training for each child separately. In this experiment, exposure duration was continually adjusted in order to maintain a constant level of accuracy. After each trial, accuracy of the current pseudoword, together with accuracy of the two previous pseudowords of the same particular orthographic structure, was evaluated. For subjects in the limited exposure condition, stimulus duration was increased when two or more errors were made, and was decreased if no errors were made. In accordance with the findings of van den Bosch's first experiment, for both groups naming latency of CVCCs and CCVCs decreased in parallel to that of CCVCCs over the training period. Adjusted exposure duration showed the same pattern of development.

The parallel improvement of words that differ in number of graphemes cannot be explained by an increase of general naming speed, because the subjects in van den Bosch's first experiment did not improve their digit naming speed.

Although the length-dependent response latency and adjusted exposure duration show that individual graphemes play a role in word identification by these subjects, an explanation for their improvement should be sought in the improvement of processes that are not grapheme-length dependent. Presumably, higher-level skills than grapheme–phoneme conversion must have been facili-tated. One explanation that was explicitly tested by van den Bosch was the following. Assume that there is a stage in the phonological decoding of a word at which all words of the types used in these experiments have the same number of elements. An example would be that the pre-vocalic phonemes would be aggregated into one cluster, and the vowel plus the next consonants into another cluster, as proposed by Treiman (1991; see below). In that case, all the monosyllabic words that were used would consist of two elements. The parallel improvement could then possibly result from improvement of the handling of those two units. As we shall see in the next section, however, van den Bosch, and others, found no evidence that Dutch readers use these particular processing units. Another explanation may be that it is processes at the level of the syllable that are facilitated in reading practice. In that case, a convergence of latency or adjusted exposure duration should be found for words that differ in number of syllables. Experiments to test this hypothesis are currently underway.

In summary, studies in which grapheme–phoneme correspondences were trained also trained other reading skills, found such training to be comparatively ineffective, or discovered training effects that cannot be explained as the result of improved grapheme–phoneme translation skill.

Multi-graphemic, sub-syllabic decoding units

In order to become competent readers of an alphabetic language and be able to decode new words, children should learn how the internal phonological structure of words relates to their orthography (e.g. Liberman *et al.*, 1989). The mapping rules need not be grapheme–phoneme correspondence rules for all stages of development.

From an instructional point of view, there are at least two possible reasons for aiming at mastery of multi-graphemic decoding rules. One is that after an initial stage of grapheme–phoneme decoding, the advanced phonological decoder acquires additional decoding units which consist of more than one grapheme. Such a new decoding unit would result from frequent encounters with the same configuration of letters, and would be associated in LTM with one or more phonological configurations, just as graphemes and phonemes are supposed to do. By applying the new translation units, phonological decoding of a word would require fewer steps and less blending activity. Examples of such higher-level decoding units which have been proposed are the 'vocalic center group' (Spoehr and Smith, 1973) and the 'spelling pattern' (Gibson and Levin, 1975). Treiman (1991) formulated a suggestion that contrasts with the previous one in that higher-level units are used for introducing the concept that written words correspond to spoken words. At a later stage, correspondences between written and spoken words at the level of the phoneme are introduced. The rationale for this sequence is that the basis of children's reading problems is a difficulty in analyzing words into phonemes, which makes it hard for them to learn to use grapheme–phoneme correspondences. Larger, more accessible units of sound would provide a means for circumventing, at least initially, this basic obstacle. Treiman refers to Rozin and Gleitman's (1977) proposal to start literacy education with syllables as the fundamental unit of analysis, but suggests the use of syllable onsets and rimes instead.

The onset of a syllable is its initial consonantal portion, e.g. *st*ar. The rime is the vowel and any following consonant, e.g. st*ar*. Not all syllables have onsets, but every syllable has a rime. Thus there are two opposing reasons for introducing multi-graphemic decoding units into the basic reading curriculum. One that suggests adoption of such units in more advanced stages of reading instruction, the other implies their initial use. Treiman's proposal has not been followed yet, as far as I know. Therefore, the discussion will be restricted to applications that are meant to promote efficient reading by furthering the development of larger decoding units.

Structured word lists of the type *can, man, tan, pan, van* are often recommended for the development of higher order decoding units, of *-an* in this example (cf. Cunningham, 1992). Reitsma and Dongelmans (1988) tested the efficacy of such word lists with poor readers. Eight lists of four high-frequency CVCs were formed. The words of each list had either the leading CV in common (e.g. *wip, wim, wil, win*), or the final VC (e.g. *mijn, lijn, pijn, fijn*). Four lists were presented as structured word lists. The words of the other four lists were mixed to form four groups of unrelated words. The structured lists and the mixed lists were presented in columns. The student repeatedly read each list aloud. A new list was only introduced after error-free reading of the current list. The acquisition of multi-letter decoding units would be evidenced by shorter latencies of words that have the repeated element in common, e.g. *wig* and *wit* in case of the *wip*, etc. list. Such pre-test/post-test differences, however, were not found, whether after structured or after mixed presentations of the practice words. There was no evidence for differential effects of CV or VC repetition. Shorter latencies were found only for the practised words themselves, again with no difference between structured and mixed presentations. A replication of this experiment with lists of CCVC words in which the final VC was held constant again provided no positive effects of structured word lists on new words containing the same VC fragments. The number of repetitions (4–16) also gave no effect. Oral reading latency of the words from the lists, however, again were shorter.

Theloosen and van Bon's (1993) first experiment in a sense replicated Reitsma and Dongelmans' mixed presentation condition. Effects of whole word and word segment repetition in poor readers were compared. Common monosyllabic words were presented for oral reading, 1, 4, or 8 times over 8 sessions. These words were mixed with other words that shared a CC, (C)CV or VC(C) fragment with 3 or 7 other words. The 4 or 8 words that had a certain fragment in common were equally distributed over the 8 sessions. Words were presented individually on a computer monitor. The subject controlled the presentation time and was instructed to keep it as short as possible. Repeated encounters with the same letter-string in 4 or 8 words did not lead to shorter response latencies for words that contained that letter-string. For example, reading *zaal, kaal, staal, baal, maal, kwaal, paal, taal* did not transfer to reading *zaal* at the post-test. (Because of a shortage of words of the required type the post-test word was also used as a practice word in the first session.) Identical repetition of a word resulted in faster recognition of that word at post-test, with a larger effect of 8 repetitions than of 4. This advantage, however, seems to be lost by the fact that orthographic neighbours of a repeated word have longer latencies. For example, after reading *heer* on each of the 8 sessions it was recognized faster, but *beer* was recognized more slowly.

In their second experiment Theloosen and van Bon increased fragment repetition frequency to 16. The experiment was designed to test the hypothesis that rime repetition is more effective than repetition of syllable segments that consist of the initial consonant(s) and the vowel. No general letter-string repetition effect or differential repetition effects of segment types were found, however.

Van Daal (1993, Experiment 5.3) contrasted segmentation at the onset–rime boundary with post-vowel segmentation. Monosyllabic words were repeatedly presented to poor readers on a computer screen. Each word was always segmented in one of two ways – for example, the word *cat* was always presented to some children as *c-at*, and to others always as *ca-t*. Visual presentation was accompanied by the correspondingly segmented spoken word. The subject's task was to blend and read the word. However, neither for the repeated (C)CV letter-strings, nor for the VC(C) letter-string transfer was found to new words that included these strings.

The absence of an advantage for onset–rime segmentation over post-vowel segmentation in these training studies is not limited to poor readers. Reitsma (1988), training with structured word lists comparable to Reitsma and Dongelmans' (1988), also found no evidence for the operation of rimes as decoding units in normal beginning readers. The critical difference may be one of language. The children studied by Reitsma (1988), Reitsma and Dongelmans (1988), Theloosen and van Bon (1993) and van Daal (1993) were native Dutch speakers, who learned to read in that language, whereas in studies of children learning to read in English an advantage for onset–rime segmentation over post-vowel and other types of segmentation was found in beginning readers (e.g. Santa, 1976–7; Goswami, 1986; Wise *et al.*, 1990), and, although the advantage was not significant, in retarded readers (Olson *et al.*, 1990). Further evidence for a difference between Dutch and English is provided by van den Bosch (1991), who could not replicate Treiman and Chafetz's (1987) finding that a separation marker after the vowel grapheme disrupted reading of monosyllabic words more than a marker at the onset–rime boundary in beginning nor in skilled readers. The task van den Bosch used, however, was oral reading, and not lexical decision as in Treiman and Chafetz. With lexical decision as the reading task and adults as subjects, van den Bosch, like Treiman and Chafetz, found an onset–rime effect. This is puzzling because phonological information is supposed to be more important for naming than for lexical decision. In these experiments, van den Bosch used an asterisk as a separation marker rather than Treiman and Chafetz's double slash, because in a pilot study subjects reported the tendency to interpret // as two letter *l*s. In a final experiment, van den Bosch manipulated letter colour and size to suggest a division of monosyllabic words in two parts. Using an oral reading task, he again found no difference between post-vowel and onset–rime segmented words in good and poor beginning readers.

Apart from van den Bosch's lexical decision experiment, the evidence points in the direction of a role of onset–rime structure in reading English, but not in reading Dutch. Even for English, however, the evidence from training studies is not so clear-cut. Fayne and Bryant (1981) compared the effectiveness of various word attack strategies and found that their learning disabled youngsters profited most from training the synthesis of CVCs according to a CV-C pattern, for instance, compared to a C-VC pattern. But, as Wise *et al.* (1990) suggest, the effects may have been produced by overlearning a few highly consistent stimuli.

The basis for this difference between languages is perhaps in orthography rather than in phonology, because Schreuder and van Bon (1989) concluded from their data on Dutch beginning readers that the onset–rime distinction is relevant for their phonemic segmentation.

If Wise *et al.* (1990) are correct that, in English, post-vocalic consonants influence the pronunciation of a vowel grapheme more than pre-vocalic consonants, it is logical that children would acquire more consistent associations between written and spoken rimes than between written and spoken onset-plus-vowel units. In Dutch words, however, only the pronunciation of the single-letter vowel graphemes – not of homogeneous vowel digraphs (like *aa* and *ee*), nor of heterogeneous vowel digraphs (like *ei* and *ui*) – is determined by the post-vocalic part of the syllable. A letter that usually denotes a short (lax) vowel is pronounced with the long (tense) counterpart of that vowel if it is not followed by a consonant grapheme. The acquisition of VC decoding units, therefore, will not be as profitable for children who learn to read in Dutch as for children who learn to read in English. The finding of more convincing onset–rime effects in reading English may thus result from the fact that some regularities in English orthography happen to coincide with the phonological onset–rime structure.

In summary, the research on remedial teaching of reading using multi-letter units does not show significant results, at least not for the Dutch language. For English, there may be an advantage for training according to an onset–rime division of the syllable, but under certain conditions repetition of other units may be even more profitable (Fayne and Bryant, 1981).

Syllables and morphemes

If the basic reading problem is in handling grapheme–phoneme correspondences, this problem could be circumvented or postponed by stressing higher-order translation units. In the preceding section we saw that this line of reasoning led Treiman to suggest the use of onset–rime units in initial (remedial) reading practice. There are, however, alternatives to onsets and rimes as higher-order decoding units.

There is evidence to suggest that syllables (e.g. Mewhort and Campbell, 1981) and morphemes (e.g. Tyler and Nagy, 1990) play a role in skilled reading. In this section we shall therefore review a number of studies on syllables and morphemes as basic decoding units.

Scheerer-Neumann (1979; see also Solle and Stümpel, 1987) discusses a German remedial reading method that has *morphemes* as the units for reading instruction, and with which the names of Schubenz and Rabe are associated. They claim that a limited number of German morphemes constitute an economic basic inventory of meaningful units for decoding numerous words.

First, children learn to recognize letters and to name them. Grapheme–phoneme correspondence rules are not taught because these rules have many exceptions in German. Next, children learn to read and write about 200 frequent morphemes. Written texts are presented with words segmented into morphemes by means of slashes. The final phase aims at learning more morphemes, the understanding of the meaning of text and making the child teacher-independent.

No large-scale study on the effectiveness of the morpheme method seems to have been undertaken.

In the absence of empirical evidence, Scheerer-Neumann's consideration of the morpheme method is worthwhile. First, although German orthography may not be strictly phonological, it is transparent enough to expect advantages of learning grapheme–phoneme correspondence rules. Second, complete morphological division of words which is supposed to provide insight into the correspondence between form and content leads to problems. Often there is no correspondence between the meaning of the entire word and the morphemes that it seems to contain: searching for morphemes a child might think that *sau/er* (sour) is derived from *sau* (sow). Elimination of grammatical morphemes from a word frequently results in meaningless stem morphemes (e.g. *gess* remaining from *ver/gess/en* [understand] has no meaning). Often the relation between different words in their lexical morphemes is only understandable along etymological or metaphoric lines (e.g. *Elt/er/n* (parents) from *alt* (old)). Moreover, although speakers of a language may have implicit morphological knowledge, it is not clear whether this implicit competence can be transformed into explicit performance. Finally, from the indications that readers use morphological aspects of written words, one cannot conclude that morphemes are the essential reading units.

Henry (1988) assumes that fluent readers of English first look for familiar morphemes in unknown words, then make decisions based on syllable division, and ultimately apply letter–sound conversion. Because dyslexic children know little about the major structural aspects of words, and literacy instruction emphasizes simple grapheme–phoneme rules, they cannot make use of the regularity that derives from the morphological aspects of English orthography.

She therefore advises that dyslexic children should be taught about the historic origins of English in order to make them look for Greek, Romance and Anglo-Saxon spelling patterns. Letter–sound correspondences and syllable and morpheme patterns should be discussed for each language of origin separately. Henry claims to have found remarkable progress with such a teaching method in an as yet unpublished study.

Her claim contrasts with the outcome of the two studies on the effects of morphemic analysis training in normal school children discussed by Johnson and Baumann (1984). In both studies children acquired the morphological competence (recognition of regular affixes, for example) that was taught, but their general reading proficiency did not improve. Henry is not alone in suggesting that the orthography of English is much more transparent if one takes account of its morphological basis. This does not necessarily mean, however, that introduction of a strong morphological component into instruction facilitates literacy acquisition. Perhaps only competent readers who know the word-specific spellings of a large number of words can profit from a structural analysis of the proposed kind. One may recognize that words are of Greek origin because of an initial or final *ph*, but how should one recognize those words as Greek if one does not know that they should be written with *ph*?

In conclusion, empirical studies on the remedial effects of morpheme-oriented reading instruction are badly needed, because in their absence one can only speculate about possible beneficial effects. In those studies attention should be given to the stage at which structural analysis is introduced.

One reason for making *syllables* the central unit in reading instruction is that they would make longer words easier to decode by breaking them up into more manageable parts (Johnson and Baumann, 1984). Another reason is that it is easier for children to segment spoken words into syllables than into phonemes (e.g. Liberman *et al.*, 1974). The second argument persuaded Rozin and Gleitman (1977) that initial reading instruction should use syllables to introduce the concept that written words stand for sounds.

Using pseudowords that were either first- or fourth-order approximations of German words, Scheerer-Neumann (1981) found that poor third-grade readers reported fewer letters correctly than good readers, and that this difference was larger for fourth-order than for lower-order approximations. From this finding she concluded that poor readers were inferior in utilizing intraword redundancy. However, breaking up the written words into syllables by inserting spaces at the syllable boundaries improved the scores of the poor readers for fourth-order approximations drastically, approaching those of the good readers. Explicit visualization of the syllable structure seems to induce in poor readers the strategy that is normal for good readers. If poor readers do not take advantage of intraword structure, then learning to recognize that structure should promote reading proficiency. Therefore, Scheerer-Neumann developed a training programme which first taught children to segment spoken words into their syllables, and next to relate the spoken syllables to their visual counterparts. The training programme contained a morphemic aspect because children were trained to recognize common affixes as units. Syllable identification in written words included first finding the vowels and then marking the syllable boundaries according to phonological rules. Poor readers in this training condition performed better at post-test than children in a no training or in a reading control condition. Whereas the reading error rate for control children increased steeply with the number of syllables, it did not for the experimental children.

An objection that one may raise against Scheerer-Neumann's training experiments is that the training condition differed from the control condition in more than one respect. Children in the control condition either were not engaged in special activities, or read comics and short stories. The experimental children not only received training in syllable identification, but also systematically practised reading long words. Thus, decoding skills of a more general kind, such as context-dependent grapheme–phoneme decoding, may have improved and may be responsible for the findings. The experiment therefore should be replicated with a more appropriate comparison condition before it can be concluded that structural analysis training is effective.

Syllable feedback was one of the speech feedback conditions in Olson *et al.* (1990; see also Wise *et al.*, 1989). While reading short stories presented on a computer monitor, disabled readers could ask for speech feedback about a particular word by targeting the word with a mouse. Segmented feedback appeared to bring about larger gains in pseudoword reading than whole word feedback or no training. Onset–rime feedback seemed to produce larger gains than syllabic feedback, but the difference between segmented feedback conditions was not significant. On a time-limited word recognition test, syllabic and sub-syllabic feedback again appeared to produce larger gains than the no training condition (with onset–rime segmentation again being the most effective), but these gains were not statistically different from those that resulted from whole word feedback. There were no differences between conditions on an untimed word recognition test, probably because of the low sensitivity of the test used. Reasoning that phonological coding skills as exhibited on the pseudoword reading task are important for independent decoding of unfamiliar words and for learning accurate orthographic representations of words, Olson *et al.* suggest that the results of the pseudoword reading task are the most significant ones. However, that the advantage of segmented speech feedback over whole word feedback did not spread to timed word reading qualifies the suggested importance of pseudoword reading skills. As whole word feedback appears to contribute to the development of reading skill, the effects of different levels of speech feedback on different aspects of reading skill should be investigated further, differentiating between reading skills, taking into account the relations between reading skills, and determining long-term effects. For the time being, Olson *et al.*'s results do not favour a specific type of segmented speech feedback, whether at the syllabic or the sub-syllabic level, or whole word speech feedback.

Johnson and Baumann (1984) point to the problem in syllable identification methods that it presupposes the availability of the word's pronunciation. But pronunciation itself is supposed to result from the method. Syllable identification of written words according to orthographic and hyphenation rules is often unsuitable for such segmentation, even for languages that have a quite transparant orthography. A further problem is the difference between syllable and morpheme boundaries. Such difficulties indeed have to be resolved in developing remedial reading methods that use syllables as a basic decoding unit, yet do not demonstrate that such a method is fundamentally ineffective.

Although neither Scheerer-Neumann's (1981) experiments nor Olson *et al.*'s (1990; Wise *et al.*, 1989) results provide conclusive evidence for the efficacy of emphasizing the syllabic structure in remedial teaching of reading, they suggest at least a potentially fruitful line of research. This is especially true given the parallel improvement in word naming speed found by van Bon *et al.* (1987) and van den Bosch (1991) for monosyllabic words of different lengths which points to the improvement of processes at the syllabic level.

Whole words

Because word recognition is likely to be a central reading skill (Gough, 1984; Stanovich, 1991), and lower-level skills like grapheme–phoneme decoding are probably only instrumental, but even then not necessarily so, in word identification, remedial training programmes are often evaluated by their effects on word recognition. Word recognition training thus has been a topic of interest in a number of training studies, some of which are reviewed here. They are grouped according to the type of training used, namely error correction, whole word recognition, speech feedback, repeated reading of single words and complete texts, and reading while listening.

In an empirical comparison of *error-correction procedures* with learning-disabled junior high school students, Jenkins and Larson (1979) found drill on words that had been read incorrectly to be more effective than other correction procedures, such as immediate supply of the correct spoken word, end of page review of the words that had been misread or discussion of their meanings. Effectiveness was evaluated by asking the students to read a list of words that had been corrected the day before. Possibly the drill procedure made the students learn set specific discriminations of the kind discussed above when we reported Olson *et al.*'s (1990) study. A comparable advantage of drill was found, however, in a situation in which set-specific learning is less probable, namely when rereading the original sentences in which the errors had occurred.

The question whether it is correct whole word association learning or the opportunity to practise word decoding that makes word-oriented error correction profitable was addressed by Meyer (1982). With younger (middle-school) poor readers as her subjects and in a word-attack context, she compared a drill procedure of the type used by Jenkins and Larson in which the correct pronunciation was supplied by the teacher with one that entailed the analysis of misidentified words in a phonics-like manner. The students in both conditions improved more on standardized reading tests than the original norm samples. Apparently, the word-oriented teaching helped these students to acquire higher generalized reading accuracy. Meyer suggests that even the students in the word supply condition had internalized a set of explicit decoding rules and strategies which could be used to re-analyze a word that they had incorrectly read. That word analysis was not inferior to whole word feedback shows that these poor readers were able to profit from analytic instruction, in contrast to the opinion that the difficulties poor readers have with phonics skills require the teaching of compensatory higher-level reading skills. The results of Meyer's study should be viewed with caution, however. Lowest scoring subjects were probably selected for participation in the study, and because no control group but change in scaled scores was used for effect evaluation, at least part of the effect is possibly due to regression towards the mean.

As we have seen earlier, the *whole word training* condition in the Vellutino and Scanlon (1986) study differed from the phonics condition in that it emphasized pronunciation and picture name learning rather than learning associations between written and spoken words. It is possible, therefore, that equalizing the amount of sight word learning in the whole word condition to that of grapheme–phoneme conversion in the phonics condition would lead to equal or even better results of the whole word condition. Moreover, the training conditions were alike in that both involved learning whole word associations between written and spoken words. Therefore, the advantages of the phonics training possibly resulted from an interaction with the concomitant whole word learning.

Indications of superiority of whole word training of regular words over word analysis-oriented training were found by Lovett *et al.* (1990) (see p. 155 above). The reading-disabled children in the whole word condition had higher post-test scores on a standardized reading measure and on spelling regular words that had not been practised. It is remarkable that these transfer effects should be found for the whole word training group and not for the word decoding group, as it is the latter group that is supposed to receive a generalizable skill training. But as no such transfer effects were found on other tests, such as the pseudoword reading test, this finding may be due to chance factors. As was argued earlier, however, the design of the Lovett *et al.* study probably promoted whole word learning even in the letter–sound training group. And because both groups made marked progress, which according to Lovett *et al.* suggests the acquisition of specific lexical knowledge, this study might show that whole word learning can be brought about successfully in reading-disabled children.

The *speech feedback* study by Olson *et al.* (1990; Wise *et al.*, 1989) did not provide unequivocal evidence that feedback at the syllabic or sub-syllabic level is more beneficial than feedback at the whole word level, or vice versa, provided that feedback is above the grapheme–phoneme level. Van Daal and Reitsma (1990) observed more reading accuracy improvement for words that had been repeatedly read than for unpractised words. They also found no difference between whole word and segmented speech feedback conditions, both giving better results than no feedback.

A few studies have investigated whether *repeated reading* of the same *single words* makes them better recognized by reading-disabled children, and whether such effects spread to other words. Van Daal *et al.* (1986), for instance, found repetition effects for repeated words, but not for their orthographic neighbours. In the training sessions, however, the same set of 48 words was presented. Testing for word-specific repetition effects also involved presentation of the same set. It is possible therefore that the subjects have learned to make set-specific discriminations which give no advantage when words are presented among others that are outside the set (van Bon *et al.*, 1986). In Reitsma and Dongelmans' (1988) study on structured word lists, positive word repetition effects were again found for the repeated words, but no transfer of training to their orthographic neighbours. As reported earlier, Theloosen and van Bon (1993) not only found faster word recognition for words after their repeated presentation, but also slower recognition of orthographically similar words, an effect that can be explained from spreading inhibition.

That the word-specific learning is not dependent on lexical features, such as meaning, that characterize real words, is evident from van den Bosch's (1991) second experiment. Frequency of pseudoword presentation (1, 4 or 8 times) was reflected in their naming accuracy, latency and adjusted exposure duration. Comparable repetition frequency effects on the recognition of pseudowords were found by Theloosen and van Bon (1993).

Indirect evidence for the importance of whole word recognition training can be deduced from Rashotte and Torgesen's (1985) study on the effects of *repeated reading* of the *same texts* by non-fluent disabled readers. Reading speed appeared to increase over (first readings of) passages most if each new text had many words in common with the texts that had been repeatedly read in earlier training sessions. If the passages shared few words, repeated reading was not more effective than non-repetitive reading. More direct evidence for improved word recognition was found by van der Leij (1983) in an investigation of the effects of repeated *reading while listening* (RwL) to the same text (exp. IIIc). Each text was practised ten times. Isolated words from the texts were read faster after practice than before; there was no concomitant improvement of reading accuracy. First readings (before practice) of the words sampled from the texts were more accurate after eight weeks' training (with other texts) than before the training period, which suggests that general word recognition skill also had improved. Transfer of improved word recognition skill to passage reading was not found, however. Van Bon *et al.* (1991) compared the effects of repeated RwL with those of non-repetitive RwL and with those of non-repetitive RwL involving the detection of mismatches between written and tape-recorded text. With all three methods, texts that had been practised and words from those texts were read faster than new texts and randomly selected words. Only for texts was there a larger practice effect in favour of one particular training condition, namely repeated RwL. That the single word familiarity effect was not larger for repeated RwL than for the non-repetitive conditions suggests that the improvement of word recognition occurs in one or only a few reading trials. But as training and testing session were only separated by one or a few days, the possibility should be ruled out in a replication study involving follow-up testing that this familiarity effect is one of short-term activation of the respective lexical entries. No transfer of training to the reading of new texts and random samples of single words was found.

The research reviewed above suggests that it is word-specific knowledge that profits most from various training situations, and that training favouring the recognition of specific words tends to produce the larger advances in reading skill. A few remarks have to be made, however, which should inhibit one from drawing drastic conclusions as to the remedial implications.

The first is that it need not be words or lexical items in general that benefit most from reading practice, because van den Bosch (1991) also found effects of pseudoword repetition. Moreover, as most words that were used in these studies will have been monosyllabic, and the studies by Scheerer-Neumann (1981) and Lovett *et al.* (1990) suggest beneficial effects of syllable-oriented training, it is possible that the effects occur at the level of the syllable rather than that of the word.

Second, one should not expect large effects from whole word recognition training. There is little evidence that growth of word-specific knowledge transfers to text reading, to reading new real words or to reading pseudowords. Negative effects on the recognition of orthographic neighbours are even found (Theloosen and van Bon, 1993). Rashotte and Torgesen's (1985) study on the effects of repeated reading may suggest that new texts are read more fluently if they contain words that have been previously practised, but Fleisher *et al.* (1979) found no improvement of text comprehension by poor readers after training them to recognize a large number of words from the texts. These latter findings undermine the strong version of the 'verbal efficiency model' (Perfetti, 1985), which predicts better comprehension as a consequence of improved word recognition. Perhaps specific instruction is needed in addition to recognition training in order to raise the level of text comprehension.

Third, no distinction has been made between different types of whole word recognition. It has been suggested that there are various ways of recognizing whole word patterns. Frith (1985), for instance, distinguishes the beginning reader's logographic identification of familiar words on the basis of salient graphic features from the orthographic letter pattern recognition, which is characteristic of the advanced reader. Whether these are the (only) types of whole word recognition is not as relevant here, as the possibility that whole words can be recognized in a variety of ways, some of which are not efficient in the long run.

One such inefficient strategy – learning to make set-specific discriminations – has previously been mentioned. A particular variety of this strategy could be responding with a high-frequency word after the identification of only a few letters. This strategy must lead to reading errors if the target word has one or more high-frequency orthographic neighbours, as is evident from the adverse effect of word repetition on words that have a letter-string in common (Theloosen and van Bon, 1993). Disabled readers may develop such inefficient strategies, either in coping with the requirements of a particular experimental task, or in trying to circumvent their basic reading problem (Frith, 1985). Training effects on whole word recognition should therefore be evaluated within a theoretical framework that differentiates between recognition strategies that are characteristic for skilled reading and compensatory, possibly inefficient, strategies that are only useful in solving short-term reading tasks.

Conclusion

The central question that this review was intended to answer was whether remedial reading instruction tailored to a certain linguistic level gives the better results. No conclusive answer, however, seems to be possible to date. There are indications that training at the phonological level is effective in preventing and reducing reading problems, but the studies permit rival explanations for such effects. Studies in which grapheme–phoneme correspondences were trained also trained other reading skills, found such training to be comparatively ineffective, or discovered training effects that cannot be explained as the result of improved grapheme–phoneme translation skill. Conflicting findings of studies that aimed at the acquisition of decoding units consisting of several graphemes brought up the interesting suggestion that training effects may differ according to the orthography of the language in question. The few studies on the effectiveness of morpheme-oriented methods hardly allow any conclusion to be drawn, but they suggest a number of theoretical and practical problems in implementing such methods. Training at the syllabic level seems to be promising, but here too the evidence is not conclusive. Knowledge at the word level seemed to profit most from various training situations, but a few caveats against drawing conclusions for remedial training from this observation were formulated.

This overview almost inevitably leads to the conclusion that too little is known about remedial reading instruction, and that additional research is badly needed. For such research to be useful, appropriate control conditions should be chosen so that important contrasts can be tested. The tendency is understandable to evaluate effects of comprehensive instruction packets, but the general implications of the findings from such studies are only limited. One more specific desideratum should be mentioned, namely that the effects of two temporal aspects of training should be investigated: the effect of training duration and the duration of the training effect. It may be, for instance, that whole word training gives better short-term effects, but that decoding-oriented training produces better long-term effects (cf. Wise, 1992). Varying training duration – and reading-disabled children can be assumed to profit only from training over long periods of time – and inclusion of both short-term and long-term follow-up testing can contribute considerably to our knowledge of the effects of remedial reading instruction.

References

Ball, E.W. and Blachman, B.A. (1991), 'Does phoneme awareness training in kindergarten make a difference in early word recognition and developmental spelling?' *Reading Research Quarterly*, *26*, 49–66.

Bender, L.A. (1957), 'Specific reading disability as a maturational lag', *Bulletin of the Orton Society*, *7*, 9–18.

Bradley, L. and Bryant, P.E. (1983), 'Categorizing sounds and learning to read – a causal connection,' *Nature*, *301*, 419–21.

Bradley, L. and Bryant, P.E. (1985), *Rhyme and Reason in Reading and Spelling*, Ann Arbor, MI: University of Michigan Press.

Chall, J.S. (1983), *Learning to Read: The great debate*, updated edition, New York: McGraw-Hill.

Cunningham, A.E. (1991), 'Explicit versus implicit instruction in phonemic awareness', *Journal of Experimental Child Psychology*, *50*, 429–44.

Cunningham, P.M. (1992), 'What kind of phonics instruction will we have?' In C.K. Linzer and D.J. Leu (eds.) *Literacy Research, Theory and Practice: Views from many perspectives. Forty-first yearbook of the National Reading Conference*, Chicago: NRC.

Elkonin, D.B. (1973), 'USSR'. In J. Downing (ed.) *Comparative Reading. Cross-national studies of behavior and processes in reading and writing*, New York: Macmillan.

Fayne, H.R. and Bryant, N.D. (1981), 'Relative effects of various word synthesis strategies on the phonics achievement of learning disabled youngsters', *Journal of Educational Psychology*, *73*, 612–23.

Fleisher, L.S., Jenkins, J.R. and Pany, D. (1979), 'Effects on poor readers' comprehension of training in rapid decoding', *Reading Research Quarterly*, *15*, 30–48.

Fox, B. and Routh, D.K. (1975), 'Analyzing spoken language into words, syllables, and phonemes: a developmental study', *Journal of Psycholinguistic Research*, *4*, 331–42.

Fox, B. and Routh, D.K. (1976), 'Phonemic analysis and synthesis as word attack skills', *Journal of Educational Psychology*, *68*, 70–4.

Fox, B. and Routh, D.K. (1983), 'Reading disability, phonemic analysis and dysphonetic spelling: a follow-up study', *Journal of Clinical Psychology*, *12*, 28–32.

Fox, B. and Routh, D.K. (1984), 'Phonemic analysis and synthesis as word attack skills: revisited', *Journal of Educational Psychology*, *76*, 1059–64.

Frith, U. (1985), 'Beneath the surface of developmental dyslexia'. In K. Patterson, M. Coltheart and J. Marshall (eds.) *Surface Dyslexia*, London: Lawrence Erlbaum.

Gibson, E.J. and Levin, H. (1975), *The Psychology of Reading*, Cambridge, MA: MIT Press.

Golinkoff, R.M. (1978), 'Phonemic awareness skills and reading achievement'. In F.B. Murray and J.J. Pikulski (eds.), *The Acquisition of Reading: Cognitive, linguistic and perceptual requisites*. Baltimore, MD: University Park Press.

Goswami, U. (1986), 'Children's use of analogy in learning to read: a developmental study', *Journal of Experimental Child Psychology*, *42*, 73–83.

Gough, P.B. (1984), 'Word recognition'. In P.D. Pearson (ed.) *Handbook of Reading research*, Vol. I, New York: Longman.

Henry, M.K. (1988), 'Beyond phonics: integrated decoding and spelling instruction based on word origin and structure', *Annals of Dyslexia, 38*, 258–75.

Hurford, D.P. (1990), 'Training phonemic segmentation ability with a phonemic discrimination intervention in second- and third-grade children with reading disabilities', *Journal of Learning Disabilities, 23*, 564–9.

Jenkins, J.R. and Larson, K. (1979), 'Evaluating error-correction procedures for oral reading', *The Journal of Special Education, 13*, 145–56.

Johnson, D.D. and Baumann, J.F. (1984), 'Word identification'. In P.D. Pearson (ed.) *Handbook of Reading Research*, New York: Longman.

Johnson, D.J. and Myklebust, H. (1967), *Learning Disabilities*, New York: Grune & Stratton.

Juel, C., Griffith, P.L. and Gough, P.B. (1986), 'Acquisition of literacy: a longitudinal study of children in first and second grade', *Journal of Educational Psychology, 78*, 243–55.

Kerstholt, M.T., Van Bon, W.H.J. and Schreuder, R. (in press), 'Training in phonemic segmentation: the effects of visual support', *Reading and Writing*.

Liberman, I.Y. (1973), 'Segmentation of the spoken word and reading acquisition', *Bulletin of the Orton Society, 23*, 65–77.

Liberman, I.Y., Shankweiler, D. and Liberman, A.M. (1989), 'The alphabetic principle and learning to read'. In D. Shankweiler and I.Y. Liberman (eds.) *Phonology and Reading Disability: Solving the reading puzzle*, Ann Arbor, MI: University of Michigan Press, pp.1–33.

Liberman, I.Y., Shankweiler, D., Fischer, F.W. and Carter, B. (1974), 'Explicit syllable and phoneme segmentation in the young child', *Journal of Experimental Child Psychology, 18*, 201–12.

Lie, A. (1991), 'Effects of a training program for stimulating skills in word analysis in first-grade children', *Reading Research Quarterly, 26*, 234–50.

Lovett, M.W., Ransby, M.J. and Barron, R.W. (1988), 'Treatment, subtype, and word type effects in dyslexic children's response to remediation', *Brain and Language, 34*, 328–49.

Lovett, M.W., Ransby, M.J., Hardwick, N., Johns, M.S. and Donaldson, S.A. (1989), 'Can dyslexia be treated? Treatment-specific and generalized treatment effects in dyslexic children's response to remediation', *Brain and Language, 37*, 90–121.

Lovett, M.W., Warren-Chaplin, P.M., Ransby, M.J. and Borden, S.L. (1990), 'Training the word recognition skills of reading disabled children: treatment and transfer effects', *Journal of Educational Psychology, 82*, 769–80.

Lundberg, I., Frost, J. and Petersen, O.-P. (1988), 'Effects of an extensive program for stimulating phonological awareness in preschool children', *Reading Research Quarterly, 23*, 263–84.

Mewhort, D.J.K. and Campbell, A.J. (1981), 'Toward a model of skilled reading: an analysis of performance in tachistoscopic tasks'. In G.E. MacKinnon and T.G. Waller (eds.) *Reading Research: Advances in theory and practice*, Vol. 3, New York: Academic Press, pp. 39–118.

Meyer, L.A. (1982), 'The relative effects of word-analysis and word-supply correction procedures with poor readers during word-attack training', *Reading Research Quarterly, 17*, 544–55.

Olson, R., Wise, B., Conners, F. and Rack, J. (1990), 'Organization, heritability, and remediation of component word recognition and language skills in disabled readers.' In T.H. Carr and B.A. Levy (eds.) *Reading and its Development: Component skills approaches*, New York: Academic Press.

Perfetti, C.A. (1985), *Reading Ability*, New York: Oxford University Press.

Rashotte, C.A. and Torgesen, J.K. (1985), 'Repeated reading and reading fluency in learning disabled children', *Reading Research Quarterly, 20*, 180–8.

Reitsma, P. (1988), 'Tussen letter en woord: het effect van oefeningen met wisselrijen' [Between letter and word: the effect of exercises with structured word lists], *Pedagogische Studiën, 65*, 321–39.

Reitsma, P. and Dongelmans, J. (1988), 'Het effect van oefeningen met wisselrijen voor leeszwakke kinderen' [The effects of exercises with structured word lists in poor readers], *Tijdschrift voor Orthopedagogiek, 27*, 248–65.

Rozin, P. and Gleitman, L.R. (1977), 'The structure and acquisition of reading II: the reading process and the acquisition of the alphabetic principle.' In A.S. Reber and D.L. Scarborough (eds.) *Toward a Psychology of Reading: The proceedings of the CUNY conferences*, Hillsdale, NJ: Lawrence Erlbaum.

Sanchez, E. and Rueda, M.I. (1991), 'Segmental awareness and dyslexia: is it possible to learn to segment well and yet continue to read and write poorly?' *Reading and Writing, 3*, 11–18.

Santa, C.M. (1976–7), 'Spelling patterns and the development of flexible word recognition strategies', *Reading Research Quarterly, 7*, 125–44.

Scheerer-Neumann, G. (1979), *Intervention bei Lese-Rechtschreibschwäche. Überblick über Themen, Methoden und Ergebnisse* [Intervention in Cases of Poor Reading and Writing. Review of themes, methods and results], Bochum: Kamp.

Schreuder, R. and Van Bon, W.H.J. (1989), 'Phonemic analysis: effects of word properties', *Journal of Research in Reading, 12*, 59–78.

Siegel, L.S. (in press), 'Phonological processing deficits as the basis of developmental dyslexia: Implications for remediation.' In J. Riddoch and G. Humphreys (eds.) *Cognitive Neuropsychology and Cognitive Rehabilitation*, Hillsdale, NJ: Lawrence Erlbaum.

Siegel, L.S. and Faux, D. (1989), 'Acquisition of certain grapheme–phoneme correspondences in normally achieving and disabled readers', *Reading and Writing, 1*, 37–52.

Snowling, M. (1987), *Dyslexia: A cognitive developmental perspective*, Oxford: Basil Blackwell.

Solle, M. and Stümpel, B. (1987), 'Die Morphem-Methode: Eine neue Chance für den Schriftspracherwerb in Schulen für Lernbehinderte?' [The morpheme method: a new opportunity for learning written language in schools for children with learning difficulties?] *Zeitschrift für Heilpaedagogik, 38*, 709–12.

Spoehr, K.T. and Smith, E.E. (1973), 'The role of syllables in perceptual processing', *Cognitive Psychology, 5*, 71–89.

Stanovich, K.E. (1986), 'Matthew effects in reading: some consequences of individual differences in the acquisition of literacy', *Reading Research Quarterly, 21*, 360–406.

Stanovich, K.E. (1991), 'Word recognition: changing perspectives'. In R. Barr, M.L. Kamil, P. Mosenthal and P.D. Pearson (eds.) *Handbook of Reading Research*, Vol. II, New York: Longman.

Theloosen, G. and Van Bon, W.H.J. (1993), 'Herhaling van woorden en lettergroepen: oefeneffecten bij zwakke lezers' [Repetition of words and letter clusters: effects of practice in poor readers], *Pedagogische Studiën, 70*, 180–94.

Tornéus, M. (1984), 'Phonological awareness and reading: a chicken and egg problem?' *Journal of Educational Psychology, 76*, 1346–58.

Treiman, R. (1991), 'The role of intrasyllabic units in learning to read.' In L. Rieben and C.A. Perfetti (eds.) *Learning to Read: Basic research and its implications*, Hillsdale, NJ: Lawrence Erlbaum, pp. 149–60.

Treiman, R. and Baron, J. (1983), 'Phonemic analysis training helps children benefit from spelling–sound rules', *Memory & Cognition, 11*, 382–9.

Treiman, R. and Chafetz, J. (1987), 'Are there onset- and rime-like units in printed words?' In M. Coltheart (ed.) *Attention and Performance*, 12, Hillsdale, NJ: Lawrence Erlbaum.

Tunmer, W.E. and Nesdale, A.R. (1985), 'Phonemic segmentation skill and beginning reading', *Journal of Educational Psychology*, 77, 417–27.

Tyler, A. and Nagy, W. (1990), 'Use of derivational morphology during reading', *Cognition*, 36, 17–34.

van Bon, W.H.J. and Duighuisen, H.C.M. (in press), 'Sometimes spelling is easier than phonemic segmentation', *Scandinavian Journal of Psychology*.

van Bon, W.H.J. Review of V.H.P. Van Daal, N.C.M. Bakker, P. Reitsma and D.A.V. Van der Leij, (1986), 'Woordfrequentie, repetitie en ernstige leesproblemen' [Word frequency, repetition and severe reading problems]. In P. Reitsma, A.G. Bus and W.H.J. van Bon (eds.) *Leren Lezen en Spellen*, Lisse: Swets & Zeitlinger.

van Bon, W.H.J., Boksebeld, L.M., Font Freide, T.A.M. and Van den Hurk, A.J.M. (1991), 'A comparison of three methods of reading-while-listening', *Journal of Learning Disabilities*, 24, 471–6.

van Bon, W.H.J., Van Kessel, A.E.G. and Kortenhorst, E.P.M. (1987), 'Beïnvloeding van woordherkenningssnelheid door middel van flash-cards' [Influencing word recognition speed by means of flash cards]. In J. Hamers and A. Van der Leij (eds.) *Dyslexie*, Lisse: Swets & Zeitlinger.

Van Daal, V.H.P. (1993), *Computer-based Reading and Spelling Practice for Young Dyslexics*, unpublished doctoral dissertation, Vrije Universiteit Amsterdam.

Van Daal, V.H.P. and Reitsma, P. (1990), 'Effects of independent word practice with segmented and whole-word sound feedback in disabled readers', *Journal of Research in Reading*, 13, 133–48.

Van Daal, V.H.P., Bakker, N.C.M., Reitsma, P. and Van der Leij, D.A.V. (1986), 'Woordfrequentie, repetitie en ernstige leesproblemen' [Word frequency, repetition, and severe reading problems]. In P. Reitsma, A.G. Bus and W.H.J. Van Bon (eds.) *Leren lezen en spellen*, Lisse: Swets & Zeitlinger.

Van den Bosch, K. (1991), *Poor Readers' Decoding Skills: Effects of training, task and word characteristics*, unpublished doctoral dissertation, Universiteit van Nijmegen.

Van den Bosch, K., Van Bon, W.H.J. and Schreuder, R. (submitted), 'Poor readers' decoding skills: effects of training with limited exposure duration.'

Van der Leij, D.A.V. (1983), *Ernstige leesproblemen: Een onderzoek naar mogelijkheden tot differentiatie en behandeling* [Severe Reading Problems: A study of possibilities for differentiation and treatment], Lisse: Swets & Zeitlinger.

Vellutino, F.R. and Scanlon, D.M. (1986), 'Experimental evidence for the effects of instructional bias on word identification', *Exceptional Children*, 53, 145–55.

Williams, J.P. (1980), 'Teaching decoding with an emphasis on phoneme analysis and phoneme blending', *Journal of Educational Psychology*, 72, 1–15.

Wise, B. (1992), 'Whole words and decoding for short-term learning: comparisons on a "talking-computer" system', *Journal of Experimental Child Psychology*, 54, 147–67.

Wise, B., Olson, R., Anstett, M., Andrews, L., Terjak, M., Schneider, V., Kostuch, J. and Kriho, L. (1989), 'Implementing a long-term computerized remedial reading program with synthetic speech feedback: hardware, software, and real-world issues', *Behavior Research Methods, Instruments, and Computers*, 21, 173–80.

Wise, B.W., Olson, R.K. and Tremain, R. (1990), 'Subsyllabic units in computerized reading instruction: onset–rime vs. postvowel segmentation', *Journal of Experimental Child Psychology*, 49, 1–19.

9

Reading comprehension instruction: where is it and how can we improve it?

Cor Aarnoutse
Department of Education, University of Nijmegen

Introduction

Reviewing the research on reading comprehension, Pearson and Gallagher (1983) divided the relevant research into four categories: existential descriptions, existential proofs, pedagogical experiments and programme evaluations. Existential descriptions are studies that describe what is going on in schools and classrooms, and what the goals and qualities of curricula or other materials are. Existential proofs attempt to prove the existence of relationships between variables. Pedagogical experiments are designed to increase the ability of pupils to comprehend and learn from a text. And programme evaluations are studies in which a curriculum, or a part of it, is assessed on the basis of certain criteria.

In this chapter we focus on two kinds of study: existential descriptions and pedagogical experiments. According to Pearson and Fielding (1991) pedagogical experiments represent the heart of reading comprehension instruction. The two questions we want to answer are: Does instruction in reading comprehension exist in the classroom? And how can instruction in reading comprehension be improved?

Our approach to designing and conducting intervention studies in the field of reading comprehension does not differ from the approach usually followed in the United States. Starting from the best developed reading theories we look for those reading tasks or aspects of reading which are relevant to teach in school and which have been investigated well enough by researchers from different disciplines such as cognitive psychology, linguistics, educational psychology and child development. Finding the main idea in an expository text is a good example of such a reading task; vocabulary is an aspect of reading. If knowledge of a relevant aspect of reading or of a reading task is insufficient, it will be difficult to design an intervention successfully. If the foundations of knowledge are not solid enough, one runs the risk of sinking into the mire.

The advantage of this approach is that our knowledge of reading tasks or reading aspects and their teaching grows. There is, however, a risk that we lose sight of the whole, the reading process. Normally, the reader is confronted with several tasks during reading and employs several strategies to perform these tasks. In the near future it will be necessary to design and conduct comprehensive intervention studies in which several strategies are trained together. Before that moment is reached, however, we have to do a lot of instructional studies.

Instruction in reading comprehension

The most influential study in the area of reading comprehension in the late 1970s was Durkin's (1978–9) investigation. This classroom observation study was designed to learn what kind and what amount of comprehension instruction was offered in the fourth grade (age 9–10 years) in the teaching of reading. Durkin and her assistants observed reading lessons in 24 classrooms throughout a year. Her data revealed that less than 1 per cent of the teacher's time was spent on instruction in reading comprehension, 10.7 per cent on assessment in reading comprehension, 10.5 per cent on the transition from one lesson to another, and 9.8 per cent on listening to oral reading. Weterings and Aarnoutse (1986) replicated this study in the Netherlands. We observed twelve fourth-grade teachers at different primary schools during eight lessons in reading comprehension. As in Durkin's study, the data revealed that almost no comprehension instruction was observed. A great deal of time was spent on assessment, non-instruction and helping with assignments in reading comprehension. Durkin's conclusion that teachers tend to be questioners (checkers) and assignment givers rather than instructors was confirmed. Other studies have analyzed reading comprehension instruction in the classroom (Duffy and McIntyre, 1982; Mason and Osborn, 1982; Duffy, 1983; Pearson and Gallagher, 1983) and reading programmes (Beck *et al.*, 1979; Durkin, 1981). From these studies it also transpired that teachers conceive reading comprehension instruction as asking questions and giving assignments; they seldom show pupils how reading tasks can be tackled and performed.

While the teachers' activities were mainly observed in the studies cited above, our second observational study focused on the activities of the pupils (Aarnoutse and Weterings, 1991). An important aspect in this context was the time pupils spend on reading tasks. This time on-task or academic learning time seemed to be an important determinant of the results of learning and an important factor for effective instruction (Rosenshine and Stevens, 1984). Since there were indications that pupils of different abilities make different use of their academic

Table 9.1 Percentage of pupils' time spent on different classroom activities

Observational category	%
Content-oriented	
Reads aloud or follows oral reading	6.1
Reads unsupervised	5.6
Listens to whole class teaching	13.8
Listens to instruction on comprehension skills	0.1
Works out reading assignments in subgroup	4.1
Applies instruction on comprehension skills in subgroup	–
Works out reading assignments individually	23.3
Applies instruction in comprehension skills individually	0.5
Is assessed during whole class discussion	11.5
Gets help during whole class discussion	3.5
Procedural	
Performs procedural activities	9.4
Waits for the teacher	0.5
Off-task activities	
Has completed the task	4.2
Is engaged in a non-appointed task	16.5
Whole class is not engaged	0.9

learning time, we selected three groups of 35 readers from the fifth grade (10–11 years) (good, average and poor comprehenders) from 18 primary schools. There were three main categories of observation: the activities of the pupils, the setting of the pupils and the activities of the teachers. The activities of the pupils and the teachers were further divided into three categories: content-oriented, procedural and off-task or non-instruction activities. The setting of the pupils was divided into whole class instruction, instruction in subgroups and individual instruction. During four lessons the pupils and their teachers ($N = 22$) were observed. Each of two observers observed three pupils per lesson. During 20 seconds the predominant activity of one pupil as well as the predominant activity of the teacher and the setting in which the student worked, were observed and coded within 10 seconds. After 30 seconds the next pupil was observed, etc.

The data revealed (see Table 9.1) that during lessons in reading comprehension pupils on average read about 12 per cent of the time, listen to whole class teaching for 13.8 per cent, work on reading assignments individually for 23.3 per cent and are assessed or listen with attention to the assessment during 11.5 per cent of the time. Table 9.1 shows that pupils receive hardly any instruction in reading comprehension skills or strategies (0.1 per cent). This percentage is very low and disadvantageous to the poor readers, who need a lot of help and explanation.

The pupils perform procedural activities (looking for a textbook, etc.) for 9.9

per cent of the time. In total the pupils are not task-directed during 21.6 per cent of the time, a relatively high percentage. With regard to the setting, it appeared that whole class teaching was dominant. Instruction in subgroups or individually scarcely occurs, despite large and expensive innovation projects concerning differentiation and individualization in the past. It is surprising that for 17.8 per cent of the time teachers are not involved in their lesson: they prepare another lesson, mark e.g. arithmetic work, or do something else. This high percentage of non-instruction indicates that teachers look on lessons in reading comprehension as easy and quiet lessons. It must be emphasized that the above-mentioned percentages are averages. There are large differences between the observed teachers.

Loglinear analysis of the data revealed that there were no significant differences between the three groups of readers with respect to the time spent on the task-directed activities (the content-oriented and the procedural activities). This means that the three groups of pupils made no different use of the academic learning time. A plausible explanation is that teachers use whole class teaching during reading comprehension lessons. In this setting teachers take no account of the differences between the children with respect to reading ability.

Research on reading comprehension instruction

The lack of instruction is due not only to the teachers and the reading programmes but also to the lack of knowledge about strategies or procedures to increase the pupils' ability to comprehend texts (cf. Tierney and Cunningham, 1984). However, several researchers have successfully attempted to extend our knowledge about strategies dealing with several reading comprehension tasks, by testing the effects of instruction in reading comprehension strategies, plans which readers apply and adapt to a variety of texts and tasks. (For reviews, see Paris *et al.*, 1986, 1991; Pressley *et al.*, 1989; Dole *et al.*, 1991; Pearson and Fielding, 1991).

In the following paragraphs we present 15 years' research in the field of reading comprehension instruction. Because this research is based on Kintsch and van Dijk (1978), the schema theory of Rumelhart (1977a), and on the direct instruction model we shall first describe these theories briefly.

Kintsch and van Dijk (1978) have developed a theory on discourse comprehension which is based on the semantic structures of discourse. The most complete description of this theory is given in van Dijk and Kintsch (1983). Their theory assumes that text comprehension is a constructive process, composed of several complex processes (strategies) which operate either serially or in parallel. Text comprehension is a process in which a coherent set of propositions and macropropositions is developed. The theory also assumes that the reading process proceeds in cycles. During one cycle the propositions of a sentence or a clause are processed. This means that some propositions are selected and retained in the buffer of the short-term memory to be connected with some propositions of the next cycle. If a connection is found between the new propositions and those in the buffer, the input is accepted as coherent. If a connection is not possible, an inference process is initiated which adds one or more appropriate propositions. In this way a coherent text base or microstructure is built up. From this text base a macrostructure is constructed by deleting, generalizing and inferring information from the propositions. The macrostructure represents the most essential information in the text base. In this process the reader's knowledge and beliefs and goals play an important role. Van Dijk and Kintsch's theory (1983) is the most comprehensive model of reading comprehension available.

According to Rumelhart (1981), a schema theory describes how knowledge is represented and how representation facilitates the use of knowledge in particular ways. In this view all knowledge is packaged into units or schemata, which represent knowledge at all levels of abstraction. Embedded in these packets is information about how this knowledge is to be used. The schema theorists assume that schemata or knowledge structures play an important role in the process of understanding and remembering discourse. In this view reading comprehension implies the activation of the appropriate schemata and the linking of these schemata with the information of the text. According to Anderson (1977), reading comprehension is an interaction between the knowledge of the reader and the characteristics (and context) of the text: 'There is the "top-down" imposition of schemata ... as well as the "bottom-up" thrust of data' (p. 417). Interpreting a written message is the same as matching the information in the text to the slots in a schema. The information entered into the slots is said to be subsumed by the schema. Reading comprehension is defined as a process of using prior knowledge and the cues provided by the writer to construct a model of the meaning of the text. The schema theory posits a major role for background knowledge in the reading process. It implies that the ease with which readers comprehend texts is directly related to the extent of their prior knowledge. If prior knowledge is considerable, then comprehension can amount to a simple slot-filling activity, minimizing the amount of active text processing required for reading. Conversely, if background knowledge is weak, more processing and difficult inferencing are required to make sense of the text. Compared to van Dijk and Kintsch (1983), the schema theorists are more interested in the role of the reader and the reader's knowledge than in the text and its characteristics.

The direct instruction model reveals that (1) pupils who receive much of their instruction from the teacher do better than those expected to learn on their own or from each other; and that (2) pupils learn to read most effectively when teachers use systematic instruction, monitor their responses and give them feedback about their performance (Rosenshine and Stevens, 1984). According to Duffy and Roehler (1982), direct instruction means an academic focus, sequence of content, modelling strategies, pupil engagement, monitoring and corrective feedback with a gradual shift from teacher-directed activities to independent work. The concept of direct instruction used in our studies parallels Duffy and Roehler's work. This concept corresponds with the ideas of the US National Commission on Reading, which states that direct instruction in comprehension 'means explaining the steps in a thought process that gives birth to comprehension. It may mean that the teacher models a strategy by thinking aloud about how he or she is going about understanding a passage. The instruction includes information on why and when to use the strategy' (Anderson *et al.*, 1985, p. 72).

In our experimental studies the lessons were developed according to the direct instruction paradigm. Each lesson consisted of four phases:

1. *Introduction*: the pupils get an idea of the purpose of the lesson. An exercise from the last lesson is repeated.
2. *Explaining the strategy with examples:* the teacher explains the strategy or procedure to be learned by telling, showing, demonstrating and modelling.
3. *Guided practice*: the strategy is learned by practice. The teacher is present for guidance and feedback. The responsibility for strategy acquisition begins to shift to the student.
4. *Application*: the pupils practise the strategy independently or within small groups. Several exercises of varying complexity are provided and evaluated.

The first study

Aarnoutse (1982) tested the effect of direct instruction in three reading comprehension strategies and tried to answer the questions whether these three strategies were empirically distinctive and whether each trained strategy had a transfer effect on reading comprehension in general. First, we expected a significant effect of the three training programmes on fourth-grade children. Second, we expected that the three strategies would not have an effect on each other. Third, one trained strategy was not expected to have a significant effect on tests of reading comprehension. The argument for the second and third expectations was that reading comprehension is a process in which several distinct strategies are used in combination with each other. The improvement of only one strategy is not strong enough to improve reading comprehension as measured by standardized reading comprehension tests.

On the basis of Kintsch and van Dijk's theory (1978), Rumelhart's schema theory (1981) and studies on inferences and inference training, we selected three reading comprehension strategies:

1. Inferring the main idea from an expository text.
2. Inferring the protagonist's intention from a narrative.
3. Drawing inferences from logical reasoning.

The concept of *main idea* was defined on the basis of Kintsch and van Dijk's (1978) theory. In this view the main idea of a text is a macroproposition which states what the writer essentially wants to say about the theme or topic. Inferring the main idea from an expository text could be defined as finding a statement about the theme of the text which allows the different statements (propositions) in the text to function as arguments. To infer the intention of the protagonist presupposes the necessary knowledge of more or less conventional patterns of actions (Miller and Johnson-Laird, 1976; Schank and Abelson, 1977).

Inferring *the intention of the protagonist* could be defined as finding the motive to act in a narrative, in which a sequence of acts is described as part of the implementation of a plan, without stating the goal of this plan.

Drawing *inferences from logical reasoning* is a strategy which is not as common in primary schools as the other two strategies. In this study we used two types of deductive reasoning: class and conditional reasoning. Class reasoning deals with propositions of the form 'All As are Bs', whereas conditional reasoning involves propositions of the form 'If A, then B'. On the basis of the investigations of several researchers (Ennis and Paulus, 1965; Carroll, 1975) the valid principles of modus ponens and modus tollens and the invalid principles of conversion and inversion were chosen. The reasoning task consisted of a text with a categorical or hypothetical major premiss, a minor premiss and some less relevant sentences. The children were asked to respond to a conclusion in terms of true, not true or maybe. The texts referred to facts that were not within the children's experience.

After defining the three strategies on reading comprehension, we operationalized them into short texts with multiple-choice items. A large number of texts and items was necessary in order to develop tests with two parallel forms for each strategy. Three tests were developed: the *main idea test*, the *intention test* and the *reasoning test*. Each item of each test was based on a separate text. For each test the same question was asked after every text. Psychometric analyses revealed that the tests met the requirements of parallelism, reliability and validity.

The next step was the development of three experimental programmes: the *main idea programme*, the *intention programme* and the *reasoning programme*. These programmes would be used for instruction in the three selected strategies. The programmes were developed on the basis of the research done in the field of main idea, story structure and reasoning, the task analysis procedure of Gagné (1977) and the direct instruction model. An example of the structure and content of the programmes is shown in Table 9.2.

Table 9.2 contains a brief description of the ten lessons of the main idea programme. Lessons 1–4 focus on the theme of a text; lessons 5–10 focus on the main idea. In these lessons the children learn to identify and infer the main idea from a short text. As Table 9.2 shows, the programme is designed according to the step-by-step approach of the direct instruction model. The texts and the tasks are arranged from simple to complex. The goal of the programme can be stated at length (see lesson 10, Table 9.2): the children can independently infer and state the main idea from texts consisting of 4–8 sentences, some relevant and some irrelevant. They can also select the irrelevant sentences. The instructional strategy consisted of four phases, which were repeated in each of the ten lessons. The lessons of the main idea programme were worked out in detail to make sure that they were taught in the same way by a number of different instructors.

Table 9.2 Objectives of the main idea lessons

Lesson	Text features	Task
1.	Relevant sentences; theme in each sentence (3–4)*	Identify theme
2.	Relevant sentences; theme not in each sentence (4–6)	Identify theme
3.	Relevant sentences; theme not in each sentence and scattered (4–9)	Identify theme
4.	Relevant and irrelevant sentences (4–7)	Identify theme and irrelevant sentences
5.	Relevant sentences (4)	Infer main idea (with teacher)
6.	Relevant sentences; main idea (sentence) in the text (5–8)	Identify main idea
7.	Relevant sentences; main idea in the text (5–8)	Find out irrelevant sentences
8.	Relevant and irrelevant sentences; main idea as title (4–6)	Find out irrelevant sentences
9.	Relevant sentences (4–9)	Infer and formulate main idea
10.	Relevant and irrelevant sentences (4–8)	Infer and formulate main idea; find out irrelevant sentences

Note:
* Size of the text in number of sentences.

Before the programme was tested in the experiment, two pilot studies were carried out. With some adaptations the procedure for developing the main idea programme was also used with regard to the two other programmes.

One hundred and eighty-two fourth-grade children from three large primary schools participated. A pre-test/post-test control group design was used in this study. Five standardized tests on decoding, reading comprehension, vocabulary and non-verbal intelligence were administered before pre-testing. Form A of the three strategy tests was administered during pre-testing; form B and again form A of these tests were administered during post-testing and retention testing. Before pre-testing, the fourth-grade pupils of each school were matched on two reading comprehension tests and divided at random into four groups. For a period of five weeks each group received instruction in one of the three experimental programmes or a control programme. The lessons of this programme were just as new as the lessons of the three other programmes; none of the selected strategies was explicitly trained in the control programme. The three experimental groups and the control group received ten lessons (two lessons a week) of 45 minutes each. The lessons were given by university students (experienced primary school teachers) who were intensively prepared for this task. Two different programmes were given by each student-teacher. Post-testing occurred five weeks after the treatment; retention testing took place after the next five weeks. During post-testing and retention testing two standardized reading comprehension tests other than those used before pre-testing were administered.

The main idea programme and the reasoning programme had a significant effect on the main idea test and the reasoning test in the post-testing. The intention programme had no significant effect on the intention test. In the retention test only the reasoning programme had a significant effect. These results indicate that the strategies to infer the main idea from a text and to draw inferences from logical reasoning can be succesfully taught. As predicted, the main idea programme and the reasoning programme had no positive effect on the tests of the other programmes. From this finding we can conclude that the strategies to infer the main idea and to draw inferences from logical reasoning are empirically distinctive. As predicted, the main idea programme and the reasoning programme did not have a transfer effect on tests which measure reading comprehension in general.

The finding in this study that the main idea strategy can be taught successfully is consistent with Baumann's (1984) study, carried out some years later. The fact that instruction in inferring the intention of the protagonist did not result in a positive effect is not in line with the findings of Gordon and Pearson (1983) and Fitzgerald and Spiegel (1983). The lack of effect may be due to the fact that the intention programme was overloaded. To grasp the structure of stories and to infer the intention of the protagonist was perhaps too much for fourth-grade pupils. The strong effect of the reasoning programme can probably be explained by the fact that the strategy to draw inferences from logical reasoning requires mainly strategic knowledge; background knowledge does not play an important part in it. The fact that the two strategies are empirically distinctive confirms our belief that reading comprehension is a process in which several distinct strategies are active. None of the programmes resulted in higher scores on standardized reading comprehension tests. Some years later other researchers (cf. Paris and Oka, 1986) were confronted with the same problem, the lack of far-transfer.

The second study

How reading comprehension strategies can be taught efficiently and effectively was once more the central question of the second experimental study (Aarnoutse and Schmitz, 1991). We were interested in the effect of direct instruction in text-based strategies, i.e. plans or procedures which readers use to solve problems directly related to the text and its structure. Finding the main idea of a text or comprehending anaphoric relationships are text-based strategies rather than reader-based strategies. Planning and controlling one's own reading activities before, during and after reading are more reader-based strategies. These strategies are more psychological than psycholinguistic in nature. In this study we wanted to know the effect of explicit, direct instruction in reading comprehension strategies under normal classroom conditions with regular teachers. Furthermore, we wanted to know which group of readers (poor, average or good readers) would profit most from the instruction. We expected that the poor readers would benefit most from the instruction.

On the basis of the theory of van Dijk and Kintsch (1983), the schema theory and the research on teaching reading comprehension (cf. Tierney and Cunningham, 1984), we selected seven strategies for this study:

1. Comprehending anaphoric relationships.
2. Finding the structure of a narrative.
3. Inferring the intention of the protagonist from a narrative.
4. Inferring the main idea from an expository text.
5. Inferring cause–effect relations from an expository text.
6. Drawing inferences from logical reasoning.
7. Summarizing an expository text of three paragraphs.

Strategies 3, 4 and 6 had already been selected in the first study. The training programmes to teach these strategies were improved on the basis of the experience of the first study and some subsequent studies. To meet the needs of the good and poor readers we developed additional exercises.

With regard to strategy 1, anaphoric relationships are language relations in which a word or phrase is used instead of another word or phrase which has been introduced previously. Anaphora play an important role in the process of understanding sentences and text (cf. Garrod and Sanford, 1977; van Dijk and Kintsch, 1983). Research has shown that children have problems with a number of anaphoric relationships (cf. Lesgold, 1974; Kameenui and Carnine, 1982; Barnitz, 1986; Oakhill and Yuill, 1986). On the basis of the experimental study of Baumann (1986) we developed a programme of eleven lessons for the third- and fourth-grade pupils. In this programme six types of anaphora were included: personal pronouns (he, she), demonstrative anaphora (this, that), locative anaphora (here, there), synonymous anaphora (boy, lad) and superordinate anaphora (dog, animal), arithmetic anaphora (one, some) and inclusive anaphora (the idea, that). In the last three lessons the distance between the antecedent and the anaphora increased systematically. To test the effect of the anaphora programme we developed the anaphora test, consisting of two parallel forms (cf. Roelofs *et al.*, 1991).

With regard to strategy 2, story grammars and structures have been described by Rumelhart (1977), Mandler and Johnson (1977) and Thorndyke (1977). According to Thorndyke a story includes a setting, a theme (a goal or problem faced by the protagonist), one or more plot episodes and a resolution. Several investigators showed that readers use their knowledge of story structure to distinguish between major and minor events, to see relationships between events, to improve memory of the text, to predict outcomes and to facilitate understanding (Kintsch, 1977; Mandler and Johnson, 1977; Thorndyke, 1977). Several studies encouraged children to use story structure as a means of increasing comprehension (cf. Bowman, 1981; Gordon and Pearson, 1983; Fitzgerald and Spiegel, 1983; Greenewald and Rossing, 1986). On the basis of these studies we developed a programme of ten lessons for teaching third- and fourth-grade pupils. In this programme the following components and their relationships were included: protagonist, setting, reaction, goal, plan, actions, obstacles and resolution. To test the effect of the structure programme we developed the structure test, consisting of two parallel forms.

With regard to strategy 5, it is important to point out that texts are frequently filled with causal relations between propositions. These relations are often signalled by terms such as because, since, so, for, hence, therefore, etc. There are instances in which both cause and effect are stated, but where the relation is not explicit; it is also possible that only the cause or the effect is stated. In that case the reader is forced to engage in forward or backward inferencing in order to understand the causal relations. Sometimes these relations are disguised as time relations, conditional relations or explanatory relations. Several researchers have investigated the causal relations between propositions (Kintsch, 1974; Thorn-dyke, 1976; Keenan *et al.*, 1984; Vonk and Noordman, 1990). There are few studies in which the cause–effect relations between propositions or sentences are taught systematically. On the basis of analyses of the cause–effect relation and studies on causal inferences, we developed a programme of eleven lessons for fourth- and fifth-grade pupils. This programme included the following steps: conceptualize cause and effect, identify signal words for cause and effect, identify cause and effect(s) with the help of signal words, infer the cause–effect relation from a short text, infer the cause–effect relation from longer texts. To test the effect of the cause–effect programme we developed the cause–effect test, consisting of two parallel forms.

With respect to strategy 7, Brown and Day's (1983) rules were important. According to Kintsch and van Dijk (1978) mature readers use three rules to construct the macrostructure of a text: deletion, generalization and construction. On the basis of these rules, Brown and Day (1983) identified six summarization rules: (1) delete trivial or irrelevant information, (2) delete redundant information, (3) substitute a superordinate term for a list of items, (4) substitute a superordinate term for a list of actions, (5) select a topic sentence or main idea, if one is available, and (6) infer a topic sentence, if none is available. In the last decade several researchers have shown that teaching students how to summarize texts has a positive effect on written summaries and/or reading comprehension (Day, 1980; McNeil and Donant, 1982; Cunningham, 1982; Hare and Borchardt, 1984; Bean and Steenwijk, 1984; Rinehart *et al.*, 1986). On the basis of the rules of Brown and Day (1983) and the above-mentioned summarization studies we developed a programme of ten lessons for fifth- and sixth-grade pupils. The programme included the following steps: (1) delete irrelevant and redundant information, (2) identify and infer a main idea, (3) write a summary of one paragraph, (4) write a summary of two and three paragraphs. To test the effect of the summary programme we developed the summary test, consisting of two parallel forms. In this test the children have to evaluate a number of summaries.

Table 9.3 Reliability coefficients of the parallel tests and the correlations between their forms

Test	Items	Form A	Form B	r (A, B)
Anaphora	31	0.89	0.86	0.89
Structure	35	0.83	0.82	0.79
Intention	24	0.83	0.82	0.85
Main idea	29	0.89	0.89	0.92
Cause–effect	26	0.85	0.83	0.79
Reasoning	40	0.87	0.87	0.90
Summary	20	0.84	0.88	0.82

The subjects were $\pm$ 500 third- to sixth-grade pupils from six primary schools. A pre-test/post-test design was used in this study. A standardized test on reading comprehension was administered in each year at the beginning and the end of the school year. During pre-testing form A of a (strategy) test was administered; during post-testing form B of the same test followed. Table 9.3 shows the reliability coefficients of the parallel tests and the correlations between forms A and B. The reliability coefficients of these multiple choice tests and the correlations between the forms are high.

Each teacher of all experimental grades received one or two programmes during a school year. A short training for the teachers preceded each programme. To help the teachers to carry out the new method of strategic reading instruction all the lessons of each programme were very detailed. After administering form A of a test the teacher started with the first lesson of the programme. After the last lesson form B was administered. After each lesson and at the end of the programme the teacher filled in a questionnaire. Inspection of the questionnaires showed that the lessons were mostly given as planned.

T-tests revealed that all the seven programmes had a significant effect in all the classes studied. Table 9.4 shows that not all programmes have the same effect. The reasoning programme has the strongest effect in both the fifth and sixth grades. The effects of the main idea, anaphora and structure programmes are strong. The effect of the summary programme is weak. From these results one can conclude that explicit instruction in reading comprehension strategies is possible under normal classroom conditions.

To answer the second question – which group of readers profits most from the instruction? – we divided the sample into three groups (poor, average and good readers) on the basis of the scores of the reading comprehension test. The analysis of the scores of these groups revealed that the average and good readers profited relatively most from the programmes. This fact does not imply a confirmation of the Matthew effect (cf. Stanovich, 1986). In four of the seven programmes the poor readers progressed more, in absolute terms, than the two other groups.

Table 9.4 Results of seven programmes designed to develop reading comprehension strategies

Grade	N	Programme	Form	M	s	t	p
3	159	Anaphora	A	18.35	6.83		
			B	22.46	5.76	9.58	0.000
4	129	Structure	A	22.24	6.28		
			B	27.03	5.33	12.18	0.000
4	129	Intention	A	15.43	4.88		
			B	17.50	4.33	6.03	0.000
4	134	Main idea	A	16.01	6.90		
			B	21.24	5.93	12.24	0.000
5	116	Cause–effect	A	19.15	4.60		
			B	20.98	3.68	5.89	0.000
5	116	Intention	A	17.87	4.55		
			B	19.16	4.14	3.98	0.000
5	118	Reasoning	A	26.66	7.21		
			B	35.03	5.49	16.92	0.000
6	121	Reasoning	A	28.31	7.40		
				35.55	4.43	13.40	0.000
6	93	Summary	A	14.18	2.42		
			B	14.76	2.96	2.71	0.008

Note:
The maximum number of items of each test is presented in Table 9.3.

The third study

The third study is concerned with the structure of expository texts and with the strategy to find the structure of a text. The best-known text analysis systems were developed by Kintsch (1974) and Meyer (1975). Meyer's approach differs from Kintsch's in so far as the unit of analysis is no longer the proposition but the idea. This allows her system to identify the structure of a text. Through application of this system, all information of a text is represented in a detailed outline or tree structure. This structure depicts three aspects: the top-level structure, the macropropositions and the micropropositions. The top-level structure is the rhetorical relationship that ties all propositions in a text together and gives it its overall organization. The macropropositions include the top-level structure of a text and the content and relationships in propositions at the top of the structure.

The micropropositions include the propositions at the middle and bottom levels of the structure. These propositions are found in clauses and sentences.

Meyer identified five rhetorical relationships or patterns authors use to structure their expository writing. These top-level organizational patterns are: description, collection, causation, problem-solving and comparison. Description has only one organizational component – grouping by association – where one element is subordinate to another. This structure gives information about a topic by presenting attributes, specifics, explanations or settings. The collection structure includes more than one grouping by association. The ideas or events are related on the basis of some commonality, such as a sequence of events organized by time or space order. A causation structure has a third organizational component – causal links between elements – in addition to grouping and sequence. A problem-solving structure is derived from, but has more organizational components than, the causation structure. The comparison structure, finally, may have any number of organizational components, depending on how many similarities and differences are presented.

Meyer *et al.* (1980) showed that students who are able to identify and use top-level structures in expository texts recalled not only more information but also more macropropositions than those who did not. Meyer *et al.* assume that readers who are aware of structure search texts for relations that link large chunks of information into a cohesive whole. According to Meyer and her colleagues these readers use the structure strategy:

> Readers employing the structure strategy are hypothesized to approach text looking for patterns which will tie together the propositions contained in the text; in addition, they search for the author's primary thesis which will provide the content to be bound by these patterns or schemata. Then, they search for relationships among this primary thesis and supporting details. (Meyer, 1984, p. 122)

Bartlett (1978) showed that the structure strategy can be taught to ninth-grade pupils. These pupils were taught explicitly to identify four top-level structures (causation, comparison, description and problem-solving) and to use them in their recall protocols. The instruction led to significant increased identification of the top-level structure used in text and its use in recall protocols. Armbruster *et al.* (1987) instructed fifth-grade pupils in using the problem-solving structure when reading social studies materials. The results of this study indicated that direct instruction of this structure can facilitate formation of a macrostructure of that type of text. In Meyer *et al.* (1989), young and old adults were taught five different top-level structures. The training programme, which was developed according to the direct instruction model, was aimed at teaching the adults a specific strategy for remembering what they read. The findings indicated that instruction in the structure strategy increased the amount of information remembered after reading. No effects were found on conventional reading comprehension tests.

On the basis of Meyer's work, the above-mentioned experimental studies and the direct instruction model, we developed two programmes intended to teach the structure strategy to seventh-grade children. The first programme consisted of fourteen lessons to be used for whole-class instruction (van Kan and Aarnoutse, 1993). The first four lessons were directed at identifying the topic and main idea of expository texts. In the other lessons the top-level structures of collection, comparison, problem-solving and causation were taught. The second programme was a computer program. The instructional software of this program consisted of five modules. Besides an instruction module for identifying the topic and main idea of an expository text, the program included the four top-level structures just mentioned. Important parts of the whole-class programme as well as the computer program were: identifying the topic of the text, recognizing signal words, identifying the rhetorical relation, building up the top-level structure of short and longer texts and identifying the main idea of the text.

In the first experiment with a pre-test/post-test control group design, the findings indicated that the whole-class programme enhanced the pupils' ability to recognize the top-level structures in texts. A positive transfer effect on a conventional reading comprehension test was not found. In the second experiment (Entken *et al.*, in press) the central question was whether explicit instruction through educational software would enhance the knowledge and use of two top-level structures as compared to the whole-class programme. A pre-test/post-test control group design was used to assess the effects of the two experimental conditions. The computer-based instruction consisted of six sessions. The first three sessions were devoted to familiarization with the programme and dealt with the module on the topic and main idea of a text. In the next three sessions the modules of problem-solving and causation were presented to the students. The whole-class programme also started with the topic and the main idea (two lessons). Then two lessons on the problem-solving structure followed and two lessons on the causation structure. Results of analysis of variance showed that seventh-grade pupils trained in the problem-solving module as well as pupils trained in the whole-class lessons in the problem-solving structure scored higher on the different measures than the pupils of the control group. A difference between the computer condition and the whole-class condition was not found for this structure. With regard to the causation structure only the whole-class lessons showed a significant effect compared with the control group. Although a sizeable part of the computer sessions and of the whole-class lessons was directed at the top-level structure of the texts and on finding the main idea of the text, no effects were found on a main idea test. It is likely that the time devoted to finding the main idea of a text was too short in both programmes to have any effect on the test. The fact that the effects of the computer sessions largely paralleled those of the whole-class lessons is in line with a general conclusion from research on the effectiveness of computer-based instruction, namely that computer-based instruction increases student achievement at least as much as more conventional modes of instruction.

The fourth study

For the last few years we have been investigating some strategies which are pre-eminently reader-based strategies, namely strategies in the area of metacognition. Metacognition refers to the knowledge and control someone has over his or her own thinking and learning activities. It can be defined as the knowledge a person has to reflect on his or her own cognitive activities, plans or strategies and the ability to monitor and control these strategies. Metacognition in reading means that readers have knowledge and control over at least four variables which play an important role in reading: their own characteristics (their knowledge of the world, interests, skills and strategies), the characteristics of the text (text structures and types), the task or goal to be achieved, and the strategies to be employed before, during and after reading.

A variety of intervention studies has been undertaken to promote reading awareness and comprehension monitoring. Paris *et al.* (1991) distinguish two approaches to interventions: interventions that teach and measure metacognition directly, and interventions that promote metacognition indirectly by teaching specific strategies. An example of the first approach is Paris and Oka's (1986) study, which was designed to promote students' metacognition about reading by teaching them declarative, procedural and conditional knowledge of a variety of comprehension strategies. Approximately 500 third-grade and 500 fifth-grade pupils received an experimental programme (Informed Strategies for Learning) that explicitly taught them to use reading strategies. In the lessons five techniques were used: (1) informed teaching (telling students what a strategy is, and how, when and why it should be used), (2) metaphors for strategies (be a reading detective), (3) group dialogue, (4) guided practice, and (5) bridging to content-area reading. After 4 months of instruction the pupils made significantly greater gains in reading awareness than control pupils, and demonstrated superior strategic skills. However, the intervention failed to change pupils' scores on a standardized reading comprehension test.

An example of the second approach is Palincsar and Brown's (1984) reciprocal teaching method. This method involves an interactive learning game in which the instructor and students alternately lead a dialogue about particular text segments. During this dialogue four strategies are used and taught: (1) predicting or activating relevant knowledge for the purpose of hypothesizing what the author will discuss, (2) questioning or framing the key content in a question, (3) clarifying or taking the appropriate steps to restore meaning, and (4) summarizing or integrating information across sentences and paragraphs. The person who is assuming the role of teacher for a segment notes or solicits points to be clarified, generates a question to which the others in the group respond, gives predictions about what might occur next and summarizes that portion of text. The role the student plays is expanded over time in training from mostly responding to instruction to mostly instructor. Several years of research conducted to evaluate the reciprocal teaching method reveal that this method is a powerful intervention.

Poor readers in the seventh grade who received 20 days of intensive instruction showed improvements in the four strategies and transferred these strategies to lessons in science and social studies. However, the effect on a standardized reading comprehension test was questionable (Palincsar and Brown, 1984). In a later study with third- and fourth-grade pupils, Brown and Palincsar (1989) showed that their method promoted significant changes in pupils' comprehension and comprehension monitoring. Lysynchuk *et al.* (1990) produced convincing evidence that reciprocal teaching can improve standardized reading comprehension performance in poor comprehenders in the fourth and fifth grades.

Following Brown and Palincsar (1989) we designed an experiment in which the four strategies of clarifying, questioning, predicting and summarizing were taught to children aged 9–11 years. The aim of this experiment was to determine the effect of an experimental programme intended for children with decoding and reading comprehension problems, and with different levels of listening comprehension. In this study the children received a programme of twenty lessons in which the reciprocal teaching method and the direct instruction model were combined. The four strategies were taught in a combined reading and listening mode.

In this experiment there were two experimental groups consisting of 45 fourth-grade pupils selected from 13 elementary schools, and 38 pupils from 4 schools of special education. Both groups of children had low scores on a decoding and reading comprehension test, and low or high scores on a listening comprehension test. These two groups received the same programme of 20 lessons: 10 reading lessons, 5 listening lessons and 5 lessons in which reading and listening were combined. The lessons were given by trained student-teachers over 8–10 weeks. The four strategies were taught and discussed in heterogeneous groups of 6 pupils. In each group 3 or 4 children were the experimental subjects, while the other 2 or 3 pupils were what we call teacher supporters – good readers who assisted both the teacher and the poor readers in conducting the discussions. Contrary to the reciprocal teaching method, the four reading comprehension strategies were not presented at the same time. The strategy of predicting was taught in the first few lessons. Then, after these lessons, the second strategy was taught, and so on.

In this experiment with a pre-test/post-test design analysis of variance with repeated measures showed that the programme had a significant effect on the following variables: a test which measured the four strategies in a reading situation, a test which measured the four strategies in a listening situation, a metacognitive questionnaire, and a standardized reading comprehension test. Two significant differences were found between the fourth-grade pupils and the children from the special schools: the fourth-grade pupils performed better on the test which measured the four strategies in a reading situation and on a standardized listening comprehension test. Although these results are promising, the gains need to be compared with a control group. Until that time we cannot draw strong conclusions from this experiment (Gruwel *et al.*, in press).

Conclusion and discussion

From the studies reviewed we can draw two conclusions:

1. Primary school children receive hardly any instruction in reading comprehension skills or strategies. This lack of instruction is due to teacher training and to the traditional reading programmes used in the school.
2. Reading comprehension strategies can be taught effectively to primary school children. By teaching and developing strategies step by step, by explaining, demonstrating and modelling the involved strategies carefully and explicitly, and by practising all steps with texts that increase in complexity, children can learn how to tackle reading tasks or problems.

This does not mean that all the questions about instruction in reading comprehension strategies have now been answered. On the contrary, experimental studies need to be carried out in the near future to explore which elements or components of a successful intervention are responsible for the effect. Intervention programmes which differ in the sequence or number of lessons, in the way a strategy is explained or modelled, in the settings used (whole classroom, group work or individual), or in the way the children are motivated need to be compared with one another. Such studies are very important because they will reveal which factor or factors cause the effect of an intervention or treatment.

As we said in the introduction, the risk of the strategy approach is that strategies are taught in isolation and that they fragment the reading process. To avoid isolation it is important that intervention studies are carried out in which several strategies are trained in connection with each other. Interventions in which the children learn when and how to apply some important strategies before, during and after the reading process. Palincsar and Brown (1989), Paris and Oka (1986) and Lysynchuk *et al.* (1990) are a good point of departure.

A question that requires a lot more research has to do with transfer. Transfer can be defined as the influence which previously learned knowledge and skills have on the use of this knowledge and these skills in new learning situations and fields of application (Simons, 1990). Mayer and Greeno (1972) differentiate between near- and far-transfer. In reading, one can speak of near-transfer when the reader can apply a learned strategy to tasks and texts that differ slightly from the tasks and texts used during the training situation. When a reader can apply the learned strategies to tasks and texts that differ strongly from the tasks and texts used during the intervention, one can speak of far-transfer. An example of far-transfer is the application of strategies to standardized reading comprehension tests. From the above-mentioned studies we know that carefully designed instruction in one or more reading comprehension strategies can result in near-transfer, measured with different instruments. In the studies that were reviewed, however, far-transfer is the greatest problem: only some of the studies could boast of far-transfer effects (Brown and Palincsar, 1989; Lysynchuk *et al.*, 1990). That certain measurement instruments, i.e. standardized reading comprehension tests, account for the failing of far-transfer effects (cf. Paris and Oka, 1986) is an argument that is not convincing enough. This does not mean, however, that the need for developing other instruments measuring reading comprehension in general is not true. We think that the real causes have to be sought in the intervention programmes themselves.

The most important failures of the intervention programmes that try to realize far-transfer are:

1. *They train too few strategies*: Since we know that reading comprehension is a complex process with several interacting subprocesses which require several strategies or actions from the reader, it is logical that teaching and developing one strategy only cannot influence reading comprehension in general. Improving reading comprehension in general involves the learning of several strategies and their application to a variety of texts.
2. *Their duration is too short*: If one wants to realize far-transfer, it is necessary to design and carry out intervention programmes that take several months to a year. Learning to use and apply higher-order strategies takes a lot of time for primary school children. Besides, we must realize that standardized reading comprehension tests are only sensitive to interventions that last several months to a year.
3. *They are not sufficiently focused on transfer*: We must stress that far-transfer needs to be trained or taught. To apply the developed strategies to different situations, to tasks and texts that are not nicely presented and not well structured or written, is a complex and difficult task that needs intensive instruction or training. For children and students it is important to become aware of the fact that a lot of (expository) texts are badly written, and that occasionally it is impossible to apply the learned strategies. A higher level of far-transfer and metacognition is hardly possible.

Another question that requires a lot of research concerns the development of several reading comprehension strategies during the elementary school years. Longitudinal studies that describe the development of these strategies are very important for the improvement of reading comprehension instruction. For some years now it has been possible to follow children in the Netherlands from the second to the sixth grade who are using a reading programme designed according to the ideas of the strategic instruction approach (Aarnoutse and Van de Wouw, 1991). The development of several reading comprehension strategies of the children using this programme could be compared with the development of the children who are using the programme *Lees je Wijzer* (Read and Get Wise) based on Bol (1982) and described in this volume by Gresnigt (Chapter 10).

References

Aarnoutse, C.A.J. (1982), *Aspecten van begrijpend lezen in het vierde leerjaar van het gewoon lager onderwijs* [Aspects of Reading Comprehension in the Fourth Grade of the Elementary School], Nijmegen: Berkhout.
Aarnoutse, C.A.J. and Schmitz, H. (1991), 'Onderwijs in begrijpend en studerend lezen'

[Instruction in reading comprehension and study skills], *Pedagogisch Tijdschrift, 4*, 219–33.

Aarnoutse, C.A.J. and Van de Wouw, J. (1991), *Wie dit leest. Een methode voortgezet lezen aansluitend bij Veilig Leren Lezen* [Who Reads This. A reading programme for the elementary school], Tilburg: Zwijsen.

Aarnoutse, C.A.J. and Weterings, A.C.E.M. (1991), *Onderwijs en begrijpend lezen* [Instruction and Reading Comprehension], Nijmegen: KUN, Vakgroep Onderwijskunde.

Anderson, R.C. (1977), 'The notion of schemata and the educational enterprise'. In R.C. Anderson, R.J. Spiro and W.E. Montague (eds.) *Schooling and the Acquisition of Knowledge*, Hillsdale, NJ: Lawrence Erlbaum, pp. 415–31.

Anderson, R.C., Hubert, E.H., Scott, J.A. and Wilkinson, J. (1985), *Becoming a Nation of Readers*, Washington, DC: National Institute of Education.

Armbruster, B.B., Anderson, T.H. and Ostertag, J. (1987), 'Does text structure/ summarization instruction facilitate learning from expository text?' *Reading Research Quarterly, 22*, 331–46.

Barnitz, J.G. (1986), 'The anaphora jigsaw puzzle in psycholinguistic and reading research'. In J.W. Irwin (ed.) *Understanding and Teaching Cohesion Comprehension*, Newark, DE: International Reading Association, pp. 45–55.

Bartlett, B.J. (1978), *Top-level Structure as an Organizational Strategy for Recall of Classroom Text*, unpublished doctoral dissertation, Arizona State University, Tempe.

Baumann, J.F. (1984), 'Effectiveness of a direct instruction paradigm for teaching main idea comprehension', *Reading Research Quarterly, 20*, 93–108.

Baumann, J.F. (1986), 'Teaching third grade students to comprehend anaphoric relationships: The application of a direct instruction model', *Reading Research Quarterly, 21*, 71–84.

Bean, T.W. and Steenwijk, F.L. (1984), 'The effect of three forms of summarization instruction on sixth graders' summary writing and comprehension', *Journal of Reading Behavior, 15*, 297–306.

Beck, J.L., McKeown, M.G., McCaslin, E.S. and Burkes, A.M. (1979), *Instructional Dimensions that may Affect Reading Comprehension: Example from two commercial reading programs*, Pittsburgh: Learning Research and Development Center.

Bol, E. (1982), *Leespsychologie* [The Psychology of Reading], Groningen: Wolters-Noordhoff.

Bowman, M.A. (1981), 'The effect of story structure questioning upon the comprehension and metacognitive awareness of sixth grade students', *Dissertation Abstracts International, 42*, 626A.

Brown, A.L. and Day, J.D. (1983), 'Macrorules for summarizing texts: the development of expertise', *Journal of Verbal Learning and Verbal Behavior, 22*, 1–14.

Brown, A.L. and Palincsar, A.S. (1989), 'Guided, cooperative learning and individual knowledge acquisition'. In L.B. Resnick, *Knowing, Learning, and Instruction. Essays in honor of Robert Glaser*, Hillsdale, NJ: Lawrence Erlbaum, pp. 393–451.

Carroll, C.A. (1975), 'Low achievers' understanding of logical inference forms'. In M.F. Rosskopf (ed.) *Children's Mathematical Concepts. Six Piagetian studies in mathematics education*, New York: Teachers College Press, pp. 173–208.

Cunningham, J.W. (1982), 'Generating interactions between schemata and text'. In J.A. Niles and L.A. Harris (eds.) *New Inquiries in Reading Research and Instruction*, Rochester, NY: National Reading Conference, pp. 42–7.

Day, J.D. (1980), *Training Summarization Skills: A comparison of teaching methods*, unpublished doctoral dissertation, University of Illinois, Urbana-Champaign.

Dole, J.A., Duffy, G.G., Roehler, L.R. and Pearson, P.D. (1991), 'Moving from the old to the new: research on reading comprehension instruction', *Review of Educational Research, 61*, 239–64.

Duffy, G. (1983), *From Turn Taking to Sense Making: Classroom factors and improved reading achievement*, Michigan State University: Institute for Research on Teaching.

Duffy, G.G. and McIntyre, C.W. (1982), 'A naturalistic study of instructional assistance in primary grade reading', *The Elementary School Journal, 83,* 15–23.

Duffy, G., and Roehler, L. (1982), 'The illusion of instruction', *Reading Research Quarterly, 17,* 438–45.

Durkin, D. (1978–9), 'What classroom observations reveal about reading comprehension instruction', *Reading Research Quarterly, 15,* 481–533.

Durkin, D. (1981), 'Reading comprehension instruction in five basal reading series', *Reading Research Quarterly, 16,* 515–44.

Ennis, R.H. and Paulus, D.H. (1965), *Critical Thinking Readiness in Grades 1–12. Phase 1: Deductive reasoning in adolescence*, Ithaca, NY: Cornell Critical Thinking Project.

Entken, M., Voeten, M., Bergmans, A. and Aarnoutse, C. (in press), 'Teaching structures of expository texts through educational software'. In F.P.C.M. de Jong and B.H.A.M. van Hout-Wolters (eds.) *Process-oriented Instruction, Verbal and Pictorial Aids & Comprehension Strategies*, Amsterdam: VU University Press.

Fitzgerald, J. and Spiegel, D.L. (1983), 'Enhancing children's reading comprehension through instruction in narrative structure', *Journal of Reading Behavior, 15,* 1–17.

Gagné, R.M. (1977), *The Conditions of Learning*, New York: Holt, Rinehart & Winston.

Garrod, S. and Sanford, A. (1977), 'Interpreting anaphoric relations', *Journal of Verbal Learning and Verbal Behavior, 16,* 77–90.

Gordon, C.J. and Pearson, P.D. (1983), *The Effects of Instruction in Metacomprehension and Inferencing on Children's Comprehension Abilities*, (Technical Report No. 277), Urbana: University of Illinois, Center for the Study of Reading.

Greenewald, M.J. and Rossing, R.L. (1986), 'Short-term and long-term effects of story grammar and self-monitoring training on children's story comprehension'. In J.A. Niles and R.V. Calik (eds.) *Solving Problems in Literacy: Learners, teachers, and researchers* (Thirty-fifth Yearbook of the National Reading Conference), Rochester NY: National Reading Conference, pp. 210–13.

Gresnigt, G. (1994), 'Learning to read and cognitive development: communication oriented teaching of reading comprehension'. In E.M.H. Assink (ed.) *Literacy Acquisition and Social Context*, Hemel Hempstead: Harvester-Wheatsheaf.

Gruwel, F.L.J.M., Aarnoutse, C.A.J. and Van den Bos, K.P. (in press), 'Reciprocal teaching on text comprehension strategies in a reading and listening situation'. In J.E. Rink, R.C. Vos, K.P. van den Bos, P.L. Friesema and R van Wijck (eds.) *Prospectives of Special Education*, Amersfoort-Leuven: Garant.

Hare, V.C. and Borchardt, K.M. (1984), 'Direct instruction of summarization skills', *Reading Research Quarterly, 20,* 62–78.

Kameenui, E.J. and Carnine, D.W. (1982), 'An investigation of fourth graders' comprehension of pronoun constructions in ecologically valid texts', *Reading Research Quarterly, 17,* 556–80.

Keenan, J.M., Baillet, S.D. and Brown, P. (1984), 'The effects of causal cohesion on comprehension and memory', *Journal of Verbal Learning and Verbal Behavior, 23,* 115–26.

Kintsch, W. (1974), *The Representation of Meaning in Memory*. Hillsdale, NJ: Lawrence Erlbaum.

Kintsch, W. (1977), 'On comprehending stories'. In M.A. Just and P.A. Carpenter (eds.) *Cognitive Processes in Comprehension*, Hillsdale, NJ: Lawrence Erlbaum, pp. 33–62.

Kintsch, W. and van Dijk, T.A. (1978), 'Toward a model of text comprehension and production', *Psychological Review, 85,* 363–94.

Lesgold, A.M. (1974), 'Variability in children's comprehension of syntactic structure', *Journal of Educational Psychology, 66,* 333–8.

Lysynchuk, L.M., Pressley, M. and Vye, N.J. (1990), 'Reciprocal teaching improves standardized reading comprehension performance in poor comprehension', *The Elementary School Journal*, *90*, 469–84.

Mandler, R.M. and Johnson, N.S. (1977), 'Remembrance of things parsed: story structure and recall', *Cognitive Psychology*, *9*, 111–51.

Mason, J. and Osborn, J. (1982), *When Do Children Begin Reading to Learn? A survey of classroom reading instruction practices in grades two through five* (Technical Report No. 261), University of Illinois at Urbana-Champaign: Center for the Study of Reading.

Mayer, R. and Greeno, J.G. (1972), 'Structural differences between learning outcomes produced by different instructional methods', *Journal of Educational Psychology*, *63*, 165–73.

McNeil, J. and Donant, L. (1982), 'Summarization strategy for improving reading comprehension'. In J.A. Niles and L.A. Harris (eds.) *New Inquiries in Reading Research and Instruction*, Rochester, NY: National Reading Conference, pp. 215–19.

Meyer, B.J.F. (1975), *The Organization of Prose and its Effect on Memory*, Amsterdam: North-Holland.

Meyer, B.J.F. (1984), 'Organized aspects of text: effects on reading comprehension and applications for the classroom'. In J. Flood (ed.), *Promoting Reading Comprehension*, Newark, DE: International Reading Association, pp. 113–38.

Meyer, B.J.F., Brandt, D.M. and Bluth, G.J. (1980), 'Use of top-level structure in text: key for reading comprehension of ninth-grade students', *Reading Research Quarterly*, *16*, 72–103.

Meyer, B.J.F., Young, C.J. and Bartlett, B.J. (1989), *Memory Improved: Reading and memory enhancement across the life span through strategic text structures*, Hillsdale, NJ: Lawrence Erlbaum.

Miller, G.A. and Johnson-Laird, P.N. (1976), *Language and Perception*. Cambridge, MA: Harvard University Press.

Oakhill, J. and Yuill, N. (1986), 'Pronoun resolution in skilled and less skilled comprehenders. Effects of memory load and inferential complexity', *Language and Speech*, *29*, 25–37.

Palincsar, A.S. and Brown, A.L. (1984), 'Reciprocal teaching of comprehension-fostering and comprehension-monitoring activities', *Cognition and Instruction*, *1*, 117–75.

Palincsar, A.S. and Brown, A.L. (1989), 'Instruction for self-regulated reading'. In L.B. Resnick and L.L. Klopfer (eds.) *Toward the Thinking Curriculum: Current cognitive research*, Yearbook of the Association for Supervision and Curriculum Development, pp. 19–39.

Paris, S.G. and Oka, E.R. (1986), 'Children's reading strategies, metacognition, and motivation', *Developmental Review*, *6*, 25–56.

Paris, S.G., Wasik, B.A. and Turner, J.C. (1991), 'The development of strategic readers'. In R. Barr, M.L. Kamil, P.B. Mosenthal and P.D. Pearson (eds.) *Handbook of Reading Research*, Vol. 2, White Plains, NY: Longman, pp. 609–40.

Paris, S.G., Wixson, K.K. and Palincsar, A.S. (1986), 'Instructional approaches to reading comprehension'. In E. Rothkopf (ed.), *Review of Research in Education*, vol. 14, Washington, DC: American Research Association, pp. 91–128.

Pearson, P.D. and Fielding, L. (1991), 'Comprehension instruction'. In R. Barr, M.L. Kamil, P.B. Mosenthal and P.D. Pearson (eds.) *Handbook of Reading Research* Vol. 2, White Plains, NY: Longman, pp. 815–60.

Pearson, P.D. and Gallagher, M.C. (1983), 'The instruction of reading comprehension', *Contemporary Educational Psychology*, *8*, 317–44.

Pearson, P.D. and Gallagher, M.C. (1983), *The Instruction of Reading Comprehension* (Technical Report No. 297), University of Illinois at Urbana-Champaign: Center for the Study of Reading.

Pressley, M., Johnson, C.J., Symons, S., McGoldrick, J.A. and Kurita, J.A. (1989), 'Strategies that improve children's memory and comprehension in what is read', *The Elementary School Journal, 90*, 3–32.

Rinehart, S.D., Stahl, S.A. and Erickson, L.G. (1986), 'Some effects of summarization training on reading and studying', *Reading Research Quarterly, 21*, 422–38.

Roelofs, E.C., Aarnoutse, C.A.J. and Voeten, M.J.M. (1991), 'Leren begrijpen van anaforische relaties in teksten: effecten van instructie in jaargroep vijf van het basisonderwijs' [Comprehending anaphoric relationships in texts: effects of instruction in grade 3], *Tijdschrift voor Onderwijsresearch, 16*, 93–106.

Rosenshine, B. and Stevens, R. (1984), 'Classroom instruction in reading'. In P.D. Pearson, R. Barr, M.L. Kamil and P. Mosenthal (eds.), *Handbook of Reading Research*, Vol. 1, White Plains, NY: Longman, pp. 745–98.

Rumelhart, D.E. (1977a), 'Toward an interactive model of reading'. In S. Dornic (ed.) *Attention and Performance*. Hillsdale, NJ: Lawrence Erlbaum, pp. 573–603.

Rumelhart, D.E. (1977b), 'Understanding and summarizing brief stories'. In D. La Berge and J.J. Samuels (eds.), *Basic Processes in Reading: Perception and Comprehension*, Hillsdale, NJ: Lawrence Erlbaum, pp. 265–303.

Rumelhart, D.E. (1981), 'Schemata: the building blocks of cognition'. In R.J. Spiro, B.C. Bruce and W.F. Brewer (eds.) *Theoretical Issues of Reading Comprehension*, Hillsdale, NJ: Lawrence Erlbaum.

Schank, R.C. and Abelson, R.P. (1977), *Scripts, Plans, Goals, and Understanding*, Hillsdale, NJ: Lawrence Erlbaum.

Simons, P.R.J. (1990), *Transfervermogen* [Transfer of Learning], Nijmegen: Quickprint.

Stanovich, K.E. (1986), 'Matthew effects in reading. Some consequences of individual differences in acquisition of literacy', *Reading Research Quarterly, 21*, 360–407.

Thorndyke, P.W. (1976), 'The role of inferences in discourse comprehension', *Journal of Verbal Learning and Verbal Behavior, 15*, 437–46.

Thorndyke, P.W. (1977), 'Cognitive structures in comprehension and memory of narrative discourse', *Cognitive Psychology, 9*, 77–110.

Tierney, R.J. and Cunningham, J.W. (1984), 'Research on teaching comprehension'. In P.D. Pearson, R. Barr, M.L. Kamil and P. Mosenthal (eds.), *Handbook of Reading Research*, Vol. 1, White Plains, NY: Longman, pp. 609–55.

van Dijk, T.A. and Kintsch, W. (1983), *Strategies of Discourse Comprehension*, New York: Academic Press.

van Kan, N. and Aarnoutse, C. (1993), *Programma Structuur van Informatieve Teksten voor het Voortgezet Onderwijs* [Programme Structure of Expository Texts for Secondary Education], Nijmegen: Berkhout.

Vonk, W. and Noordman, L.G.M. (1990), 'On the control of references in text understanding'. In D.A. Balota, G.B. Flores d'Arcais and K. Rayner (eds.) *Comprehension Processes in Reading*, Hillsdale, NJ: Lawrence Erlbaum.

Weterings, A.C.E.M. and Aarnoutse, C.A.J. (1986), 'De praktijk van het onderwijs in begrijpend lezen' [Reading comprehension practices], *Pedagogische Studiën, 63*, 387–401.

10

Learning to read and cognitive development: communication-oriented teaching of reading comprehension

Giel Gresnigt
Department of Experimental Psychology, University of Utrecht

This chapter discusses the theoretical and empirical results of a research project aimed at the development of reading comprehension in primary school education (informative texts) in Dutch schools. An experimental reading curriculum entitled *Lees je Wijzer* (LJW) [Read and Get Wise] was developed, based on Bol (1982). This theory is inspired by neo-Vygotskian developmental and educational theory on the stimulation of cognitive development. Drawing on Bol's theory a series of teaching experiments investigating the teaching of reading informative texts was developed. In this chapter we give an account of Bol's theory and the results of the teaching experiments.

Introduction

Historically, there has been hardly any specific teaching of reading comprehension in primary schools in The Netherlands. The basic philosophy of current reading education consists of on-the-job learning. Most attention is paid to reading, with poorly explained exercises, such as retelling the story and summarizing (Weterings and Aarnoutse, 1986), and with much time spent on the technical aspects of reading and language development. In short, reading comprehension is tested rather than taught (Boonman and Kok, 1986), and pupils have to discover for themselves how to acquire the various skills that underlie the required achievements. Furthermore, the endless testing of skills that have never been taught is not unique to The Netherlands (e.g. Durkin, 1979). What is more, many pupils never reach an acceptable level of reading comprehension. A not uncommon explanation for this unsatisfactory situation is that little is known about the reading process, and for that reason it is not clear how reading comprehension should be improved.

In this chapter we shall discuss the theoretical background and testing in the primary school setting of an experimental curriculum in reading comprehension of informative texts. The reading curriculum is based on Bol (1982). Bol starts from a communication-oriented approach to reading comprehension. The curriculum, *Lees je Wijzer* [Read and Get Wise], assumes that a number of problems with reading and studying can be avoided if the usual achievement tasks are part of an approach that is directed at the provision of a specific orientation base (Gal'perin, 1969; Van Parreren and Carpay, 1980). Pupils must first be properly introduced to a learning task before they can reasonably be expected to perform the task on their own.

First, we shall discuss the theoretical basis of the course. This concerns the question of what pupils should learn in order to meet the demands of informative texts. Then, we shall discuss the question of how the relevant skills can be taught efficiently. Finally, we shall give a short account of the results of the experimental course.

Task analysis

Reading is a complex skill. In order to read it is, of course, first necessary for a pupil to be able to decode reasonably well. Second, a sufficient knowledge of the language is necessary: i.e. its grammar and vocabulary. Third, the reader must possess sufficient knowledge of the world in order to be able to understand texts. Finally, the reader must have the capacity to think and reason in order to detect and solve problems in relation to the meaning of what is written. We refer to the prominent role of thinking, conceived as the active interpretation of the information by the reader, the development of a conscious awareness in relation to these problems and the development of the ability to solve such problems. Because the active analysis of statements in texts as a rule constitutes the biggest problem in reading and learning, the theoretical analysis of the factors that can obstruct or promote this reasoning is of great importance.

Before investigating this matter further, we want to point out that the importance of learning to think and interpret texts in the context of thinking and reasoning skills is not emphasized by all researchers. Traditionally, the concept of reading ability has been restricted to a narrow, psycholinguistic sense. Advocates of such an approach assume that comprehension of decontextualized written language can be reached primarily on the basis of the processing of linguistic information. As a rule, cognitive psychological analyses are confined to linguistic structures and the rules of transformation from these to other structures, usually postulated as psychological (for instance, concepts, schemata, structures of logical relations). Perfetti (1985, p. 8), for instance, explicitly supports the psycholinguistic view that 'reading ability can be understood in terms of linguistic processes'. Word decoding, lexical access, working memory and knowledge of the world are believed to be the ultimate factors that determine the level of reading ability. As a consequence of psycholinguistic concepts of meaning, communication ability is rarely recognized as a factor in reading comprehension. Moreover, for Perfetti – as for most information processing theorists – reading is regarded as a purely individual process, not a social activity, because 'there is no communication partner' (*ibid.*). The assumption that meaning is conventionalized in the text itself further implies that written language is essentially decontextualized.

We have chosen another approach, which is associated with Vygotsky (1962, 1978) and Wittgenstein (1971). According to both Vygotsky and Wittgenstein, language utterances only have meaning when they are seen as speech-acts, which have their place in a wider frame of human activity. The concept of speech acts is also clearly stated by Austin (1962). The reading of texts is seen in the framework of the communication between intentionally acting subjects (Hörmann, 1976, 1986). The possibility of communication between intentionally acting subjects is closely connected with shared knowledge and experience (Leon'tev, 1979).

We conceive reading comprehension to be a goal-directed activity, aimed at the understanding of the intention of the author. The reader sees words and sentences. The significance of these words and sentences can become clear as soon as a connection can be established with the writer's underlying plan. But this interpretation process can only succeed when the reader accepts that the writer has a plan and motive for his or her language. Speech as such is not sensible, but becomes sensible by virtue of the general consideration that speech *must* be sensible. This is what Hörmann (1976) calls *Sinnkonstanz* (sense constancy). Hörmann illustrates this in a number of instances; e.g. the statement 'The theory of relativity is blue' gives rise to a thinking activity which may lead to the conclusion that a book must be meant.

This point of view implies that a text can only be understood when the reader assumes that the text has been written by a writer who intends to make a sensible statement. The conflict between what appears not to be sensible and the general idea that language is being used in a sensible way prompts the thinking and reasoning which is characteristic of competent reading. The competent reader's thinking is not only determined by language rules, actualized cultural scripts and cognitive schemata, but also by the way the reader *works* with the information. A linguistic and logical manipulation is necessary, but not sufficient. The competent reader is a very active authority, who at the same time gives meaning to the text. As opposed to psycholinguistic and cognitive views, where texts are considered as things in themselves, we see texts as a social phenomenon, as something between people.

In our conception, the understanding of words, passages and texts as a whole necessarily rests on a creative intellectual activity which differs from strict psycholinguistic processing. This activity is directed towards the solving of communicative problems. Reading is seen as a problem-solving process, in which the reader makes use of all sorts of linguistic and non-linguistic information. The reader is engaged in an internal dialogue with the writer (Bol, 1982; Hörmann, 1986) or a 'long distance discussion with the author' (Goodman and Burke, 1980) to make sense of the text.

It is apparent that advocates of the two different language-to-meaning conceptions agree that during the development of language and/or language proficiency a stage exists when the comprehension of utterances is dependent on the extralinguistic communicative context. The point of disagreement is whether this context in the case of decontextualized written texts vanishes completely as an independent factor in the processing of information – and is absorbed by sophisticated linguistic structures and knowledge of the world – or remains active at an internal level. Following Vygotsky's internalization hypothesis we assume that, in the case of decontextualized written texts, the extralinguistic context of the activity involved (including the actor role of the subject) can be transposed to an internal, conceptualized plane. Reading and writing are activities which involve a discourse or discussion on an internal plane, with someone not actually present, performed 'in the head' of the writer or the reader. The process of fitting textual information and internally depicted context of activity to each other, therefore, is the core activity of the mind in the case of text comprehension (Bol, 1988).

Results of an inquiry concerning the relation between communication ability and reading comprehension (Bol *et al.*, 1991) indicate, that – along with factors such as technical reading and language ability (grammar, vocabulary) – communication ability plays an important and independent role in reading comprehension and that pupils with a higher communication ability score higher in reading comprehension tests. By communication ability we mean the ability to put oneself in the place and the way of thinking of the other (the writer, what he or she wants and thinks) in decontextualized situations.

The crucial point is that statements only acquire meaning against the background of this inter-mental cooperation. The writer as a rule tries to be as lucid as possible. The reader is the partner who thinks with him or her. Communication as the 'making' of meaning implies that the communication partners try to reach a common 'field' of attention and interpretations, the common 'making' of thoughts, emotions, ideas, values, plans, norms, and so on. This requires the capacity to analyze the communication situation and to place oneself in the position of the writer: what he or she wants, thinks and does, and his or her viewpoint. In order to do this it is necessary for the participants in the communication to have a basic mental model of cooperation at their disposal, which Bol (1982) calls the *communicative triangle* (see Figure 10.1).

In Figure 10.1 the horizontal line represents a social directedness and the fact that people approach each other as intentionally acting *subjects* directed towards cooperation. By 'domain' a more or less delineated area of human *activity* is implied.

The way in which this scheme develops is of some interest. During the first years of their lives, children experience a multitude of situations in which

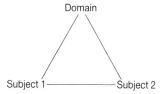

Figure 10.1 Communicative triangle.

common activity takes place according to relatively fixed, ritualized patterns (e.g. eating, bathing, playing). Within the framework of such situations, social roles, actions and intentions form the anchor points, on the basis of which the language can be learned. At first the language in the communication can only be used to point out persons and actions in concrete situations. In doing so, it is characteristic that the people and essential facts involved are present in the situation – the elementary linguistic usage functions within the 'here and now' of an actual situation. An important step forward is made when the child learns to use language to describe factual and intended topics.

On the basis of such descriptions it becomes possible to exceed the direct here and now action context, so that the participants can speak and think about matters that are situated elsewhere in time and place. The situation about which they speak then lies on a verbal and inner plane, rather than on a material one. The top of the communicative triangle (the domain) is, in this case, not on a material but on a mental level. This development makes high demands on language development and imaginative faculties.

In the case of oral messages, the communication situation (the horizontal part of the communicative triangle) is still physically present. However, with written texts this is no longer the case. Not only is the situation absent, there is also no eye contact with the communication partner. In the case of a written text, the acting human being is hidden behind the text. The communicative triangle lies completely on an inner level, via a process of internalization. In the same way writing differs from speaking.

Writing as well as reading requires a fundamentally different relation to the communication situation. That is to say that in the case of written language, the communicative context must be imagined. 'It is a conversation with a white sheet of paper, with an imaginary or conceptualized interlocutor. Still, like oral speech, it is a conversational situation. Written speech requires a dual abstraction from the child. It requires an abstraction from the auditory aspects of speech and an abstraction from the interlocutor' (Vygotsky, 1987). Writing and reading are therefore much more difficult for the 8-year-old child than speaking and listening.

In the case of common daily communication, an intuitive notion of the communication situation involved (or an intuitive mental model of the communicative triangle) is sufficient. However, giving meaning to written texts requires a more profound and conceptualized 'metacommunicative' understanding in the communication situation. Flavell (1977, 1979) has defined metacognition as a growing consciousness of psychological processes and argued that 'meta-communication' is of crucial interest for success in school. He suggests that communicative competence is not only concerned with the communication itself but also with reflection on the communicative activity as such.

Such an insight arises partly from spontaneous experiences with written utterances and other forms of more indirect communication. However, it appears that primary school children are only partly able to form an inner picture of the communicative setting of written texts. The text appears to them as an isolated thing, discrete from the writer as interlocutor. The deliberate regulation falls out, so to speak, resulting in passive reading. In our opinion a large component of the problem with the understanding of texts originates from the fact that there is little attention to this question in the current reading comprehension courses.

Without a sufficiently profound and conceptualized metacognitive insight into the written communication situation, it is meaningless to present informative texts in educational settings. However, this is a necessary but not a sufficient condition. It will be clear that with respect to content informative texts do not relate to the ordinary daily situations pupils are used to. To that end a further explanation of the communicative setting of informative texts is necessary, to create the possibility for the pupil to comprehend the nature of the activity of the writer.

In order to work with this more conceptualized knowledge, it is necessary for pupils to make themselves familiar with the elementary 'methods of inquiry' (Bol, 1982) that are used by the writers of informative texts. The author makes use of methods like analysis, comparison, classification, models of change-processes and causality. These methods are used for the development of constructions, by means of which knowledge can be fixed (Lompscher *et al.*, 1975). In a text about an eclipse of the moon, for instance, the writer analyzes (the earth is round), describes change-processes (the moon circles the earth), cause and effect, and the like. The meaning of the concept 'whale' can be explained in a text. The description can be linked to the more general concept 'mammal'. Some whales can be described and compared, so that the concept 'whale' can be fitted into a conceptual system (classification).

These 'knowledge operations' (Lompscher *et al.*, 1975) are conceived as the most elementary thinking operations in the function of the acquisition of coherent knowledge, for reading as well as research in a broader sense. In order to cope with informative texts, it is necessary for pupils to be systematically introduced into these more developed and intentionally applied forms of inquiry.

Against the theoretical background briefly described here, it should now be clear that reading education does not end with technical mastery, the development of knowledge and language ability. Along with demands which are made on the lexical, grammatical and semantic aspects, the point at issue with regard to reading education is the addition of communicative competence.

A relatively small number of essential insights and mental skills are at issue here. First, the reader must be able to build up clear images of written statements. This has to do with the fact that the domain of written texts lies at the mental level. Second, in order to understand the meaning of these images the pupil must come to understand that a text is not only a series of sentences on a sheet of paper but also the product of a purposefully thinking and acting person, who turns towards the reader with a certain intention. A reader must be able to orient within the intersubjective communicative settings of texts and intentions of writers. Third, in the case of informative texts, a further elaboration of these communicative settings is required, in the course of which the pupil learns to orient him or herself to the nature of the activity of the writer, what he or she thinks and does, and why. To that end, it is essential that the reader is reasonably familiar with the elementary methods of inquiry used by the writer.

The strategy of education

In this section we shall briefly discuss the education strategy of the reading curriculum *Lees je Wijzer* [Read and Get Wise]. The central issue is the principle with which the learning goals can be reached. A first general characteristic of our reading curriculum is that pupils are not confronted with ready-to-use reading strategies as in *direct instruction*, but that the aim is to create meaningful general arrangements in a joint venture search process by teacher and pupils, beginning on a concrete and material level. So the starting point is not the teaching of abstractions by making them concrete, but concrete phenomena and experiences that require systematization. Moreover, the children's own activity must trigger the didactic activity of the teacher.

As a result, the emphasis must not be put on associatively connected forms of knowledge but on the acquisition of generalized 'educational schemes' or theoretical knowledge (Davydov, 1977, 1983, 1988). According to Davydov, traditional forms of education are unduly directed at empirical relationships instead of being focused on theoretical constructions, which refer to fundamental inner coherences. Such theoretical insights have the form of schemes in the curriculum. We shall discuss some of them below.

A central question in this respect is how general insights can grow out of the numerous concrete experiences of children. This question is of great theoretical and practical importance. The starting-point of our learning strategy is Vygotsky's internalization hypothesis, which states that the development of thinking operations as important elements of the structure of intelligence emanates from guided external activities of the child. Building on this interiorization hypothesis, Gal'perin developed a theory of stepwise formation of mental actions. The essence of his learning strategy is that mental actions and insights are developed from material actions, with verbal actions as a necessary intermediate stage. The verbal action has the function of generalizing the action.

Figure 10.2 General scheme of oral communication.

Figure 10.3 General scheme of written communication.

Stepwise formation of mental actions stresses the rich material and varied experience as the fundamental of stimulation of cognitive development. The actual experience with material, visible, tangible phenomena and the joint discussion about it allows pupils to become familiar with a richer, sharper and elaborated representation. That is why we take the view that reading courses that start at a verbal level with texts and schemes begin to build on the third floor instead of starting with the foundations.

The theme 'communication', for instance, starts with 8-year-olds on a material level: the investigation of oral, direct communication of the pupils themselves. The intended goal of this reflection on their own language usage and that of others via games, talks and representations in schemes is to make the communicative triangle explicit on a material level. The pupils get acquainted with the scheme shown in Figure 10.2. There are games in which pupils must explain things without using language. The pupils consequently acquire insight into the function of language. With the goal-directed exploration of the oral communication situation via common reflection, the foundation is laid for the inquiry of written language. It must become clear that writing is speaking with a pen and that reading is analogous to listening. The pupils learn that it is sometimes useful to speak and sometimes to write. The scheme for written texts is represented in Figure 10.3. In this way pupils learn that every text has a writer who has composed a text with a certain intention. This intention gives the central theme of the text. Moreover, the pupils themselves carry out the role of being writers. By being writers themselves they experience how a text comes into being and what the context of it is.

Later, pupils explore various communicative settings of simple short texts. The

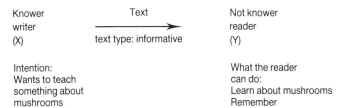

Figure 10.4 Specific scheme for informative texts.

pupils learn that there are different kinds of text, dependent on the various general intentions of writers, e.g. stories, informative texts, advertisements.

Next, great attention is paid to the function of informative texts (theme: becoming a 'knower'; in Dutch, *'weter'*). Pupils reflect on the question of what they (or the teacher) already know and what they do not yet know, what others know and do not know, etc. Special attention is paid to the fact that informative texts contribute to knowledge in the context of questions and activities such as: 'What do you already know about x and what don't you know yet?' 'What is the best way to find out what you want to know about x?' (reading an informative text, finding out for yourself, asking). 'Did we succeed in finding out what we wanted to know about x?' 'What can we do with this information?' etc. In this phase children also learn to handle sources of information.

The abstract basic Figure 10.3 is detailed for the various communicative settings. In fact, such schemes are generalized thinking models, which help pupils to orient themselves in the deep structure of the message. This concerns not only the question 'What is the text about?' but also what the writer wants and why – and what the reader wants and why. The final scheme for informative texts is shown in Figure 10.4.

It is important that children are able to attach a rich meaning to the schemes. That is why it is important that they develop the schemes by themselves in cooperation with and under the direction of the teacher (guided discovery). What they 'discover' for themselves is generally more effective than what is told to them by direct instruction. (This does not mean, however, that direct instruction has no place in the curriculum.) The scheme can be used for the further analysis of the structure of the communication and the exploration of texts, in and outside classroom settings.

In this way, the social background (communication triangle) of written informative texts is made explicit on a 'metacognitive' level for the pupils (cf. Ajdarova *et al.*, 1979). The next step is that the pupils learn to apply mental operations in methods of inquiry and description, by investigating and describing objects on the basis of common questions according to visualized schemes (see Figure 10.5).

From the elementary scheme, other schemes have been derived for the inquiry

Questions about mushrooms	Features of mushrooms
What colour is it?	_____
What shape is it?	_____
What does it taste like?	_____
What does it smell like?	_____

Figure 10.5 Inquiry and description of object features.

and description of composition of objects, comparison of objects, classification of objects, changes of objects, processes and activities of objects. Finally, schemes are introduced for reasoning and explanation.

The essence of this programme is that the pupils learn to operate with written information in a communicative setting, on the basis of first, performing research activities themselves, putting them into the scheme; then, describing the results of their inquiries in an informative text; and finally, reading informative texts in which the same methods of inquiry and description are used as they learned to apply themselves. As a reader, the pupil tries to reconstruct the inquiry performed by the writer/investigator (in fact, an imaginary dialogue with the writer). The reader/pupil must try to reconstruct the questions the writer/ researcher has put him or herself and what conclusions the writer has arrived at. The same schemes can be used to analyze other people's texts. Following Gal'perin, the schemes of inquiry and description are interiorized to a mental level of command. The mental operations are then integrated within mental acts of inquiry and description.

An important theme in *Lees je Wijzer* is the exploration of causal relationships. This first occurs at the material level. A number of very clear and concrete examples of cause and effect in the classroom are chosen in order to construct and give significance to the scheme (pupils in the role of investigator). Because the cause-and-effect scheme is used in all kinds of different situations, pupils learn that the scheme expresses a general principle of cause and effect (generalization). Next, the children report on their investigations (pupils in the role of writer), and finally the scheme is used to analyze other people's short texts in terms of cause and effect (pupils in the role of reader). Initially, very short texts of just a few lines are used, with clear instances of cause and effect. Next, more complicated instances can be chosen. By means of the continuous alternation of roles (researcher, writer, reader), it becomes clear how informative texts originate and what their purpose is: a researcher has questions, makes inquiries, finds answers, and finally reports these answers in a text in order to inform readers. In short, the activities of the teacher are directed to the following:

1. The teacher should open up new possibilities in the pupils' acquisition of new forms of culture. The 'zone of proximal development' (Vygotsky, 1987) marks the area in which the child can and wishes to develop.

What is happening here?

process 1   process 2

causes

Figure 10.6 Representing causal relationships.

2. The pupils develop for themselves the systematic supervision of research. The role and significance of the schemes in the learning process must be very clear to the teacher.
3. What the pupils are doing and why and what is discovered in discussion (verbal stage, reflection of own activity).
4. In *Lees je Wijzer* pupils are stimulated to reconstruct the results of their thinking and why they come to certain conclusions. Verbalizing for themselves, reasoning and arguing, the legitimation of ideas and insights into others' thinking and learning to listen to others are central activities throughout the course. The teacher must supervise this process of systematization, listening, verbalizing and arguing.
5. The effectiveness and purposefulness of the various exercises, teaching methods and examples that are proposed are assessed, in the light of the underlying principles of the curriculum. Although the course is highly detailed, the teacher must be able to choose new goals or adapt the means to meet the basic goals of a (series of) lessons, linked to the daily experiences and interests of the children.
6. Surveying, with the other pupils, the correspondences between their own activities as a researcher and writer and the activities of writers of informative texts. Because the pupils have acted in the role of researcher and writer themselves, they are able to communicate with the writer, and assess what he or she is actually doing, what questions were asked and what was discovered.

The teaching experiment

The aim of the teaching experiment is to answer the questions: to what extent can the learning models or schemes associated with the development of communicative competence be fruitfully taught in the primary school; and to what extent can the experimental reading course *Lees je Wijzer* lead to significantly improved learning outcomes? In order to measure the results of the course with pupils from grades 5 to 8 (8–12-year-olds) their reading progress was organized to conform to this strategy over a period of four years.

The experimental curriculum consists of five learning units. Unit I (designed for grade 5; 9-year-olds) consists of an orientation in communicative settings, in which spoken and written texts are important. The first step is that the social-cultural background of (simple) texts should be made explicit to the pupils. In Unit II (grades 5 and 6; 9–10-year-olds) the pupils are introduced to an analytical method by which the distinctive features of objects and the mental images of them can be systematically investigated and conceptualized. This method of analysis should help the pupils build a clear picture of the things described in informative texts. In Unit III (grades 6 and 7; 10–11-year-olds) the pupils are taught to make comparisons in a systematic way (Feuerstein, 1980), then to place objects in classification schemes and use these for the analysis of texts (e.g. definitions). In Unit IV (grades 7 and 8; 11–12-year-olds) the pupils are introduced to the analysis of (patterns of) change processes which are frequently used by writers of informative texts (e.g. the concept of development). In Unit V (grade 8, 12-year-olds) the students learn to cope with causal and final relationships in texts and certain interpretations the writer gives for the phenomena involved.

Two experimental schools and one control school participated in the project. Two cohorts of pupils have followed the experimental reading curriculum for a period of four years (grade 5 to grade 8). About 3 per cent of the school timetable was taken up by these lessons. The first run of the experiment (Group 1) started in 1979 with two experimental classes (fifth graders, 8–9-year-olds; N = 29) and two control classes (N = 31). The second run of the experiment (Group 2) started in 1980 with the same experimental and control schools (experimental pupils, N = 27; control pupils, N = 34). In the preceding years pilot studies were set up in order to try out learning materials and find control classes that matched the experimental classes. The lessons were given by the teachers in the experimental classes following a teacher manual in which detailed scripts were given for all the lessons.

Participation in an experiment such as this demands a lot of instruction and supervision, aimed at the teacher's activity. In order to acquaint the teachers with the rationale of the curriculum, a series of conferences was organized for all the teachers of the experimental schools, in which the teaching materials relating to the underlying principles, the nature of the teaching schemes, etc. were discussed. In addition, most of the lessons were observed and commented on by a member of the research team.

For each of the five learning units (I–V) parallel pre- and post-tests were designed (pre-test/post-test design). Each test consists of very short texts. These mini-texts require a command of the basic intellectual operations discussed, e.g.

Today, Rose's eyes are small and sleepy.

In which text is it stated why this is the case?

1. Yesterday Rose was reading late into the night, so that she has small, sleepy eyes now.
2. Rose has very small, sleepy eyes today, although she normally has very bright eyes.
3. Because Rose has small, sleepy eyes today, she has to go to bed very early, without watching television.
4. Rose has very small, sleepy eyes today, although this morning she took a cold shower for an hour and a half.

Figure 10.7 Sample test item.

Table 10.1 Overview of the duration of the experiment

Unit	Implementation Group 1 class	duration (months)	Implementation Group 2 class	duration (months)
I	5	6	5	7
II	5/6	14	5/6	13
III	6/7	11	6/7/8	19
IV	7/8	8	–	–
V	8	6	8	6

communicative setting, analysis, causality, reasoning, comparison, classification. A sample test item on causal and final relationships is presented in Figure 10.7.

Table 10.1 gives an overview of the actual duration of the various learning units in months. From this table, it appears that Groups 1 and 2 needed about the same amount of time for Units I, II and V. In the case of Unit III (comparison and classification), however, there was a substantial time difference of more than 6 months. This was caused by a delay in the programme for Group 2. For this reason it was not possible to teach the whole of Units IV and V, and it was therefore decided to drop Unit IV. With the exception of the tests in Unit IV, Group 2 performed all the tests. Group 1 performed all the tests, with the exception of the pre-tests for Units 1 and II, as these tests were not available at the time; and, in the case of the control group, the post-test for Unit V.

Table 10.2 gives the reliability scores for the pre- and post-tests. The reliability scores are not high but acceptable, with the exception of the very low reliability coefficient of Unit III, in the case of Group 2. The reliability of the pre-test of Unit I is also fairly low. The reason for the low probability of the pre-test for Unit III is probably that this test is too difficult (see Table 10.3). Because

Table 10.2 Summary of the reliability of the tests (Lambda-2)

Unit	Group	Pre-test grade	N	Rel.	Post-test grade	n	Rel.
I	1	5	–	–	5	95	0.70
	2	4	144	0.64	5	134	0.72
II	1	5	–	–	6	107	0.81
	2	5	140	0.79	6	138	0.79
III	1	6	109	0.75	7	104	0.71
	2	6	153	0.45	8	161	0.77
IV	1	7	106	0.72	8	102	0.71
	2	7	–	–	8	–	–
V	1	8	108	0.72	8	62	0.79
	2	8	154	0.75	8	157	0.79

Table 10.3 Summary of the results of Group 1*

Block	Cond.	Pre-test m	sd	Post-test m	sd	Covariate F	P	Main effect F	P	R^2
1	ex	–	16.3	3.0	–	–	10.2	0.002	–	
	co	–	–	11.0	3.3					
2	ex	–	–	11.0	3.3					
	co	–	–	12.6	3.5					
3	ex	13.9	3.0	11.3	2.8	39.8	0.001	27.0	0.001	0.54
	co	10.4	3.9	6.8	2.0					
4	ex	13.0	2.9	15.6	2.1	36.2	0.001	20.2	0.001	0.50
	co	10.3	3.5	11.8	2.8					
5	ex	15.0	2.6	17.3	2.0	–	–	–	–	–
	co	12.1	3.2	–	–					

Notes:
* ex = experimental group, N = 29; co = control group, N = 31.

the pre-test of Unit III was performed very well by some pupils in Group 1, we anticipated a possible ceiling effect when it came to the post-test. That is why the test was made more difficult for Group 2. It seems, however, that the test was made too difficult, so that the scores for the pupils performing at the poorest level are subject to chance.

Table 10.3 presents the mean and standard deviations of Group 1 for every test. The scores on the post-test are analyzed by means of an analysis of covariance with the scores on the pre-test as covariate, where possible. Scores are included of only those pupils who did all the tests and who undertook the whole curriculum, so that the calculations are not skewed by a selective loss of subjects.

Table 10.4 Average scores of the pre- and post-tests of the
experimental and control pupils in Group 1 (%)

	Exp. (N = 29)	Contr. (N = 31)	P
Average sum pre-tests	67.3	51.8	0.001
Average sum post-tests	67.3	46.5	0.001
Difference	0	−5.3	

Table 10.3 shows that the difference in means between the experimental and control groups for Unit I is statistically significant. Since there is no pre-test, it is not clear whether this difference can be attributed to the experimental programme. For Unit II, pre-test data are also missing for Group 1. However, the scores for the post-test of Unit I can serve as a covariate. In that case it appears that the experimental group scored significantly higher compared with the control pupils. For Units III and IV we have both pre- and post-test data. For both learning units, a significant main effect favours the experimental group. We do not have post-test data for Unit V for the control group in Group 1. Scores on the post-test appear to be significantly higher than scores on the pre-test. However, it is not clear whether this difference can be attributed to the experimental curriculum.

Table 10.4 gives the average total scores of the pre- and post-tests of Group 1. Only the results of pre- and post-tests are used. In the case of Group 1, these are the combined pre- and post-tests of Units III and IV (40 items). The reliability coefficient (Lambda - 2) of the added pre-tests is 0.79 and of the added post-tests 0.80 (60 pupils).

The scores for control groups' post-tests are somewhat lower than for the pre-tests. This is a result of the fact that the post-test for Unit III was made more difficult. The experimental group scored higher than the control group on the pre-tests as well as the post-tests. The difference in the case of the post-tests is larger, indicating a learning effect for at least two of the five learning units of Group 1.

Table 10.5 shows an analysis of covariance for the data in Table 10.4. There is a good correspondence between the tests and there is a very significant main effect.

Table 10.6 presents a summary of the results of Group 2 by learning unit. The scores of the post-tests are analyzed by means of a covariance analysis, with the pre-tests as a covariate. In the case of Group 2, the difficulty of pre- and post-tests was held as equal as possible.

When we look at the level of reading ability, as measured by the pre-test for Unit I, at the start of the experiment for Group 2, we see that the experimental group did not score significantly higher than the control group (F = 0.11,

Table 10.5 Analysis of covariance of the scores, pre- and post-test, Group 1

	SS	F	P
Covar. sum pre-tests	1,051.2	90.4	0.001
Main effect	284.5	24.5	0.001
Residue	662.9		
Total	1,998.6		
Test homogeneity of variances			R = 0.82
Bartlett-Box $F = 0.000$; $P = 0.989$			$R^2 = 0.67$

Table 10.6 Results by Unit, Group 2*

Block	Cond.	Pre-test m	sd	Post-test m	sd	Covariate F	P	Main effect F	P	R^2
1	ex	9.7	3.1	14.0	3.0	17.2	0.001	6.9	0.111	0.29
	co	9.4	2.9	11.9	3.4					
2	ex	11.9	4.3	16.6	3.1	26.0	0.001	5.0	0.029	0.35
	co	10.3	3.9	14.0	3.7					
3	ex	8.7	3.0	11.3	4.0	13.6	0.001	2.1	0.154	0.21
	co	10.4	3.9	6.8	2.0					
5	ex	14.2	2.6	15.4	3.2	48.4	0.001	0.9	0.348	0.46
	co	13.0	3.1	13.9	3.5					

Notes:
* ex = experimental group, N = 27; co = control group, N = 34.

p = 0.741). The post-test measures a significant main effect in favour of the experimental group (see Table 10.6). For Unit II, the experimental group also shows significantly better results. However, there are no significant main effects for Units III and V, indicating that the experimental programme had no additional effect for these units.

Table 10.7 presents the average total scores for Group 2 over the four pre- and post-tests. The reliability (Lambda – 2) for the combined pre-tests is 0.86 and for the combined post-tests 0.92 (N = 61). The experimental pupils scored higher on the pre-tests, but not significantly so. The combined post-tests show a significant difference. The control pupils also scored higher on the post-test, which could be expected on the basis of spontaneous learning effects rather than the experimental programme. In so far as a part of the learning effects may be incorporated in the combined pre-tests, then the established difference in increase certainly is not inflated.

Table 10.8 gives an analysis of covariance performed on these data. There is

Table 10.7 Average scores, pre- and post-test, of the
experimental and control pupils of Group 2 (%)

	Exp. (N = 27)	Contr. (N = 34)	P
Average sum pre-tests	55.6	50.9	0.125
Average sum post-tests	71.6	61.6	0.009
Difference	16.0	10.7	

Table 10.8 Analysis of covariance of the scores, pre- and
post-test, Group 2

	SS	F	P
Covar. sum pre-tests	5,425.99	109.1	0.001
Main effect	275.91	275.9	0.002
Residue	2,885.12		
Total	8,587.02		
Test homogeneity of variances			R = 0.82
Bartlett-Box F = 0.08; P = 0.78			R^2 = 0.66

once again a good coherence between pre- and post-tests. The main effect is significant. Such a learning effect can be measured in the case of both Group 1 and Group 2.

Discussion

Like authors who advocate a metacognitive approach, in our curriculum we pay great attention to stimulating *systematically* thinking and reasoning models in relation to reading. As in our programmes, in a number of metacognitive curricula (e.g. Palincsar and Brown, 1984; Paris *et al.*, 1984) sufficient space is provided for guided exploration and thinking activity of children. In metacognitive programmes, important educational aims – such as the development of goals for reading, the critical appreciation of what is read, self-correction, the use of context, the integration of causal and temporal sequences, and the like – have a place. These programmes are principally directed at teaching children about the nature and purpose sense of reading strategies, and when and how they can be used. The metacognitive approach corresponds to a large degree with our thesis. However, there is an important difference. In metacognitive programmes the systematic orientation on the behaviour of writers usually does not appear to its full advantage. In our view, no reading strategies or procedures, such as the marking of sentences, rules for summarizing, etc., can replace this insight in communicative settings.

Another question we want to discuss here refers to the effects of the experimental programmes on the knowledge and control of the learning schemata dealt with. From Tables 10.3 and 10.6 it appears that all learning units produce positive effects, and most of the units show a significant main effect, with the exception of Units III and V in the case of the experimental pupils in Group 2. In general, the experimental pupils in Group 1 seem to have done somewhat better than the experimental pupils in Group 2. This may be accounted for by the fact that the Group 1 teachers were more intensively supported than was possible with Group 2 teachers. Nevertheless, we found a significant main effect over the whole programme in both experimental groups (see Tables 10.5 and 10.8).

The next point concerns the significance of the effects. At first observation, an additional learning gain of 7–8 per cent due to the experimental programme – as measured by our tests – over four school years does not seem very large. A review of the results of programme tests by pupils receiving a traditional education in learning comprehension (Gresnigt, 1992) – to which there is no systematic or explicit attention to schemata hidden in descriptions – reveals a fairly constant picture.

In primary school, per year scores increase by about 7 per cent. These data point to the possibility that the final level of the experimental pupils will be reached by the control pupils about one year later. The learning gain of our experimental pupils would then be about one year. However, we should be careful with the application of cross-sectional data when making the prognoses of a developmental process. Nevertheless, the results do not seem unsatisfactory when we take into account that during the investigation only 2–3 per cent of the total school day was spent on the experimental programme.

There is somewhat more to say about the magnitude of the effect of the experimental programme. On the basis of our theoretical analysis (see Bol, 1982), we assume that the skills aimed at by the experimental curriculum are closely connected with general cognitive development. This means that the programme must have a positive influence on cognitive development. It is clear that this goal of developmental education is not a simple business and that one cannot expect spectacular effects.

Our theoretical analysis is supported by the fact that there is a strong coherence between the results of our own reading tests and other tests of verbal intelligence (OTIS and ISI). Our tests explain 55–75 per cent of the variance of such intelligence tests (Bol and Verhelst, 1985; Gresnigt, 1992). This result is all the more impressive given the fact that there are sometimes several years between these test performances. This indicates that our tests measure reasonably stable cognitive features. Against this background the results of our inquiries may be considered very acceptable.

It seems that the pupils' cognitive development in the experimental schools was speeded up in comparison with the control school pupils'. It cannot be excluded, however, that the effects may be the result of other factors, e.g. because systematically different instruction is given in the control school. Dutch schools may differ in the rate of cognitive development (Boland, 1991). However, in a pilot study such differences between our experimental and control schools were not found (Bol, 1979).

We now want to pose the question: To what extent does the effect of the programme cohere with the pupils' performances on external reading comprehension tests? These tests – together with a number of other tests, e.g. on arithmetic and spelling – are performed at the end of primary school in Dutch schools. The results of the experimental groups on these various tests were compared with the scores of previous groups at the same school. This has the advantage that possible between-school differences will not skew the results. In line with our expectations, the experimental pupils scored better on reading comprehension tests than the control groups from the same school, while scores on tests that are unrelated to our programme, such as arithmetic, spelling and grammar, did not suffer (Bol and Gresnigt, 1986).

In summary, we find in these empirical data reasonable support for the theoretical expectation that the ability of schematization of data at the mental level forms an important factor in the process of reading comprehension of informative texts. Next, we demonstrated that these skills can be speeded up via systematic education. With some reservation, we may conclude that the control of the schemata at the mental level can be brought to a higher level in pupils with the help of the experimental programme. This means that the pupils learn to observe and read more systematically and that they are better equipped to relate data and to place them in reference frames.

On the basis of the experimental programme, a commercial version of *Lees je Wijzer* was developed (Werkgroep Bol, 1988). The commercial version was extended with programmes for younger pupils (4–8 years). The result is a curriculum for grades 1–8 (4–12 years). The curriculum comes with background information (Gresnigt, 1988) and comprehensive instructions for the teacher. In addition, a modified version of the curriculum was developed and tested for special education (mentally retarded and learning-disabled pupils); and a reading comprehension test battery was developed as an integral part of the curriculum.

Taking into account the experiences with the experimental version developed in the 1980s, the commercial version is now in use in more than 1,000 primary schools and special education schools in the Netherlands. At the time of writing, the experience with this commercial version is too limited to demonstrate whether the level of reading education has risen significantly at the end of the primary school period, as measured by external tests. As indicated above, this was the case with the experimental curriculum, but here there was much more intensive support of teachers by experts than can be the case with the commercial version. Our research and experience has led us to believe that pupils can be taught to learn reading comprehension at a higher level than in traditional education. However, although a good curriculum is a necessary condition, in itself it is

218 Giel Gresnigt

not sufficient. In the end, it will always be the teacher who determines the progress of the educational learning process.

References

Ajdarova, L.I., Gorskaja, L.J. and Cukerman, G.A. (1979), 'Eersteklassers onderzoeken hun moedertaal' [First graders investigate their native language], *Pedagogische Studiën*, *56*, 25–36.
Austin, J.L. (1962), *How to do Things with Words*, Oxford: Oxford University Press.
Bol, E. (1979), *Onderzoeksopzet voor Begrijpend Lezen op de Basisschool* [Research Programme Reading Comprehension], Utrecht University: Psychology Department.
Bol, E, (1982), *Leespsychologie* [The Psychology of Reading], Groningen: Wolters-Noordhoff.
Bol, E. (1988), 'Struktur der Tätigkeit'. In J. Lompscher, W. Jantos and S. Schönian (eds.) *Psychologische Methoden und Analysen der Ausbildung der Lerntätigkeit*, Berlin: Kongress- und Werbedruck.
Bol, E. and Gresnigt, G. (1986), 'Effekten van een leergang begrijpend Lezen,' [Effects of a reading comprehension course], *Pedagogische Studiën*, *63*, 49–60.
Bol, E. and Verhelst, N.D. (1985), 'Inhoudelijke en statistische analyse van een leestoets' [Content analysis and statistical analysis of a reading comprehension test], *Tijdschrift voor Onderwijsresearch*, *2*, 49–68.
Bol, E., Gresnigt, M.A. and de Haan, J.M. (1991), *Lees je Wijzer. Toetsen voor Begrijpend Lezen* [Read and Get Wise. Reading Comprehension Tests], Baarn: Uitgeverij Dijkstra.
Bol, E., Gresnigt, M.A. and de Haan, J.M. (1992), 'Speech activity theory and reading comprehension assessment', in L.Verhoeven and J.H.A.L. de Jong (eds), *The Construct of Language Proficiency*, pp. 61–70, Amsterdam/Philadelphia: John Benjamins.
Boland, T. (1991), *Lezen op Termijn* [Long-term Reading Effects], Unpublished PhD dissertation, Katholieke Universiteit Nijmegen.
Boonman, J.H. and Kok, W.A.M. (1986), *Kennisverwerven uit Teksten* [The Acquisition of Knowledge from Texts], unpublished PhD dissertation, Utrecht University.
Davydov, V.V. (1977), *Arten der Verallgemeinerung im Unterricht*, Berlin: Volk und Wissen.
Davydov, V.V. (1983), 'De relatie tussen abstracte en concrete kennis in het onderwijs' [Relationships between abstract and concrete knowledge in education]. In J. Haenen and B. van Oers (eds) *Begrippen in het Onderwijs. De theorie van Davydov*, Amsterdam: Uitgeverij Pegasus.
Davydov, V.V. (1988), 'Problems of developmental teaching', *Soviet Education* August–October.
Durkin, D. (1979), 'What classroom observations reveal about reading comprehension instruction', *Reading Research Quarterly*, *14*, 481–533.
Feuerstein, R. (1980), *Instrumental Enrichment: An intervention program for cognitive modifiability*, Baltimore, MD: University Park Press.
Flavell, J.H. (1977), *Cognitive Development*. NJ: Prentice-Hall.
Flavell, J.H. (1979), 'Metacognition and cognitive monitoring: a new area of cognitive – developmental inquiry', *American Psychologist*, *34*, 10.
Gal'perin, P. J. (1969), 'Stages in the development of mental acts.' In M. Cole and I. Malzman (eds.) *A Handbook of Contemporary Soviet Psychology*, New York: Basic Books.
Goodman, Y. and Burke, C. (1980), *Reading Strategies: Focus on comprehension*, New York: Holt, Rinehart & Winston.
Gresnigt, M.A. (1988), *Achtergronden en Uitgangspunten van Lees je Wijzer: Begrijpend en studerend lezen* [Background Information for 'Read and Get Wise'], Baarn: Dijkstra.

Gresnigt, M.A. (1992), *Communicatief Leesonderwijs*. [Communication-oriented Reading Instruction], unpublished PhD dissertation, Amsterdam: Vrije Universiteit.

Hörmann, H. (1976), *Meinen und Verstehen. Grundzüge einer Psychologischen Semantik*, Frankfurt: Suhrkamp.

Hörmann, H. (1986), *Meaning and Context*, New York: Plenum Press.

Leont'ev, A.N. (1979), *Tätigkeit, Bewusstsein, Persönlichkeit*, Berlin: Volk und Wissen.

Lompscher, J. *et al.* (1975), *Theoretische und experimentelle Untersuchungen zur Entwicklung geistiger Fähigkeiten*, Berlin: Volk und Wissen.

Palincsar, A.S. and Brown, A.N. (1984), 'Reciprocal teaching of comprehension fostering and monitoring activities', *Cognition and Instruction, 1,* 117–75.

Paris, S., Cross, D. and Lipson, M. (1984), 'Informed strategies for learning: a program to improve children's reading awareness and comprehension', *Journal of Educational Psychology, 76,* 1239–52.

Perfetti, C.A. (1985), *Reading Ability*, New York: Oxford University Press.

van Parreren, C.F. and Carpay, J.A.M. (1980), *Sovjetpsychologen over Onderwijs en Cognitieve Ontwikkeling* [Soviet Psychologists on Instruction and Cognitive Development], Groningen: Wolters-Noordhoff.

Vygotsky, L.S. (1962), *Thought and Language*, New York: John Wiley & Sons.

Vygotsky, L.S. (1978), *Mind in Society*, Cambridge, MA: Harvard University Press.

Vygotsky, L.S. (1987), *Collected Works*, Part 1, New York: Plenum Press.

Weterings, A.C.E.M. and Aarnoutse, C.A.J. (1986), 'De praktijk van het begrijpend lezen' [Practices of reading comprehension], *Pedagogische Studiën, 63,* 387–400.

Werkgroep Bol (1988), *Lees je Wijzer. Een leergang begrijpend lezen van groep 1 t/m groep 8 van de basisschool* [Read and Get Wise: A course for reading comprehension], Baarn: Dijkstra.

Wittgenstein, L. (1971), *Philosophische Untersuchungen*, Frankfurt: Suhrkamp Verlag.

11

Literacy acquisition and social context: approaches, emphases and questions

Jan J.F. ter Laak
Department of Developmental Psychology, Utrecht University

Introduction

Literacy is a highly valued and unique human phenomenon. To study this phenomenon, psychology continually (re)defines and (re)analyzes this concept. In this concluding chapter, the two basic research orientations to literacy – the information processing approach and the socio-cultural approach – will be outlined and illustrated with examples taken from the extensive research. The meaning of 'social context' in both approaches will be analyzed. Next, the contributions presented in this volume will be confronted with these two basic orientations to literacy, and some of their accents and limitations will be discussed. Literacy research, including the empirical work presented in the present volume, not only aims to resolve current issues in the field, it also generates theoretical questions. The last section of this chapter will focus on some of these questions.

Literacy conceived as an information processing skill

In the Anglo-Saxon psychological literature, literacy is almost exclusively studied as a complex skill, acquired by individuals. Such a skill can be conceived as a functional whole, a 'Gestalt'. More often, however, skills are decomposed into subskills, using various criteria derived from disciplines such as logic, linguistics and psychology. Among the psychologically defined criteria are perceptual and representational processes, and specific information processing skills. The information processing paradigm is dominant in recent empirical literacy research, and it has the following themes:

1. There is a preference for assessing a skill in its pure form, i.e. not confounded with another skill. For example, consider grammatical awareness, which must not be confounded with semantic knowledge or with automatic speech processes (see Bowey, Chapter 7 in this volume).

2. Skills, once specified and successfully broken down, require an internal organization principle, a taxonomy of some sort. For example, one specified skill is considered to constitute the core for the acquisition of, say, reading. Empirical research often supports phonological skills as a good candidate (Cardoso, 1991; De Gelder and Vroomen, 1991; Wimmer *et al.*, 1991; Griffith *et al.*, 1992; Landerl *et al.*, 1992; Spector, 1992; Goswami, Chapter 4, this volume, but not consistently so; see Van Bon, Chapter 8, this volume). Changes in the internal organization demand that the child uses the different skills in a hierarchical way. For example, the child starts logographically and, because long-term success fails to come, continues with segmenting words into syllables and/or phonemes. Still another possibility is that the child acts in a strategic way, for example, by using different skills simultaneously in order to reach a given criterion. To make things even more complex, it is possible that the organization varies as the child grows older. Knight and Fisher (1992) detected three developmental sequences in phonemic and visual-graphic domains for single words in a group of first-, second- and third-graders (7–8 year olds), containing normal and backward readers. The most common sequence was the integration of visual-graphic and phonological domains. The two remaining sequences lacked integration of these domains; backward readers were over-represented here. The organization of skills can be defined theoretically and tested with the help of (linear) statistical techniques. (See, for example, Goetz *et al.*'s (1992) review of seven articles which used causal models for explaining literacy acquisition. They concluded that phonological skills contributed consistently to the variance explained by reading ability. As usual in methodological research, the authors complain that the constructs (phonological, orthographic and other skills) were not uniformly defined and that statistical assumptions of the path analysis techniques were at times violated.)

3. There are individual differences in literacy skills. Psychologists can assess these differences, study their origins and compute correlations with many other interesting variables. A well-known way to study the origins of the differences is the use of behavioural genetics. Olson *et al.* (1989), for example, compared backward reading, monozygotic twins with respect to their orthographic and phonological skills. The latter skills explained a significant proportion of hereditary variance. However, the genetic origin of literacy skills has not received as much attention as the origin of intelligence. It is possible that future research will change this picture, owing to the popularity of studying genetical origins of individual differences. More often, individual differences in literacy skills were related to all kinds of behavioural, cognitive and environmental variables which

theoretically made sense or, alternatively, because someone simply happened to be interested in them. In addition to this dimensional approach to individual differences with respect to some literacy operationalization, various types of persons have been distinguished. Purcell and Dahl (1991) revealed four patterns of success/non-success pupil types with regard to their literacy development in the classroom. These were the independent explorer, the curriculum-dependent, the passive nonweaver and the deferred learner.

4. Literacy acquisition refers to the mastery of spoken language, reading and writing (cf. Garton, 1992). The emphasis is, however, on reading (and writing), possibly in order to circumvent difficult questions regarding spoken language acquisition – a topic that is indeed taken care of abundantly in linguistic developmental studies. In order to assess reading (and writing) ability, several different measures have been used. The emphasis, however, seems to be on context-free words. Words are sometimes supposed to be at the core of language and literacy. Snow (1991), for example, used word recognition, word comprehension and vocabulary in her research into literacy acquisition in low-income families.

5. Not everyone becomes a competent reader. Assessment of backward reading (see Sutherland and Smith, 1991; and Stanovich, 1991 for discussion about appropriate ways) and the determination of the distribution of reading ability over different socio-economic classes continue. Assessment of functional illiteracy in children and adults is regularly readjusted because of the nature of the changing society we live in (Venezky *et al.*, 1990). Literacy, and especially reading skills, are highly valued in today's world, and an unsatisfactory mastery level of these is consequently a matter of serious concern for individuals and society. For this reason, numerous training programmes have been developed to remediate backward reading (see Van Bon, Chapter 8, this volume).

6. Literacy can be studied over the lifespan. The emphasis here, however, is on children between the ages of 5 and 12 years, the initial period of formal schooling. Traditionally, formal schooling is considered vital for reading and becoming literate. In one way or another, there has to be a place and a time for a person to learn explicitly the completely arbitrary but highly compulsory symbols and symbol groups which refer to sounds. The individual must understand that these symbols and sounds refer to things and people. This does not imply that societies without formal schooling are illiterate (Graff, 1987).

Input for the literacy skills

Although there is much theoretical controversy (Bloom, 1993) about whether literacy is 'there' from the beginning in one way or another, it is obvious that the baby does not speak, read or write. These skills have to be acquired with the use of input and processing mechanisms.

First, recent research continues to analyze the effects of specific input for reading and reading comprehension. In this research, code-oriented vs. whole language-oriented approaches are distinguished. The following selection of studies gives an impression of this research: Byrne and Fielding (1993) trained pre-schoolers' phonemic awareness and the alphabetic principle for 12 weeks, and claimed that this had an effect on later decoding and spelling. Griffith *et al.* (1992) compared a whole language-oriented curriculum (shared book experiences and writing activities) with traditional instruction (containing little writing) with respect to decoding and spelling skills and writing fluency. The effect of these two methods was, however, surpassed by the role of initial level of phonemic awareness of the first-graders (6 year olds). Schunk and Rice (1992) compared different instruction types of reading comprehension. They found that strategy modification and strategy feedback were more effective than comprehension instruction for 9–12 year olds. Sawyer and Butler (1991) recommended training in all sorts of specific language roots, i.e. phonology, syntax, short- and long-term memory and auditory segmentation, in order to prevent reading disability. Lie (1991) trained first-graders in word analysis and phoneme isolation, segmentation, position and blending. He claimed that metaphonological skills were trained and that there was a facilitating effect on reading and spelling. Vellutino (1991) reviewed the code-oriented approach (alphabetic coding and phoneme awareness) and the whole language-oriented approach (word identification and role of the context in word identification). There was support for the code-oriented approach to reading instruction. This approach was, however, according to Vellutino not contradictory to theoretical premises of the whole language-oriented approach. This author propose a balanced position with respect to the specific input.

Second, the effects of general social and non-social input on literacy acquisition are assessed. This research is relevant, but diverse. It reflects the fact that we live in a world full of lasting, non-specific social and non-social stimuli, which in many situations contain unknown effects. We learn not only for and from school, but for and from life. The following selection of studies offers an overview.

Snow's (1991) study of eighty low-income families assessed several characteristics of parents and the home environment. These characteristics were supposedly correlated with literacy development – for example, the education of the parents, their involvement in helping with homework, the creation of opportunities to learn, possibilities to read at home and story-reading, their expectations, etc. This type of study is one of the last in a long tradition, beginning with Head Start (the well-known enrichment programme for pre-schoolers). The results resembled those of Head Start. After a promising start, the benefit from the programme began to wane, with the children from the low-income families falling behind by approximately three years, compared to their middle-class peers. These results have been replicated in other Western countries. In this tradition, the hardly redeemed conviction dictates that retarded language ability can be eradicated and that literacy level is an important predictor of future school success.

Which input variables correlate with reading (dis)ability? All kinds of variables have been put forward in the prediction formulas. For example, Dickinson and Tabors (1991) predicted literacy achievement at age 5 with measures borrowed from the co-construction of a story by mother and child, explanatory talk and narratives during meals, book-reading, quality of adult language and exposure to adult speech. Scarborough *et al.* (1991) found relations of parental literacy behaviour with the reading achievement of children in the second grade (7 year olds). Significant variables included: frequency of adult reading, parent–child reading and children's solitary book activities at home. In print-rich environments pre-schoolers were observed by Neuman and Roskos (1991). The environment elicited conversations about literacy, for example, naming, negotiating on meaning and helping other children in literacy topics.

In addition to this parental input, one source of partly non-social literacy input – print exposure – has recently drawn much attention. Progress in reading was significantly correlated with the amount of print exposure in fourth- and fifth-grade pupils (9 and 10 year olds) (Cipielewski and Stanovich, 1992). Cunningham and Stanovich (1991) first assessed the construct validity of their print exposure instrument and then found that this variable was an independent contributor to the development of verbal abilities in fourth- and sixth-grade (9 and 11 year old) children.

Processing literacy input

An organism processes input. There has been a long tradition in language acquisition research to try to define the quality and structure of the specific and general, social and non-social input, as well as trying to assess the nature of the equipment of the organism. Bloom (1993) argued for a hybrid view in which the richness and possibilities of the well-organized organism as well as the (social) environment are taken into account. Recent literacy research shows interest in perceptual and cognitive processes of the organism in reading and reading comprehension, as some examples show.

Bialystok (1992) argued that symbolic representation is needed in order to understand the properties of letter and number sequences. The recurrent argument is that some cognitive processes are conditional for reading. Roberts (1992) described the development of the concept of a word related to reading. Connectionist and structural models of natural language processing and learning were compared. Connectionist models are considered as an important alternative to the symbolic and representational structures (Bever, 1992). Perfetti (1992) launched a theory of word reading that specified the form of the lexical representations in memory. The child develops an autonomous lexicon in its (in)formal literacy encounters by assessing the redundancy and the specificity of words. Cognitive processes involved in text processing are studied: Van den Broek (1993) argued that children and adults create a coherent representation of a text by means of inferential processes, like backward and forward inferencing and making causal connections.

Literacy conceived as a socio-cultural phenomenon

Advocates of this approach usually start by rejecting the individualistic skill-oriented information processing approach. Convictions concerning characteristics of the socio-cultural approach are then described, followed by empirical descriptive research which reports literacy behaviour in real life situations. Some literacy behaviours have received consistent attention and so the study of some topics is emerging.

First, testing of individual differences in skills is rejected. One of the main arguments is that skills of children are tested that have never been taught.

Second, some characteristics of literacy are set forth: to read is to communicate, good readers are good communicators, to read is to construct a shared meaning with and about people and the non-social world, to read is to take part in the intentional world of a writer and to read is not learning from another, but through another. As the Dutch poet and biologist Vroman (1964) puts it: reading a poem is to awaken the words. The child takes on an active role in becoming literate. Bruner (1990, 1993) even refused to use the concept 'acquisition' because of its connotation of passivity. Tomasello *et al.* (1993) claimed that culture and literacy are not a set of responses to be mastered, but a way of knowing and construing the world and others. To enter a literate world is not the addition of some element, but is a transformation. Heymans (1994) considers becoming literate as a developmental task, containing the construction of the child's identity as 'reader' by its own achievements and by the 'jury' of teachers and parents. Gee (1990) even reproached the skill-oriented authors as being naive, because literacy is more than sequential speech or writing. It contains cultural models consisting of words, acts, beliefs, attitudes, social identities, gestures, bodily postures, clothes, etc. Literacy earned a political dimension in his opinion, because it could play a role in changing or consolidating existing social hierarchies. Brandt (1990) emphasized the reader–writer involvement in creating a shared context. Robinson (1990) considered literacy as the ability to participate in a set of social practices and rejected the depersonalized and decontextualized study of literacy in children.

The socio-cultural approach sounds plausible and is intuitively attractive. Who would dare argue against it? But there is the problem of what and how to investigate. How does one investigate the ill-defined concept 'sharedness of meaning'? Interpersonal cognitive representations and co-construction of meaning by participants are difficult to assess and consequently problematic to study (Velichkofsky, 1993). The only way out of this is simply to start with empirical research. This forces researchers to choose both a topic and a method.

Dyson (1992) used an ethnographic method in kindergarten children and first-graders to describe as fully as possible the activities of children with regard to literacy. On request and spontaneously, children engage in producing a literacy product, for example, oral and written texts. The products of the children reflected genres and discourse traditions they were already familiar with. In the socio-cultural approach there is interest in phenomenological description of what children say and do in literacy topics, for example story-telling, dialogues and reading. Troyer (1991) observed children working together in reading and writing activities. The 6–7 year olds took responsibilities which traditionally belonged to the teacher. Kantor *et al.* (1992) used videotapes and field notes with 3–5 year olds. They reported that the children used literacy ability as a social tool. They are purposive and adapted to different social situations of peer and teacher interaction. Fishman (1992) used an ethnographic method in two eighth-graders (13 year olds) and helped them to understand what literacy was in the concrete context of the school setting. Neuman and Roskos (1991) studied the spontaneous literacy-related conversational episodes of 4 and 5 year old preschoolers. They analyzed the content of the episodes and found instances of naming, meaning, negotiating and helping each other to achieve goals, which were literacy connected. Cothern and Collins (1992) provided a theoretical description of the attitudes of children and related this to questions about reading instruction. They argue that attitudes are a result of beliefs, and that these beliefs originated in home and school cultures.

This research shows that daily purposive behaviour of preschool and school children is observed. Topics include literacy activities such as conversations, story-telling, negotiation of meaning, naming, communicative exchange and attitudes. A taxonomy of literacy activities is, however, lacking.

Social context in the two approaches

Every theory of human behaviour is at the same time a theory of the environment. In psychology, the commonly used definitions of environment are subjected to criticism. For example, in behaviourism the environment is reduced to an objective stimulus. In trait theories of personality and structural cognitive developmental theories, the role of the immediate environment is underestimated, as Kagan (1984) convincingly argued. In behavioural genetics studies, one can state with some simplification that environment is considered a rest or remainder category. There are proposals for transactional theories (Pervin, 1978). However, these theories have generated a relatively limited amount of research.

The two approaches to literacy differ in their definition of the environment. In the discussion of the information processing approach the environment is described as input. General/specific and social/non-social input were distinguished and extensively studied. In the socio-cultural approach, the environment is a co-construction of the individual and his social and cultural environment. The expression 'social context' usually refers to the last notion of environment. As argued above, this conception is plausible, but difficult to operationalize. Saegert and Winkel (1990) distinguished three paradigms in the study of person–environment interactions. The first is adaptation and refers to the micro-environment of an individual. The environment is descibed in terms of complexity, level of stimulation and (un)predictability. The individual person tries to control, to explore and to adapt. In the second, environment is described as a source of possibilities for the purposive actions of an individual. The environment is usually conceived as a temporal/spatial structure with facilities and possibilities to fulfil the needs of an individual, who plays his roles and realizes his long-term projects. The third paradigm is the notion of environment as a socio-cultural field of forces. It consists of settings and systems, in which the person is born, which he co-constructs and which he will, eventually, reproduce. The two approaches to literacy do not fit neatly into any one of the three paradigms. The information processing approach contains features of the first two paradigms; the socio-cultural approach would fit in the last two. The second paradigm is possibly one in which they can meet each other.

Emphases and limitations

In this section the emphases and limitations on literacy acquisition in general and in particular as reflected by the authors of this book are discussed. It is impossible to cover literacy in ten chapters. It is sensible, however, to emphasize important approaches. Starting from my reflection on the literature, reported in earlier sections, some emphases and limitations, as I see them, are examined.

The two approaches to literacy acquisition are present in this volume. Bus and Gresnigt, respectively, partly pursue the socio-cultural approach and reject some elements of the information processing and/or individual differences approach. Bus attacks the recent research on print exposure because it presupposes a passive child. Children are not (in the first place) exposed to literacy, they participate actively in it. For example, she observed that a very young child is willing to share toys with other children, but not to share the 'book reading' with its mother with another child. Gresnigt states that reading is not (only) a technical problem. The main difficulty is to discover and solve problems. According to him, the reader creates, together with the writer, a common field of meaning. He reproaches the information processing view as being too narrow.

The authors did not leave it at that and presented empirical research to clarify and illustrate their view. Therefore, they had to choose a topic and method. Bus has studied interactive book reading of mother and child and detected a scaffolding sequence in this interaction. Moreover, individual differences in mothers, depending on their own level of literacy and individual differences in children, depending on their type of attachment, are taken into account. Gresnigt rejects direct instruction and uses, according to his theory, a programme containing stepwise interiorization in learning to read and to comprehend texts.

This method of designing instruction is widely used by Russian educational psychologists for various kinds of academic skills (see, for example, Ter Laak *et al.*, 1994). The author claims that the programme stimulates reading comprehension, because pupils control schemata at a mental level. The author states that the programme has to be further evaluated. It is worth mentioning that the training programme took a very limited instruction time.

Bus analyzes a daily situation that is conceptually literacy-oriented. She emphasizes, however, that for the child the motive of this interactive book reading is not literacy-oriented but to create a sphere of intimacy. It is not clear whether there is, or is to be expected, a relation with later literacy and how this relation must be conceptualized. Gresnigt designed a complete programme for reading. Future research results can clarify the question whether this programme exceeds the results of other programmes. As the claim is that mental operations are changed, i.e. the formal- and not merely a domain-specific learning content is trained, the programme can and must, in my opinion, produce transfer to other learning domains. Gresnigt found only transfer in the reading domain and not in the domain of arithmetics. The question of general versus specific transfer of programmes, developed according to the Russian conception of the forming of fully developed mental actions, deserves further theoretical attention and empirical research.

The socio-cultural approach is plausible and intuitively attractive and has generated a vast amount of publications, but has, as yet, serious limitations. Theoretical assumptions partly do not exceed the level of convictions. There is no classification of literacy situations and there is no accepted assessment of, for example, the concept of 'construction of shared meaning'. There are, as yet, only descriptions of potentially important situations. More (theoretical) statements are needed as to 'why' these situations are important and for 'what'. In other words, how are these situations created in the interaction; how are they related and how do they change (or not) during the acquisition of literacy? Finally, there are no studies in which this approach is combined or is confronted with the information processing approach. An example of such a kind of confrontation is Donaldson's (1978) work on Piagetian conservation phenomena. She demonstrated that not only cognitive structure (or information processing skills) were relevant for the child's achievement, but also the child's interpretation of the interaction between the experimenter and the child.

The information processing approach is better elaborated than the socio-cultural approach and is predominant in this book. The advantage of this approach is that it offers an analytical scheme to study phenomena, while leaving at the same time room for different theoretical processing concepts. Several implications of the approach, as explained in the introductory section, are present. There are, however, also some limitations.

First, in trying to determine the contribution of grammatical awareness to reading, Bowey deals with the problem of assessing this refractory formal characteristic. This turns out to be complex, and alternative interpretations cannot be excluded.

It is not an easy task to assess formal features, such as grammatical awareness and consequentially to train them and determine effects of such a training. Grammatical awareness is not a clear-cut case. This contribution is critical and the author concludes that an acceptable solution has yet to be found. Grammatical awareness is a concept which originated from psycholinguistics. It is reasonable to ask whether one can expect this concept to have direct psychological reality. In general, one cannot expect a perfect fit between concepts derived from linguistics, logic and psychology.

Second, Goswami, Assink and Kattenberg, Bowey, and Van Bon search for basic mechanisms and units in learning to read. Goswami introduces an interesting new unit of analysis for learning to read: onsets and rimes. The psychological (or functional) reality of this unit has been empirically demonstrated. Moreover, the author connects phonemic and orthographic elements in an analogy theory. In this theory it is hypothesized that children immediately start by making analogies between spelling patterns and phonemic awareness of onsets and rimes. This is an interactive conception of learning to read. Assink and Kattenberg, Bowey, and also Van Bon, used psycholinguistic processing levels in order to find out empirically which units and/or skills are responsible for backward reading. They predicted and found differences in the initial levels of decoding and not on the contextual level. Backward readers are not just the lower part of a normal distribution and demonstrate specific failures. The reading problems are located in the initial phases of learning to read, i.e. at the word and subword level. There appears to be a difference in strategy: Goswami proposes to search for a central or core unit for the development of reading ability. Assink and Kattenberg, Van Bon, and Bowey tried to assess empirically which unit(s) are critically involved in reading (dis)ability. Both strategies can contribute to the construction of a theory of learning to read and to the discovery of the basic mechanisms. A comprehensive theory of reading acquisition, however, cannot confine itself to locating differences between normal and backward readers and a choice for one promising processing unit.

Third, individual differences in reading are discussed. Training can be organized according to distinctions founded on logical, linguistic or psychological grounds. Van Bon uses psycholinguistic processing levels at the sub-syllabic and the whole word level and examines which levels were successful for the remediation of the reading skills of backward readers. The author reports positive effects, but remains critical about the results. Training at the syllabic and word levels turned out to be useful for this group, but the training programmes often contained lengthy instructions, which makes unclear what specific element contributed to the results. The critical attitude of Van Bon is the attitude of an experimentalist versus a teacher who uses broad spectrum 'remedies' in remedial teaching. Aarnoutse, being interested in reading comprehension, adopts elements from what he calls the most elaborated text processing theories to design training programmes. Surely, different remediations are appropriate for different reading skills. Aarnoutse claims success with his training ('pedagogical experiments').

Questions concerning transfer are pervasive both from a theoretical and practical point of view. Van Bon is dissatisfied because he gets no grip on the specific contributing elements. Aarnoutse is eclectic in his selection of text processing theories and finds positive effects of training. Both authors, justly, address the question of the lack of (far) transfer. Finally, a thorough discussion on the (im-) possibilities of the remediation of substantial individual differences is lacking and would be welcomed by the reader.

Fourth, Cunningham *et al.* study a general and non-specific but massive factor in literacy acquisition: print exposure. Not only reading achievement, but also general cognitive development over a longer period of time (ten years) is studied and presented. They use statistical techniques to assess the independent contribution of print exposure to reading achievement and cognitive development. They were able to show a long-term effect. This is impressive, and the question is what caused that prolonged effect or what sustained it over the long period? Such information is very important for everyone designing curricula and trying to accomplish lasting effects and changes.

Finally, Berninger tries to build a bridge between the two traditions. Following the work of Vygotsky and his pupil Luria, she argues for a biological/neurological basis of phonological and orthographic codes. It is not difficult to see a gap between the traditions, although everyone admits that behaviour has a biological basis and is impressed by the findings that different areas of the brain correlate with behavioural differences. The traditions, however, differ even more than the information processing and socio-cultural approaches. It is a complex and unquestionably long chain from neural connections to the co-construction of shared meaning, and such a chain is as strong as its weakest link. There are many opponents to the idea of linking neurological and psychological processes. Reese (1993) stated that psychology will not profit from neurological and physiological knowledge. Berninger justly draws our attention to the fact that there is a developmental dimension which causes the integration of different skills and of neurobiological processes at different ages.

To summarize, the chapters of this volume reflect two central approaches of literacy acquisition. The emphases of recent research are also considered. Moreover, the approaches are supported by empirical research. Availability of research is a criterion for scientific fruitfulness. Both approaches have their specific (dis)advantages. The complexity of the phenomenon of literacy acquisition allows different perspectives with their own value. Sometimes, paradigms elucidate different but equally relevant parts of complex psychological phenomena.

Concluding remarks and questions

Literacy research in this volume emphasized an empirically-oriented social scientific approach. Linguistics, logic and epistemological issues were justly left out of consideration. Theoretical and practical questions prevailed. Literacy acquisition was limited to reading and reading comprehension. Some questions dealing with determinants of emergent literacy, reading achievements and effects of training programmes were dealt with. The contributions of authors with a variety of specialisms not only addressed current issues, they also introduced relevant questions.

First, the question of the input for literacy acquisition has a long history and diverse answers have been suggested. This volume on literacy acquisition brings this question once more into the limelight. In the contributions, the characteristics of the relevant input varied. Gresnigt proposes a stepwise instructional reading system in order to realize text comprehension at a mental level. There is a supposed path from the concrete input to the mentally adequately represented input, i.e. the text. Aarnoutse derives the input from concepts adapted from text processing theories and directly instructs these concepts to the pupils. The training programmes for backward readers discussed by Van Bon contained very specific input, based on multiple psycholinguistic processing levels. He assumes that specific input has specific effects and that one has to start from the beginning, i.e. from the smallest unit. Assink and Kattenberg followed the same approach. At this point we are prompted to ask: Do specific inputs always have specific effects? Are there not examples of simple inputs with complex effects, and complex inputs with simple effects?

A second question concerns the effect of the duration and massivity of the input. The assumption is that strong input has a strong impact. This is one of the decision heuristics, used by Tversky and Kahneman (1974) in their research. Cunningham *et al.* (Chapter 5, this volume) highlighted massive print exposure as a powerful factor, which was resistant to genetically-based variability. Effects of print exposure, as related to reading disability, have also recently been presented by Assink and Kattenberg (1993). Authors who developed curricula and training programmes often attributed the lack of effects to the short duration of the training period.

Input and output are implicitly supposed to be linearly related. Cunningham *et al.* undoubtedly assessed long-term effects. Snow (1991), however, was disappointed to find that long-term effects of her powerful programme for the low-income families did not persist. Implicitly, she assumed a linear relation between her efforts (and the efforts of the parents and children) and the output. Linearity between input and output is too easily accepted a priori by literacy researchers. Bates and Carnevale (1993) convincingly pointed to the existence of non-linear dynamics in aspects of language acquisition. Connectionist models, for example, for the acquisition of word meaning, gave way to the idea of a non-linear relation between the semantic input and acquisition of meaning. It is possible that the old Gestalt notion of insight will adopt a new technically sophisticated foundation. The comment that literacy researchers adhere too easily to the 'the more, the merrier' philosophy when investigating effects of general, specific, social and non-social infuences, is, therefore, justified.

Related to the idea of linearly related input and output comes a third point, the assumption that all kinds of input accumulate. Influences simply add up to one powerful force. This issue can be dealt with only empirically and there are plausible alternatives. Snow (1991), for example, considered the differences in literacy input between home (of low income families) and school as opposing forces.

A fourth point concerning input is that different inputs are relevant at different ages. It is obvious that one can study book reading interaction in mother–child couples, but not in the same way in a second-grader (7 year olds). It is clear that the inputs are not the same for children of different ages. Every training programme implicitly accounts for age differences. Seldom is this founded in the theory of literacy development. It is analogous to intelligence testing, where age norms are constructed by using a representative sample to account for age differences, while a theory about the development of intelligence is lacking. In this volume Berninger (Chapter 3) points to the fact that, while growing older, neurobiological systems can integrate or become independent. The causes of literacy achievement can differ at different ages. The experimental and educational literacy researchers make their point in this volume, but the developmental point of view is not strongly represented here.

One possible way to introduce a developmental perspective is to consider literacy as a life-long developmental task (Heymans, 1994). An outline of such an approach will be given below. It is inspired by the research of Bus and by Assink's introductory chapter to this volume. Assink describes the child as being introduced into a literate world by the mother. The mother acts as if the child joins in an orderly world, consisting, among others, of books and dialogues. The mother determines the input and introduces, or even seduces, the child to take part in the world of books, stories and dialogues.

Books are unfamiliar to the child, as are the letters and words for the pre-schooler. It is mandatory, however, for the child to get involved in this world of symbols and to become literate, appropriate for its age. People have beliefs as to what is adequately literate for certain ages (Cruts, 1991) and act accordingly. 'Book reading' at the age of about 2–4 years is considered by most mothers in the prosperous West as an element of the literacy of the child. Therefore, the mother must create a frame of reference in which the child can participate. Intimacy creating activities such as 'Come and sit with me, I'll tell you a story; I'll show you something very exciting and beautiful' create such a frame of reference. The child has to agree, just like the mother, that something is going to happen. At the end of such an episode, the child is praised for its 'reading'. It can be argued that story-telling has a broader function than only to create intimacy, as proposed by Bus. It may be true that it starts with intimacy creation, but thereafter creates its own momentum. Telling stories is universal and creates a frame in which a child can easily participate. Later in development, other inputs are necessary.

In order to become a competent reader, everyone has to learn the completely arbitrary, but compulsory, and in the end quite efficient system of symbols and associated sounds. Children can be frightened by these symbols, just as adults can be frightened, when having to learn to operate a computer for the first time. Some children therefore need help to overcome this barrier. Besides the input of the framing of a world, in which this symbolic, arbitrary sign system appears promising, other kinds of input are also necessary if the child is to master the system. The information processing approach has offered much knowledge with regard to these inputs, as is shown in the introductory section. The input in literacy must therefore be both technical and 'framing and eliciting'. The same input can signify different things at different ages. The question as to which input fits for a given developmental level is not systematically addressed in the present volume.

A fifth point concerns the search for one simple cause for one simple element of the reading ability. One simple cause was not found, however. Phonological skill training seemed a good candidate both in this volume and in the literature, but the issue is still not settled. Van Bon saw himself confronted with an empirical paradox with respect to training of phonological skills. Wimmer *et al.* (1991) doubted the causal direction and asked whether phonemic awareness was the cause or the consequence of literacy. This is not a clear-cut case. The question is whether one should try harder to find one simple cause, or should one assume multiple causes, which in addition can also vary at different ages? It may be argued that simple causes do not exist.

Besides questions concerning inputs, there are questions addressing the level of analysis. What are acceptable units for the subject in the process of becoming literate? Units can be defined analytically, they can be adopted from linguistics and logic or from psychology. As a consequence, they varied from stories and book reading to the perception of letters. It is, of course, acceptable to investigate any unit in research. It is, however, not self-evident that all units are psychologically relevant in a cognitive representational sense. In the research on concept acquisition there is some support for the existence of 'natural' units for concepts (Rosch *et al.*, 1976). Is it possible that a 'natural' processing level also exists? There appeared to be a preference for selecting the word as a unit.

The concept of literacy is not systematically analyzed. This is not always necessary, because the meaning is sometimes clear from the context. However, as it turned out, there was hardly room for literacy as a factor which predicts future behaviour. At the same time, however, it is suggested that this factor has long-term effects. Why should one invest so much effort in literacy acquisition, starting so early and persisting for such a prolonged period, if there are only a few, empirically supported, hints of the reward for these efforts?

The term 'social context' is not systematically analyzed. This would be superfluous if the meaning were evident in the various chapters. It is not, however. This becomes particularly clear in the suggestion of the social context as a co-construction of at least two persons and a group or society. The definition of the social context offers special problems, which are ignored too easily.

There is an organism – a baby, a toddler, a child, an adolescent, an adult and an elderly person – who is becoming or continues to be literate. Which processes and which levels are involved? It is true that some levels have been discussed – neurobiological, information processing and cultural levels – but how can these levels be integrated? Or does this question make no sense? How should one respond to Reese's (1993) criticism?

Methodologically, literacy research may appear confusing to a non-expert public. To investigate basic processes, backward readers are compared to normal readers, theoretically crucial factors are manipulated and experimental and pedagogical training studies are conducted. What are the appropriate designs for what kind of questions?

Finally, a practical concern is the effect of training programmes for backward readers. Backward reading is a serious problem. Despite many studies there is no (even very complicated) answer to the question of middle- and long-term effectiveness and near–far transfer of training programmes. Van Bon calls for more research, but reading has already been researched so thoroughly that this may sound meaningless. Why not look for new approaches?

The contributions not only address questions, they also generate questions. In 1984, a colleague in my own Developmental Psychology Department had a discussion with Harry Beilin of New York University about the topic of research she should choose after finishing her PhD. Beilin's advice was: 'Well, one thing, don't start reading research, because so much has been done by so many talented people. And the success? That's no better than it should be'. However, literacy acquisition deserves further research and new concepts. The complexities of the phenomenon and the importance of the subject will create new theoretical and particularly practical challenges in our changing society. If we want to enter the twenty-first century with confidence, everyone has to be literate, irrespective of the content of literature at that point in time. Research can analyze literacy and help people become literate.

References

Assink, E.M.H. and Kattenberg, G.P.A. (1993), 'Computerized assessment of verbal skill', *Journal of Psycholinguistic Research, 22*, 427–44.

Bates, E. and Carnevale, G.F. (1993), 'New directions on language research', *Developmental Review, 13*, 436–71.

Bever, T.G. (1992), 'The demons and the beast: modular and modular kinds of knowledge', In R.G. Reilly and N.E. Sharkey (eds.) *Connectionist Approaches to Natural Language Processing*, Hove: Lawrence Erlbaum.

Bialystok, E. (1992), 'Symbolic representation of letters and numbers', *Cognitive Development, 7*, 301–16.

Bloom, P. (ed.) (1993), *Language Acquisition: Core readings*, New York: Harvester-Wheatsheaf.

Brandt, D. (1990), *Literacy as Involvement: The acts of writers, readers and texts.* Carbondale, Ill: Southern Illinois University Press.

Bruner, J. (1990), *Acts of Meaning*, Cambridge, MA: Harvard University Press.

Bruner, J. (1993), 'Do we "acquire" culture or vice versa?' *Behavioral and Brain Sciences 16*, 515–16.

Byrne, B. and Fielding, R. (1993), 'Evalution of a program to teach phonemic awareness to young children: a 1-year follow-up', *Journal of Educational Psychology*, *85*, 104-11.

Cardoso, C. (1991), 'Awareness of phonemes and alphabetic literacy acquisition', *British Journal of Educational Psychology*, *61*, 164–73.

Cipielewski, J. and Stanovich, K.E. (1992), 'Predicting growth in reading from children's exposure to print', *Journal of Experimental Child Psychology*, *54*, 74–89.

Cothern, N.B. and Collins, M.D. (1992), 'An exploration: attitude acquisition and reading instruction', *Reading Research and Instruction*, *31*, 84–97.

Cruts, A.A.N. (1991), *Folk Developmental Psychology*, unpublished PhD dissertation, Utrecht University.

Cunningham, A.E. and Stanovich, K.E. (1991), 'Tracking the unique effects of print exposure in children: associations with vocabulary, general knowledge and spelling', *Journal of Educational Psychology*, *83*, 264–74.

De Gelder, B. and Vroomen, J. (1991), 'Phonological deficits: beneath the surface of reading-acquisition problems', *Psychologische Forschung*, *53*, 88–97.

Dickinson, D.K. and Tabors, P.O. (1991), 'Early literacy: linkages between home, school and literacy achievement at age five', *Journal of Research in Childhood Education*, *6*, 30–46.

Donaldson, M. (1978), *Children's Minds*, New York: W.W. Norton.

Dyson, A.H. (1992), 'Whistle for Willie, lost puppies and cartoon dogs: the sociocultural dimensions of young children's composing', *Journal of Reading Behavior*, *24*, 433–62.

Fishman, A.R. (1992), 'Ethnography and literacy: learning in context', *Topics in Language Disorders*, *24*, 65–75.

Garton, A.F. (1992), *Social Interaction and the Development of Language and Cognition*, Hillsdale, NJ: Lawrence Erlbaum.

Gee, J.P. (1990), *Social Linguistics and Literacies: Ideology in discourses*, New York: The Falmer Press.

Goetz, E.T., Parsons, J.L. and Wilson J.J. (1992), 'Causal models of literacy acquisition', *Reading Research and Instruction*, *21*, 1–10.

Graff, H.J. (1987), *The Labyrinths of Literacy: Reflection on literacy past and present*, London: The Falmer Press.

Griffith, P.L., Klesius, J.P. and Kromrey, J.D. (1992), 'The effect of phonemic awareness on literacy development of first grade children in a traditional or a whole language classroom', *Journal of Research in Childhood Education*, *6*, 85–92.

Heymans, P.G. (1994), 'Developmental tasks: a cultural analysis of development'. In J. ter Laak, A. Podol'sky and P. Heymans, *Developmental Tasks: Toward a cultural analysis of human development*, Dordrecht: Kluwer Scientific Publishers, pp. 1–34.

Kagan, J. (1984), *The Nature of the Child*, New York: Basic Books.

Kantor, R., Miller, S.M. and Fernie, D.E. (1992), 'Diverse paths to literacy in a preschool class room: a sociocultural perspective', *Reading Research Quarterly*, *27*, 184–201.

Knight, C.C. and Fisher, K.W. (1992), 'Learning to read words: differences in developmental sequences', *Journal of Applied Developmental Psychology*, *13*, 377–404.

Landerln, K., Lintortner, R. and Wimmer, H. (1992), 'Phonologische Bewusstheit und Schriftspracherwerb im Deutschen', *Zeitschrift für Pedagogische Psychologie*, *6*, 17–83.

Lie, A. (1991), 'Effects of a training program for stimulating skills in word analysis in first-grade children', *Reading Research Quarterly*, *26*, 234–50.

Neuman, S.B. and Roskos, K. (1991), 'Peers as literacy informants: a description of young children's literacy conversations in play', *Early Childhood Education Research Quarterly 6*, 233–48.

Olson, R., Wise, B., Connors, F., Rack, J. and Fulker, D. (1989), 'Specific deficits in component reading and language skills: genetic and environmental influences', *Journal of Learning Disabilities*, *22*, 339–48.

Perfetti, C.A. (1992), 'The representation problem in reading acquisition'. In P.B. Gough, L.C. Ehri and R. Treiman (eds.) *Reading Acquisition*, Hillsdale NJ: Lawrence Erlbaum, pp. 145–74.

Pervin, L.A. (1978), 'Person–environment congruence in the light of the person–situation controversy', *Journal of Vocational Behavior*, *31*, 222–30.

Purcell, V. and Dahl, K.L. (1991), 'Low SES children's success and failure at early learning in skills-based classrooms', *Journal of Reading Behavior*, *23*, 1–34.

Reese, H.W. (1993), 'Developments in child psychology from the 1960's to the 1990's', *Developmental Review*, *13*, 503–24.

Roberts, B. (1992), 'The evolution of the young child's concept of word as a unit of spoken and written language', *Reading Research Quarterly*, *27*, 124–38.

Robinson, J.L. (1990), *Conversations on the Written Word: Essays on language and literacy*. Portsmouth, NH: Heinemann.

Rosch, E., Mervis, C.B., Gray, W.D., Johnson, D.M. and Boyes-Brahm, P. (1976), 'Basic objects in natural categories', *Cognitive Psychology*, *7*, 573–605.

Saegert, H. and Winkel, G. (1990), 'Environmental psychology', *Annual Review of Psychology*, *44*, 441–77.

Sawyer, D.J. and Butler, K. (1991), 'Early language intervention: a deterrent to reading disability', *Annuals of Dyslexia*, *41*, 55–79.

Scarborough, H.S., Dobrich, W. and Hager, M. (1991), 'Pre-school literacy experience and later reading', *Journal of Learning Disabilities*, *24*, 508–11.

Schunk, D.H. and Rice, J.M. (1992), 'Influence of reading-comprehension strategy information on children's achievement outcomes', *Learning Disability Quarterly*, *15*, 51–64.

Snow, C.E. (1991), 'The theoretical basis for relationships between language and literacy development', *Journal of Research in Childhood Education*, *6*, 5–10.

Snow, C.E., Barnes, W.S., Chandler, J., Goodman, I. and Hemphill, L. (1991), *Unfulfilled Expectations: Home and school influences on literacy*, Cambridge, MA: Harvard University Press.

Spector, J.E. (1992), 'Predicting progress in beginning reading: dynamic assessment of phonemic awareness', *Journal of Educational Psychology*, *84*, 353–63.

Stanovich, K.E. (1991), 'Conceptual and empirical problems with discrepancy definitions of reading disability', *Learning Disability Quarterly*, *14*, 269–80.

Sutherland, M.J. and Smith, C.D. (1991), 'Assessing literacy problems in mainstream schooling: a critique of three literacy screening tests', *Educational Review*, *43*, 39–48.

Ter Laak, J., Podol'sky, A. and Heymans, P. (eds) (1994), *Developmental Tasks, Towards a Cultural Analysis of Human Development*, Dordrecht: Kluwer Scientific Publishers.

Tomasello, M., Kruger, A.C. and Horn-Ratner, H. (1993), 'Cultural learning', *Behavioral and Brain Sciences*, *16*, 495–552.

Troyer, C.R. (1991), 'From emergent literacy to emergent pedagogy: learning from children learning together', *National Reading Conference Yearbook*, *40*, 119–26.

Tversky, A. and Kahneman, D. (1974), 'Judgment under uncertainty: heuristics and biases', *Science*, *184*, 1124–31.

Van den Broek, P. (1993), 'Comprehension and memory of narrative texts: inferences and coherence'. In M.A. Gernsbacher (ed.) *Handbook of Psycholinguistics*, New York: Academic Press.

Velichkovsky, B.M. (1993), 'From intra- to interpsychological analyses of cognition: cognitive science at a developmental crossroad', *Behavioral and Brain Sciences*, *16*, 537–38.

Vellutino, F.R. (1991), 'Introduction to three studies on reading acquisition: convergent findings on theoretical foundations of code-oriented versus whole-language oriented approaches to reading instruction', *Journal of Educational Psychology*, *83*, 437–43.

Venezky, R.I., Wagner, D.A. and Ciliberti, B.S. (1990), *Toward Defining Literacy*. Newark DE, International Reading Association.

Vroman, L. (1964), *126 gedichten* [126 Poems], Amsterdam: Querido.

Wimmer, H., Landerl, K., Lintortner, R. and Hummer, P. (1991), 'The relationship of phonemic awareness to reading acquisition: more consequence than precondition, but still important', *Cognition*, *40*, 219–49.

Index

Aarnoutse, C.A.J. 7, 176–98, 199, 229
Aaron, P.G. 43
Abbott, R. 34, 35, 36, 37, 38–9, 42
Adams, M.J. 41, 86
Adult Attachment Interview 20
  see also story-book reading by parent
Ahrens, M. 86
Ajdarova, L.I. 207
Allen, L., *et al.* 1992 74, 86
Allington, R.L. 71, 86
alphabetic coding and principle 223
Alwin, D.F. 70
analogy training *see* onset-rime analogies
anaphoric relationships 185, 187
Anderson, R.C. 71, 73, 86, 180
  et al. 1985 181
  et al. 1988 71, 73, 75, 86
Armbruster, B.B., *et al.* 1987 189
arousal unit, brain 27
artificial intelligence 25
Assink, E.M.H. 4–5, 35, 91–121, 229, 231, 232
attentional control 125
auditory processing 34
Austin, J.L. 201
Author Recognition Test (ART) 74, 80, 81, 82, 83, 85, 86
automatized processing 117

Backman, J.E., *et al.* 1984 92, 132
backward readers 65–6, 91–118, 162, 165–6, 222, 229, 231, 234
Baddeley, A.D. 73

Baker, H.J. 130
Ball, E.W. 151
Barnitz, J.G. 185
Baron, J. 151
Bartlett, B.J. 189
Bates, E. 231
Bates, J.E., *et al.* 1985 21
Baumann, J.F. 165, 166–7, 184, 185
Bean, T.W. 186
Beck, J.L., *et al.* 1979 177
behavioural genetics 221
Bender, L.A. 155
Bentin, S., *et al.* 1990 131, 139
Berninger, V.W. 2–3, 25–46, 230, 232
  Cartwright, A. *et al.* 1992 35
  et al. 1988 26, 37, 38
  et al. 1990 37
  Yates, C. *et al.* 1992 35
Besner, D., *et al.* 1984 93
Bever, T.G. 224
Bialystok, E. 125, 139, 144, 224
Biddle, B.J. 36, 140, 141
Biemiller, A. 71, 86
biological factors 230
Blachman, B.A. 151
Blachowicz, C. 41
blending 155, 156, 223
Bloom, P. 222, 224
Bohannon, J.N. 126
Bol, E. 200, 202, 204, 216, 217
Boland, T. 217
book-reading 224
Boonman, J.H. 199

stem morphemes 110
stepwise training 231
Sternberg, R.J. 73
Stevens, R. 177, 180
story,
  co-construction by mother and child 224
  structure 185–6
  telling 232
story-book reading 10, 223
story-book reading by parents 2, 10–21
structural equation modelling 36
structure programmes 187
Stuart, M. 59
Studdert-Kennedy, M. 34
Stumpel, B. 164
sub-lexical high frequency letter clusters 113–14
sub-syllabic decoding units 160–3
sub-syllabic level 229
subword level, orthographic processing 114
Sulzby, E. 9, 10, 11, 12, 14, 20
syllable feedback 166
syllable identification methods 165–7
syllable level training 171
syllable segmentation 35
syllables 3, 6, 49, 106, 164, 165, 221, 229
  structure *see* onsets; rimes
symbolic representation 224

Tabors, P.O. 224
Taft, M. 106
Tager-Flusberg, H. 125, 143
Taylor, B.M., *et al.* 1990 73
Teale, W.H. 9, 10, 11, 12, 74
ter Laak, J.J.F. 220–37
  et al. 1994 228
Test of Awareness of Language Segments (TALS) 62
text processing theories 229, 231
Theloosen, G. 161–2, 169, 170, 171
Thorndyke, P.W. 185, 186
Thornton, A. 70
Tierney, R.J. 179, 185
time diary methods 73
Title Recognition Test 74, 75–6, 77, 78–9
Tizard, J. 70
Tomasello, M., *et al.* 1993 225
Torgesen, J.K. 170

Torneus, M. 151
training duration 171–2
training studies 229
transfer 193
  effects 135
  far 193–4
  near 193
  in reading 228
Traweek, D. 40, 41
Treiman, B. 97
Treiman, R. 3, 5, 51, 62, 63, 79, 106, 117, 151, 160–1, 162
  et al. 1990 3, 63
Troyer, C.R. 226
Tsai, S. 72
Tulviste, P. 1
Tunmer, W.E. 122, 123, 124, 125, 129, 131, 133–4, 139, 140–1, 142, 143, 151
  et al. 1984 122
  et al. 1987 131, 132, 134
  et al. 1988 125, 131, 133, 139, 140, 141, 142, 143, 144, 145
Tversky, A. 231
Tyler, A. 164

uppercase 94–7

van Bon, W.H.J. 6, 150–75, 221, 223, 229, 230, 234
  et al. 1986 169
  et al. 1987 158, 167
  et al. 1991 169
van Daal, V.H.P. 162, 168–9
  et al. 1986 169
van de Wouw, J. 194
van den Bos, K.P. 72, 86
van den Bosch, K. 158–9, 162, 167, 169, 170
  et al. 1993 159
van der Leij, D.A.V. 169–70
van Dijk, T.A. 7, 179–80, 181, 185, 186
van Ijzendoorn, M.H. 11–12, 19–20
van Kan, N. 190
van Parreren, C.F. 200
van Rijnsoever, R.J. 97
Velichkofsky, B.M. 225
Vellutino, F.R. 35, 92, 140, 152–3, 154, 156–7, 168, 223
Venezky, R.I. 222
verbal intelligence 133